PLAYS
BY MOLIÈRE

THE PUBLISHERS WILL BE PLEASED TO SEND, UPON
REQUEST, A BROCHURE SETTING FORTH THE PURPOSE AND
SCOPE OF THE *Modern Library College Editions,*
AND LISTING EACH VOLUME IN THE SERIES.

MOLIÈRE

Plays

Introduction by Francis Fergusson
Associate Professor of Literature,
Princeton University

THE MODERN LIBRARY
NEW YORK

Random House IS THE PUBLISHER OF

THE MODERN LIBRARY

BENNETT A. CERF · DONALD S. KLOPFER · ROBERT K. HAAS

Manufactured in the United States of America

CONTENTS

CHRONOLOGY OF THE PRINCIPAL PLAYS
OF MOLIÈRE
(born, Paris, 1622—died, Paris, 1673)

La Jalousie de Barbouillé	(before 1650)
L'Etourdi	1653
Le Dépit Amoureux	1656
Les Précieuses Ridicules	1659
Sganarelle	1660
Don Garcie de Navarre	1661
L'École des Maris	1661
Les Fâcheux	1661
L'École des Femmes	1662
La Critique de L'École des Femmes	1663
Le Mariage Forcé	1664
Don Juan	1665
Le Misanthrope	1666
Le Médecin malgré lui	1666
Le Tartuffe	1664-1667
Amphitryon	1668
George Dandin	1668
L'Avare	1668
Monsieur de Pourceaugnac	1669
Le Bourgeois Gentilhomme	1670
Les Fourberies de Scapin	1671
La Comtesse D'Escarbagnas	1671
Les Femmes Savantes	1672
Le Malade Imaginaire	1673

INTRODUCTION

by Francis Fergusson

"Englishmen have always loved Molière," said Lytton Strachey. The same may be said of Americans and Germans, of Russians and Italians and Spaniards. For Molière is the most universally intelligible of all the great artists who form our image of the human animal. He has the divine gift of making men laugh in any language and in any period, even our own rather morose one. His comic sequences have the formal beauty of music or ballet; his art has an axiomatic quality, which makes it as fresh, inevitable and surprising as the truth. When we read his plays or see them on the stage we feel that his common sense, the basis of his laughter, really is common to civilized mankind, and therefore humane in the best sense of the word. The absurd, logical and delightful world of his theatre is always there, whenever we look at it: a bright spot in our troubled awareness of the human, with the charm, and the rare value, of sanity.

Molière's comedies are in their very essence theatrical, but they come alive on the printed page for any reader with a little willingness to make-believe. But for all their clarity, we cannot really explain their magic. Molière is ultimately as enigmatic as any genius. Yet one may come to know him intimately as one learns to know a friend or a piece of music. And for this purpose it helps to know something about his theatre; some of the ways in which his art has been understood and enjoyed in different periods, and the main facts of his life, which partakes of the gusto and gallantry of the comedies themselves.

3

MOLIÈRE'S LIFE

Molière (whose real name was Jean-Baptiste Poquelin) was born in Paris in 1622, of a substantial bourgeois family. His father was an upholsterer, and a man of some importance, for he was upholsterer to the King: *tapissier du roi.* The elder Poquelin was thus able to secure the worldly advantages for his children, and young Molière was sent to the fashionable Jesuit school of Clermont, where he studied from 1635 to 1641. The Jesuits gave him the good classical education of the time, which included a study of the Roman comic authors Terence and Plautus. The Jesuits used the theatre in their educational scheme, and it is believed that Molière was taught to perform Roman comedy while still in school. At Clermont he also made "good connections," as boys are supposed to do still when their fathers spend money on their education. Thus Molière found himself, from the very first, in the middle of French life, in the healthy growing time of the great age of Louis XIV.

Molière's father expected him to carry on the family business, but Molière became interested in the theatrical profession through the Béjart family. The Béjarts were also *bourgeois de Paris,* but they were interested in the arts; they had a touch of what was later to be called Bohemianism. Madeleine Béjart became Molière's mistress; later in life he married Armande Béjart, her daughter by another man. Molière seems to have had the usual dispute with his father about his choice of profession, but Poquelin senior relented in time, and helped his son out with money for his theatrical ventures.

Molière's first attempts were with the Béjarts in Paris. But their "Illustre Théâtre," as they called it, was a financial failure. They abandoned Paris, and from 1646 to 1658 Molière with several members of the Béjart family toured the provinces with a small acting company. This was Molière's fertile apprenticeship as actor-manager, and as author also, for his first farces were written in this period. He acquired his sure knowledge of the public, and his extraordinary mastery of the stage itself, in the only way, the hard way. Our information on this period is not extensive or certain, but we are safe in imagining Molière working very hard, suffering the risks and disappointments of the profession, reaching, at last, success and prosperity, and all the while taking his share of the pleasures of this life. It has often been pointed out that he was the unmarried leader of a troupe with several attractive women in it, and that he was by nature "very amorous."

In 1658 Molière moved his company to Paris under the patronage of the Court. *The Highbrow Ladies,* the first play in this collection, was presented in 1659. It is, among other things, a humorous picture of the literary ladies of the Hôtel de Rambouillet. It delighted Paris—all but the Hôtel de Rambouillet—and its success assured his place in the capital. From that time until his death in 1673 his plays followed one another with great rapidity, as one may see by looking over the list of his principal works on page 2.

In Paris, between the city and the Court, in the center of the power and culture of all France, Molière's life was lived in public, and a great deal is known about his last fourteen years, the summit of his career. He had an unparalleled opportunity to live and to observe the life of "man in society." No wonder he worked with such speed to catch the fascinating image in the mirror of his comedy. But his position was extremely perilous, maintained only by ceaseless fighting. Every play he produced had to please the audience, if he was to support his players. The King helped him, but not enough to make his company independent of their city following. Each of his own plays had to be defended from the machinations of those who felt attacked: *Tartuffe,* for instance, from many implacable churchmen, and *The Highbrow Ladies* from the literary coteries. Molière had very thorny relations, all this time, with his rivals and his colleagues, notably Racine and the composer Lully. He was always obliged to cultivate the King, who was his friend from the first, but required frequent doses of flattery. His marriage with Armande Béjart, with whom he was deeply in love but who was almost young enough to have been his daughter, was full of suffering.

All of this and much more is known about the troubles of Molière's illustrious career in Paris, and his admirers often seek the clue to the depth of his comedy in Molière's own sufferings. But that lively spirit never wore his heart on his sleeve, either in his writings or in his life. His public controversies reveal his pleasure in combat, his wit, objectivity, and balanced intelligence, but no bitterness or self-pity. His life, like his art, was based upon the kind of self-evident truth which may be made publicly clear. Purely private troubles, others' or his own, he disregarded. He was playing the title role in the last, and one of the greatest, of his comedies, *The Imaginary Invalid,* two hours before he died of a disease, probably tuberculosis, which was not imaginary. Molière and his real disease have departed, but his imagined invalid lives on, to our perennial delight.

MOLIÈRE'S THEATRE

I have remarked that Molière's theatre has proved both intelligible and delightful to all civilized mankind. At the same time it is, of course, extremely French. It has that alert and worldly pep which is properly called the *esprit gaulois.* Rabelais revealed it before Molière, and so did the late medieval farces which prepared his way on the French stage. This spirit still lives so unmistakably among the French that one is tempted to say Molière created it in the forms we know, instead of merely expressing it. And yet his theatre, in its essential humanity and its peculiar charm, floats free, alive beyond his time and race.

The charm of Molière's theatre is not the charm of his characters, if one thinks of them as real people. Molière off stage was probably fond of young lovers, and of the formidable race of serving-maids who castigate their masters with such frank enjoyment. But in his theatre these types are to be laughed *at* as well as *with:* they are seen in the same clean, steady light as his hypocrites, hypochondriacs and social climbers. Molière never tries to ingratiate himself with the luxury market through the glamour of tweeds, Scotch, and an insolent Junior League drawl, like the writers of our advertisements and light comedies. His lightness is of a different order. He is addressing the impersonal and disinterested good sense which no income group, class, or individual owns: the sanity of humanity at large. "I beg you to learn, Marquis," he wrote in *La Critique de l'École des Femmes,* "that good sense has no fixed place in the theatre, and that the difference between a *louis d'or* and fifteen *sols* has nothing to do with good taste." In the light of this good sense, all of his characters are comic, and the charm is in the whole lively scene.

Molière flattered no one but the King, who was both his good friend and the official recipient of literary adulation. But he offended many in his audiences who could not get his humorous perspective and thought they recognized their own portraits on his stage. This was not his intention, any more than flattery was. "Nothing displeases him so much as being accused of intending particular people in the portraits he makes," he has Brécourt say of himself in *L'Impromptu de Versailles*; "his purpose is to picture manners without touching individuals, and all the characters he represents are characters in the air, fantoms really, which he dresses according to his whim to delight the audience."

When one considers the Paris of Louis XIV, that dangerous focus of vanity, envy, and the thirst for power, it seems almost miraculous that Molière should have been able to put his free and clear-eyed comedy there, in the very center—and even make the public laugh at the mirror image he showed it. "C'est une étrange entreprise que de faire rire les honnêtes gens," he remarked with characteristic humor and courage: "It is a strange project—to make the honest laugh." Strange indeed: for the people Molière wanted to make laugh were no more honest than we are, before they saw his show. It is his own sturdy faith in common sense which creates the ideal audience, makes it honest, and makes it laugh. We can know this, whether Molière did or not, for his comedy has this effect upon us: our laughter makes us, for the moment, humane. This, I suppose, is the mysterious property of much great comedy, but especially of Molière's.

It helps one to appreciate the peculiar quality of this theatre—the sharpness of its characters, which so often dismayed the contemporary audience, combined with their impersonal, abstract, legendary scope—if one remembers that it was the outgrowth of an ancient popular tradition, that of the Commedia dell'Arte. The Commedia spread from Italy all over Europe in the late Renaissance, revivifying the theatre, giving the great dramatists of the 17th Century—Shakespeare and Molière among them—their opportunity, much of their theatrical skill, and much of their material. The players of the Commedia improvised their words and performances on the basis of familiar scenarios, often derived from Roman comedy: stock intrigues, and broad comic situations which skilled performers could build on. Each of the players was professionally identified with a traditional character, or "mask": Harlequin, Pantalone (the rich old man), or the Doctor of Bologna (the classic stage pedant). This theatre lived only in performance, since it was improvised. But we still sense its vitality and glamour in contemporary accounts of the performances, in pictures of the players from Callot to Tiepolo, and in the traces it left in dramatic literature.

Molière began to absorb the Commedia as a child in

Paris, watching the Italian players. When he went into the theatre himself, he took lessons from one of the masters, Tiberio Fiorilli, and there is a picture of him, which is often published, imitating a dancelike gesture of Fiorilli's Scaramouche. From his earliest farces to his last play, *The Imaginary Invalid*, the great tradition of the Commedia lives in Molière's works.

"The types of the Commedia," M. Ramon Fernandez wrote in his excellent *Vie de Molière*, "come down to us, thanks to their masks, their costumes and their gestures, endowed with an individuality which is both typical and concrete, very much like that of the animals in the Fables. . . . If it is true that a dramatic poet must base his creations upon creations which are collective and anonymous, the Commedia can explain (in part, of course) the marvellous sharpness of Molière's creations. Thanks to it, 17th Century Comedy had a mythology, not literary like tragic mythology, but alive and real." The comic mythology of the Commedia helps one to understand Molière's own description of his characters as "fantoms to delight the audience." His old men tormented by young women, his pedants with their resonant dog latin, may have struck home among the Parisians of his day, but at the same time they partake of the legendary life of the popular theatre. Molière found himself by perceiving afresh, and revivifying in his own Paris, this legendary world, the comic picture of Man in Society which the folk-theatre of Latin Europe had been making, off and on, for two thousand years—since Menander the Greek.

It is even more important to remember that he learned his wonderful mastery of the theatrical medium itself—the performer on the boards before an audience—from the Italian improvisers. Molière's plays are conceived as *performances* before the words are written at all. His scenes could be mimed, or danced, or set to music; and they would be intelligible theatrically as music or dance or gymnastic clowning. *The School for Wives* contains some of the subtlest, wittiest language ever written for the stage; but beneath its rhymes and its verbal play there are the rhythms of slapstick: the mock duel, the beating, the chase, the skillful parry. Beneath the spiritual agility of an Arnolphe or Alceste there is the visible gymnastic agility of the comedian, actor and dancer in one, who improvises his laughable stratagems before an audience which sees, laughs, and understands at once.

It is this farcical basis of Molière's great comedy which seems so fresh and wonderful to us, but his contemporaries and his successors seem to have taken that for granted. What interested them was Molière's ideas, language, and contemporary social satire. Hence the notion of Molière as the Classic Author and the satirist of French manners, the counterpart in comedy of Racine and Corneille in tragedy. And one must remember that Molière did share the literary culture of French Classicism. If he could build the scenarios of the Commedia into literary works, it is partly due to his early education in Terence and Plautus, from whose plays the Commedia's scenarios were derived. If he could live up to the rationality, verbal elegance and refinement of feeling of neoclassic literary taste; if he could reflect the types, language and manners of the salons, it is because he had begun to acquire some of the literary culture early. He had, for instance, acted Corneille's tragedy when he first formed an acting company. A hundred years after Molière, Goldoni, in Venice, wishing to reform Italian comedy, proposed to emulate this development of Molière's toward contemporary satire and literary sophistication, by writing realistic character parts for the actors who were still playing the traditional masks of the Commedia: "Yes," he said to himself, "you must handle character subjects, they being the source of all good comedy. This is what Molière did, thus developing his art to a degree which the ancients only indicated, and which the moderns have not yet equalled."

Goldoni is only one of many writers of comedy all over Europe, in the seventeenth and eighteenth centuries, who followed Molière. And they all followed him in the same direction: away from the folk tradition of farce, and toward rationality, literature, and the realistic imitation of contemporary characters; in short, toward modern drama as we know it. If you remove from Molière's theatre the legendary scope of the traditional masks of farce, and the peculiar mastery of the performer's art which goes with it, the way is clear for the thesis plays, the talky and sedentary parlor comedies, the well-made entertainments of our commercial theatre. Molière is the father of the great form of neoclassic comedy, which lighted the theatres of Europe for a hundred and fifty years; and by the same token he is the grandfather of the modern theatre. When one reads Molière now, one can still see the various aspects of his art which different generations have appreciated, and used for their purposes. These perspectives help one to come to know Molière. But his art is his own, and his comic genius, for all its clarity and universality, is unique.

Fortunately the cult of Molière's own plays has never died out. He is performed wherever the culture of Europe has spread, but especially, of course, in France. After his death his company was fused with that of the Hôtel de Bourgogne to make the Comédie Française. That most brilliant of state theatres, the "House of Molière" as it is often called, has survived all of the terrible vicissitudes of its native France. It flourishes still, with a more tenacious life than any other institution except the Church, or (as Henry James suggested) Parliament. James saw Molière performed there in 1872, and reported as follows: "Molière is played at the Théâtre Français as he deserves to be—one can hardly say more—with the most ungrudging breadth, exuberance, and *entrain,* and yet with a kind of academic harmony and solemnity. Molière, if he ever drops a kindly glance on MM. Got and Coquelin, must be the happiest of immortals. To be read two hundred years after your death is something; but to be acted is better." Thus Molière's own comedy plays still, a continuing source of the lore and the arts of the theatre, and also, as Henry James put it, a "school of manners": for Molière is one of those great artists with the power to form the spirit which we call humane.

NOTES ON THE PLAYS IN THIS COLLECTION

The present collection contains samples of the main types of comedy which Molière wrote. It does not include any of the entertainments, like *Psyché* and *Pastorale Comique*, which he wrote in collaboration with musicians and designers, to please and flatter the King and the Court. And it does not include the controversial pieces, like *La Critique de l'École des Femmes* and *L'Impromptu de Versailles*, in which he answered his enemies and explained the nature of his comedy. His most characteristic work extends from pure farce at one extreme to the most serious high comedy, in verse, at the other.

The Physician in Spite of Himself was written rather late in Molière's short career, in 1666, but it is a good example of the theatrical art which he learned from the Commedia, and which, as I have suggested, underlies all his work. It is based upon the Commedia's ancient comic themes: the old man with a troublesome daughter; the lusty and gymnastic clown; the sinister nonsense of the Doctor of Bologna. The reader should imagine it played with the lightness of the trapeze artist, in costumes suggesting the timeless masks of Pantalone, Zani, and the Doctor of Bologna.

The Highbrow Ladies and *The Miser* are among the plays in which the contemporary satire is most clear. *The Highbrow Ladies,* wonderfully good-natured, full of the honey and sunshine of Molière's youth, was certainly inspired by the highbrow Hôtel de Rambouillet. *The Miser,* a play of his maturity, is harder, and has a wider theme: the nonsense to which avarice reduces a whole family. The miser himself reincarnates the penny-pinching graybeards of the classical tradition of farce, but he is also a *bourgeois de Paris,* perhaps akin to Molière's own father.

The comedies of this type piqued the Parisians with their contemporary satire, but pleased them, perhaps, because of their clarity, rationality, and literary urbanity. In them one may understand Molière as one of those who formed the style of the period; a style, or taste, in which reason, in several senses, is so important a criterion: in Descartes's geometric method; in Racine's absolute and crystalline tragedy; in the symmetrical architecture and the rigidity of official manners. Molière's use of reason is singularly free for his age, because it is based upon common sense. In the light of common sense Molière's ideal "honnêtes gens" can see at once that his literary ladies, and his avaricious old man, are absurd: their ways of life are based upon glaringly false, and therefore laughable, premises. But upon these false premises they pursue their careers with the most perfectly logical consistency, until the inevitable débâcle, the practical *reductio ad absurdum* which even they must face. The texture of these comedies is rational: logical exposition and nimble dialectic. At the same time they are joyful celebrations of the absurdity to which rationalizing itself is pushed.

The other three plays in this collection, *The Misanthrope, Tartuffe,* and *The School for Wives,* were written in verse, rhymed couplets with twelve syllables to the line, the famous *Alexandrines* in which Corneille and Racine wrote their tragedies. They are all high, or serious, comedy, and some have even said that they were tragic. It would be foolish to argue about the terms "comedy" and "tragedy" in this case; one certainly would not wish to say that Molière's comic vision did not have the depth usually attributed to tragedy. And yet one is likely to miss their peculiar greatness unless one sees that, whatever their implications, these plays are all, in their immediate effect, comedy.

The Misanthrope has been called a self-portrait, Molière's *Hamlet.* The comparison reveals something; and yet, as one reads the play, one must think of it as played, with energy and exactitude, before a laughing house.

This point is well explained by Coquelin, the great French actor, in his study of the play published in 1881. He says that to make Alceste a tragic character, a Hamlet, a Faust, a Jansenist, or Molière himself, would be a mere sentimental literary theory which would miss the values of the play on stage: an interpretation more in accord with 19th Century taste than with Molière's own practice. Molière could have understood misanthropy from his own experience, but he does not make Alceste the mouthpiece for his own philosophy. On the contrary, he presents him as the "atrabilious lover," irrationally but unmistakably caught by his love for Célimène, and therefore subject to the requirements of human intercourse as we all know them. In this tight and revealing situation he is funny, for all the depth of his hatred for the worldly game. The humor is very deep; but it is the greatness of the play that it keeps the perspective of comedy.

Behind *Tartuffe* you may, if you like, feel the chill of treachery itself. But that would come later, with afterthoughts. While the comedy is played on stage, Tartuffe's falseness looks like impudence and paradox: an impossibility, a farce, for the sane audience which sees and enjoys it. And Tartuffe's impudence, like Madame Pernelle's peevishness and Orgon's blind infatuation, is fed by Molière's own love for shameless human energy in all its forms.

The School for Wives is less likely than the other two to be mistaken for a tragedy in disguise, but it is certainly a play of equal depth. Behind Arnolphe's desperate efforts to confine Agnès's love within the rules of reason, one feels Molière's delicate sense of the mystery of love itself. This comedy has all its worldly wits about it. Molière himself never surpassed the lightness and formal beauty of its dialogue: arabesques of thought and feeling, the perfection of comic play. All this is in the foreground; but behind or beneath the wit there is a *douceur* akin to Shakespeare's tenderness, or to the modest sweetness of 17th Century music.

BIBLIOGRAPHY

This list is intended primarily for the reader of English, though a few titles in French are included. It is introductory and suggestive, in no sense complete.

MOLIÈRE'S LIFE

Mantzius, Karl, *A History of Theatrical Art*. Vol. 4, *Molière and His Times*. London: 1905.
A very readable account of Molière's career in the theatre, which is, however, no longer up to date.

Fernandez, Ramon, *La Vie de Molière*. Paris: 1929.
A stimulating study of Molière and his comedy by a very good critic.

Michaut, Gustave, *La Jeunesse de Molière*. Paris: 1922.
———, *Les Débuts de Molière à Paris*. Paris: 1923.
———, *Les Luttes de Molière*. Paris: 1925.
Michaut's studies are the latest monument of Molière scholarship. They are not light reading, but contain a great deal of valuable lore.

MOLIÈRE THE FRENCH CLASSIC AUTHOR

Strachey, Lytton, *Landmarks in French Literature*. New York: 1912.
Strachey's book is still one of the best introductions to French literature for readers of English. It contains illuminating passages on Molière and his art.

Turnell, Martin, *The Classic Moment*. London: 1947.
A study of Molière, Racine and Corneille, which is very useful and suggestive as an introduction.

15

Borgerhoff, E. B. O., *The Freedom of French Classicism*. Princeton: 1950.
An illuminating discussion of the theory and practice of literature in Molière's time.

Peyre, Henri, *Le Classicisme Français*. New York: 1942.
A learned, but clearly written discussion of the literary tastes and standards of Molière's period.

MOLIÈRE IN THE THEATRE

Both Mantzius and Fernandez, listed above, explain the theatre for which Molière wrote.

Duchartre, Pierre Louis, *The Italian Comedy*. London: 1924.
A study of the Commedia dell'Arte, with many good pictures.

Van Steenderen, F. C. L., *Goldoni on Playwriting*. New York: 1919.
A collection of Goldoni's *obiter dicta* on playwriting, in which one may sample the progress of the tradition founded by Molière.

James, Henry, *The Scenic Art*. ed. Allan Wade. New Brunswick: 1946.
James's writings on the theatre, including a great deal on the French stage and French acting. Useful for the reader who wishes to understand Molière on the stage.

Coquelin, Charles, *Molière et le Misanthrope*. Paris: 1881.
The great French actor's illuminating discussion of *The Misanthrope* as a theatrical comedy.

THE HIGH-BROW LADIES

(LES PRÉCIEUSES RIDICULES)

DRAMATIS PERSONÆ

LA GRANGE, } *repulsed Lovers.*
DU CROISY,

GORGIBUS, *a good citizen.*

THE MARQUIS DE MASCARILLE, *valet to* LA GRANGE.

THE VISCOUNT JODELET, *valet to* DU CROISY.

ALMANZOR, *footman to the pretentious ladies.*

TWO CHAIRMEN.

MUSICIANS.

MADELON, *daughter to Gorgibus,* } *the pretentious*
CATHOS, *niece to Gorgibus,* } *young ladies,*

MAROTTE, *maid to the pretentious young ladies.*

LUCILE. } *two female neighbours.*
CÉLIMÈNE.

SCENE—GORGIBUS' HOUSE, PARIS.

ACT I

SCENE I.—LA GRANGE, DU CROISY.

Du Croisy. M. La Grange.

La Grange. What?

Du Croisy. Look at me for a moment without laugh,
ing.

La Grange. Well?

17

Du Croisy. What do you say of our visit? Are you quite pleased with it?

La Grange. Do you think either of us has any reason to be so?

Du Croisy. Not at all, to say the truth.

La Grange. As for me, I must acknowledge I was quite put out about it. Pray now, did ever anybody see a couple of country wenches giving themselves more ridiculous airs, or two men treated with more contempt than we were? They could hardly make up their mind to order chairs for us. I never saw such whispering as there was between them; such yawning, such rubbing of the eyes, and asking so often what o'clock it was. Did they answer anything else but "yes," or "no," to what we said to them? In short, do you not agree with me that if we had been the meanest persons in the world, we could not have been treated worse?

Du Croisy. You seem to take it greatly to heart.

La Grange. No doubt I do; so much so, that I am resolved to be revenged on them for their impertinence. I know well enough why they despise us. Affectation has not alone infected Paris, but has also spread into the country, and our ridiculous damsels have sucked in their share of it. In a word, they are a strange medley of coquetry and affectation. I plainly see what kind of persons will be well received by them; if you will take my advice, we will play them such a trick as shall show them their folly, and teach them to distinguish a little better the people they have to deal with.

Du Croisy. How can you do this?

La Grange. I have a certain valet, named Mascarille, who, in the opinion of many people, passes for a kind of wit; for nothing now-a-days is easier than to acquire such a reputation. He is an extraordinary fellow, who has taken it into his head to ape a person of quality. He usually prides himself on his gallantry and his poetry,

and despises so much the other servants that he calls
them brutes.

Du Croisy.   Well, what do you mean to do with him?

La Grange.   What do I mean to do with him?   He
must . . . but first, let us be gone.

Scene II.—Gorgibus, Du Croisy, La Grange.

Gorgibus.   Well, gentlemen, you have seen my niece
and my daughter. How are matters going on? What
is the result of your visit?

La Grange.   They will tell you this better than we
can. All we say is that we thank you for the favour you
have done us, and remain your most humble servants.

Du Croisy.   Your most humble servants.

Gorgibus (*alone*).   Hoity-toity!   Methinks they go
away dissatisfied. What can be the meaning of this?
I must find it out. Within there!

· Scene III.—Gorgibus, Marotte.

Marotte.   Did you call, sir?

Gorgibus.   Where are your mistresses?

Marotte.   In their room.

Gorgibus.   What are they doing there?

Marotte.   Making lip salve.

Gorgibus.   There is no end of their salves. Bid them
come down. (*Alone.*) These hussies with their salves
have, I think, a mind to ruin me. Everywhere in the
house I see nothing but whites of eggs, lac virginal, and
a thousand other fooleries I am not acquainted with.
Since we have been here they have employed the lard
of a dozen hogs at least, and four servants might live
every day on the sheep's trotters they use.

Scene IV.—Madelon, Cathos, Gorgibus.

Gorgibus.   Truly there is great need to spend so much
money to grease your faces. Pray tell me, what have

you done to those gentlemen, that I saw them go away with so much coldness. Did I not order you to receive them as persons whom I intended for your husbands?

Madelon. Dear father, what consideration do you wish us to entertain for the irregular behaviour of these people?

Cathos. How can a woman of ever so little under-standing, uncle, reconcile herself to such individuals?

Gorgibus. What fault have you to find with them?

Madelon. Theirs is fine gallantry, indeed. Would you believe it? they began with proposing marriage to us.

Gorgibus. What would you have them begin with— with a proposal to keep you as mistresses? Is not their proposal a compliment to both of you, as well as to me? Can anything be more polite than this? And do they not prove the honesty of their intentions by wishing to enter these holy bonds?

Madelon. Oh, father! Nothing can be more vulgar than what you have just said. I am ashamed to hear you talk in such a manner; you should take some lessons in the elegant way of looking at things.

Gorgibus. I care neither for elegant ways nor songs. I tell you marriage is a holy and sacred affair; to begin with that is to act like honest people.

Madelon. Good Heavens! If everybody was like you a love-story would soon be over. What a fine thing it would have been if Cyrus had immediately espoused Mandane, and if Aronce had been married all at once to Clélie.

Gorgibus. What is she jabbering about?

Madelon. Here is my cousin, father, who will tell as well as I that matrimony ought never to happen till after other adventures. A lover, to be agreeable, must under-stand how to utter fine sentiments, to breathe soft, ten-der, and passionate vows; his courtship must be accord-ing to the rules. In the first place, he should behold the fair one of whom he becomes enamoured either at a place of worship, or when out walking, or at some public ceremony; or else he should be introduced to her by a relative or a friend, as if by chance, and when he leaves her he should appear in a pensive and melancholy mood. For some time he should conceal his passion from the object of his love, but pay her several visits, in every one of which he ought to introduce some gallant subject to exercise the wits of all the company. When the day comes to make his declarations—which generally should be contrived in some shady garden-walk while the company is at a distance—it should be quickly followed by anger, which is shown by our blushing, and which, for a while, banishes the lover from our presence. He finds afterwards means to pacify us, to accustom us gradually to hear him depict his passion, and to draw from us that confession which causes us so much pain. After that come the adventures, the rivals who thwart mutual inclination, the persecutions of fathers, the jealousies arising without any foundation, complaints, despair, running away with, and its consequences. Thus things are carried on in fashionable life, and veritable gallantry cannot dispense with these forms. But to come out point-blank with a proposal of marriage,—to make no love but with a marriage-contract, and begin a novel at the wrong end! Once more, father, nothing can be more tradesmanlike, and the mere thought of it makes me sick at heart.

Gorgibus. What deuced nonsense is all this? That is high-flown language with a vengeance!

Cathos. Indeed, uncle, my cousin hits the nail on the head. How can we receive kindly those who are so awkward in gallantry? I could lay a wager they have not even seen a map of the country of *Tenderness,* and that *Love-letters, Trifling attentions, Polite epistles,* and *Sprightly verses,* are regions to them unknown. Do you not see that the whole person shews it, and that their external appearance is not such as to give at first sight a good opinion of them. To come and pay a visit to the object of their love with a leg without any ornaments, a hat without any feathers, a head with its locks not artistically arranged, and a coat that suffers from a paucity of ribbons. Heavens! what lovers are these! what stinginess in dress! what barrenness of conversation! It is not to be allowed; it is not to be borne. I also observed that their ruffs were not made by the fashionable milliner, and that their breeches were not big enough by more than half-a-foot.

Gorgibus. I think they are both mad, nor can I understand anything of this gibberish. Cathos, and you Madelon . . .

Madelon. Pray, father, do not use those strange names, and call us by some other.

Gorgibus. What do you mean by those strange names? Are they not the names your godfathers and godmothers gave you?

Madelon. Good Heavens! how vulgar you are! I confess I wonder you could possibly be the father of such an intelligent girl as I am. Did ever anybody in genteel style talk of Cathos or of Madelon? And must you not admit that either of these names would be sufficient to disgrace the finest novel in the world?

Cathos. It is true, uncle, an ear rather delicate suffers extremely at hearing these words pronounced, and the name of Polixena, which my cousin has chosen, and that of Amintha, which I took, possesses a charm, which you must needs acknowledge.

Gorgibus. Hearken; one word will suffice. I do not allow you to take any other names than those that were given you by your godfathers and godmothers; and as for those gentlemen we are speaking about, I know their families and fortunes, and am determined they shall be your husbands. I am tired of having you upon my hands.

Looking after a couple of girls is rather too weighty a
charge for a man of my years.

Cathos. As for me, uncle, all I can say is, that I
think marriage a very shocking business. How can one
endure the thought of lying by the side of a man, who
is really naked?

Madelon. Give us leave to take breath for a short
time among the fashionable world of Paris, where we
are but just arrived. Allow us to prepare at our leisure
the groundwork of our novel, and do not hurry on the
conclusion too abruptly.

Gorgibus (*aside*). I cannot doubt it any longer; they
are completely mad. (*Aloud.*) Once more, I tell you,
I understand nothing of all this gibberish; I will be
master, and to cut short all kinds of arguments, either
you shall both be married shortly, or, upon my word,
you shall be nuns; that I swear.

Scene V.—Cathos, Madelon.

Cathos. Good Heavens, my dear, how deeply is your
father still immersed in material things! how dense is his
understanding, and what gloom overcasts his soul!

Madelon. What can I do, my dear? I am ashamed
of him. I can hardly persuade myself I am indeed his
daughter; I believe that an accident, some time or other,
will discover me to be of a more illustrious decent.

Cathos. I believe it; really, it is very likely; as for
me, when I consider myself . . .

Scene VI.—Cathos, Madelon, Marotte.

Marotte. Here is a footman asks if you are at home,
and says his master is coming to see you.

Madelon. Learn, you dunce, to express yourself a
little less vulgarly. Say, here is a necessary evil inquiring if it is commodious for you to become visible.

Marotte. I do not understand Latin, and have not learned philosophy out of *Cyrus,* as you have done.

Madelon. Impertinent creature! How can this be borne! And who is this footman's master?

Marotte. He told me it was the Marquis de Mascarille.

Madelon. Ah, my dear! A marquis! a marquis! Well, go and tell him we are visible. This is certainly some wit who has heard of us.

Cathos. Undoubtedly, my dear.

Madelon. We had better receive him here in this parlour than in our room. Let us at least arrange our hair a little and maintain our reputation. Come in quickly, and fetch us the Counsellor of the Graces.

Marotte. Upon my word, I do not know what sort of a beast that is; you must speak like a Christian if you would have me know your meaning.

Cathos. Bring us the looking-glass, you blockhead! and take care not to contaminate its brightness by the communication of your image.

SCENE VII.—MASCARILLE, TWO CHAIRMEN.

Mascarille. Stop, chairman, stop. Easy does it! Easy, easy! I think these boobies intend to break me to pieces by bumping me against the walls and the pavement.

First Chairman. Ay, marry, because the gate is narrow and you would make us bring you in here.

Mascarille. To be sure, you rascals! Would you have me expose the fulness of my plumes to the inclemency of the rainy season, and let the mud receive the impression of my shoes? Begone; take away your chair.

Second Chairman. Then please to pay us, sir.

Mascarille. What?

Second Chairman. Sir, please to give us our money, I say.

Mascarille (*giving him a box on the ear*). What, scoundrel, to ask money from a person of my rank!

Second Chairman. Is this the way poor people are to be paid? Will your rank get us a dinner?

Mascarille. Ha, ha! I shall teach you to keep your right place. Those low fellows dare to make fun of me!

First Chairman (*taking up one of the poles of his chair*). Come, pay us quickly.

Mascarille. What?

First Chairman. I mean to have my money at once.

Mascarille. That is a sensible fellow.

First Chairman. Make haste, then.

Mascarille. Ay, you speak properly, but the other is a scoundrel, who does not know what he says. There, are you satisfied?

First Chairman. No, I am not satisfied; you boxed my friend's ears, and . . . (*holding up his pole*).

Mascarille. Gently; there is something for the box on the ear. People may get anything from me when they go about it in the right way. Go now, but come and fetch me by and by to carry me to the Louvre to the *petit coucher*.

Scene VIII.—Marotte, Mascarille.

Marotte. Sir, my mistresses will come immediately.

Mascarille. Let them not hurry themselves; I am very comfortable here, and can wait.

Marotte. Here they come.

Scene IX.—Madelon, Cathos, Mascarille, Almanzor.

Mascarille (*after having bowed to them*). Ladies, no doubt you will be surprised at the boldness of my visit, but your reputation has drawn this disagreeable affair upon you; merit has for me such potent charms that I run everywhere after it.

Madelon. If you pursue merit you should not come to us.

Cathos. If you find merit amongst us, you must have brought it hither yourself.

Mascarille. Ah! I protest against these words. When fame mentioned your deserts it spoke the truth, and you are going to make *pic, repic,* and *capot* all the gallants from Paris.

Madelon. Your complaisance goes a little too far in the liberality of its praises, and my cousin and I must take care not to give too much credit to your sweet adulation.

Cathos. My dear, we should call for chairs.

Madelon. Almanzor!

Almanzor. Madam.

Madelon. Convey to us hither, instantly, the conveniences of conversation.

Mascarille. But am I safe here?

(*Exit* ALMANZOR.)

Cathos. What is it you fear?

Mascarille. Some larceny of my heart; some massacre of liberty. I behold here a pair of eyes that seem to be very naughty boys, that insult liberty, and use a heart most barbarously. Why the deuce do they put themselves on their guard, in order to kill any one who comes near them? Upon my word! I mistrust them; I shall either scamper away, or expect very good security that they do me no mischief.

Madelon. My dear, what a charming facetiousness he has!

Cathos. I see, indeed, he is an Amilcar.

Madelon. Fear nothing, our eyes have no wicked designs, and your heart may rest in peace, fully assured of their innocence.

Cathos. But, pray, Sir, be not inexorable to the easy chair, which, for this last quarter of an hour, has held

out its arms towards you; yield to its desire of embrac‚
ing you.

Mascarille (after having combed himself, and adjusted the rolls of his stockings). Well, ladies, and what do you think of Paris?

Madelon. Alas! what can we think of it? It would be the very antipodes of reason not to confess that Paris is the grand cabinet of marvels, the centre of good taste, wit, and gallantry.

Mascarille. As for me, I maintain that, out of Paris, there is no salvation for the polite world.

Cathos. Most assuredly.

Mascarille. Paris is somewhat muddy; but then we have sedan chairs.

Madelon. To be sure; a sedan chair is a wonderful protection against the insults of mud and bad weather.

Mascarille. I am sure you receive many visits. What great wit belongs to your company?

Madelon. Alas! we are not yet known, but we are in the way of being so; for a lady of our acquaintance has promised us to bring all the gentlemen who have written for the Miscellanies of Select Poetry.

Cathos. And certain others, whom, we have been told, are likewise the sovereign arbiters of all that is handsome.

Mascarille. I can manage this for you better than any one; they all visit me; and I may say that I never rise without having half-a-dozen wits at my levee.

Madelon. Good Heavens! you will place us under the greatest obligation if you will do us the kindness; for it is certain we must make the acquaintance of all those gentlemen if we wish to belong to the fashion. They are the persons who can make or unmake a reputation at Paris; you know that there are some, whose visits alone are sufficient to start the report that you are a *Connaisseuse*, though there should be no other reason for it. As for me, what I value particularly is, that by means of these ingenious visits, we learn a hundred things which we ought necessarily to know, and which are the quintessence of wit. Through them we hear the scandal of the day, or whatever niceties are going on in prose or verse. We know, at the right time, that Mr. So-and-so has written the finest piece in the world on such a subject; that Mrs. So-and-so has adapted words to such a tune; that a certain gentleman has written a madrigal upon a favour shown to him; another stanzas upon a fair one who betrayed him; Mr. Such-a-one wrote a couplet of six lines yesterday evening to Miss Such-a-one, to which she returned him an answer this morning at eight o'clock; such an author is engaged on such a subject; this writer is busy with the third volume of his novel; that one is putting his works to press. Those things procure you consideration in every society, and if people are ignorant of them, I would not give one pinch of snuff for all the wit they may have.

Cathos. Indeed, I think it the height of ridicule for any one who possesses the slightest claim to be called clever not to know even the smallest couplet that is made every day; as for me, I should be very much ashamed if any one should ask me my opinion about something new, and I had not seen it.

Mascarille. It is really a shame not to know from the very first all that is going on; but do not give yourself any farther trouble, I will establish an academy of wits at your house, and I give you my word that not a single line of poetry shall be written in Paris, but what you shall be able to say by heart before anybody else. As for me, such as you see me, I amuse myself in that way when I am in the humour, and you may find handed about in the fashionable assemblies of Paris two hundred songs, as many sonnets, four hundred epigrams, and more than a thousand madrigals all made by me, without counting riddles and portraits.

Madelon. I must acknowledge that I dote upon portraits; I think there is nothing more gallant.

Mascarille. Portraits are difficult, and call for great wit; you shall see some of mine that will not displease you.

Cathos. As for me, I am awfully fond of riddles.

Mascarille. They exercise the intelligence; I have already written four of them this morning, which I will give you to guess.

Madelon. Madrigals are pretty enough when they are neatly turned.

Mascarille. That is my special talent; I am at present engaged in turning the whole Roman history into madrigals.

Madelon. Goodness gracious! that will certainly be superlatively fine; I should like to have one copy at least, if you think of publishing it.

Mascarille. I promise you each a copy, bound in the handsomest manner. It does not become a man of my rank to scribble, but I do it only to serve the publishers, who are always bothering me.

Madelon. I fancy it must be a delightful thing to see one's self in print.

Mascarille. Undoubtedly; but, by the by, I must repeat to you some extempore verses I made yesterday at the house of a certain duchess, an acquaintance of mine. I am deuced clever at extempore verses.

Cathos. Extempore verses are certainly the very touchstone of genius.

Mascarille. Listen then.

Madelon. We are all ears.

Mascarille.   *Oh! oh! quite without heed was I,*
      As harmless you I chanced to spy,
         Slily your eyes
         My heart surprise.
    Stop thief! stop thief! stop thief I cry!

Cathos. Good Heavens! this is carried to the utmost pitch of gallantry.

Mascarille. Everything I do shows it is done by a gentleman; there is nothing of the pedant about my effusions.

Madelon. They are more than two thousand miles removed from that.

Mascarille. Did you observe the beginning, *oh! oh!*? There is something original in that *oh! oh!* like a man who all of a sudden thinks about something, *oh! oh!* Taken by surprise as it were, *oh! oh!*

Madelon. Yes, I think that *oh! oh!* admirable.

Mascarille. It seems a mere nothing.

Cathos. Good Heavens! How can you say so? It is one of these things that are perfectly invaluable.

Madelon. No doubt on it; I would rather have written that *oh! oh!* than an epic poem.

Mascarille. Egad, you have good taste.

Madelon. Tolerably; none of the worst, I believe.

Mascarille. But do you not also admire *quite without heed was I? quite without heed was I,* that is, I did not pay attention to anything; a natural way of speaking, *quite without heed was I, of no harm thinking,* that is, as I was going along, innocently, without malice, like a poor sheep, *you I chanced to spy,* that is to say, I amused myself with looking at you, with observing you, with contemplating you. *Slily your eyes.* . . . What do you think of that word *slily*—is it not well chosen?

Cathos. Extremely so.

Mascarille. Slily, stealthily; just like a cat watching a mouse—*slily.*

Madelon. Nothing can be better.

Mascarille. *My heart surprise,* that is, carries it away from me, robs me of it. *Stop thief! stop thief! stop thief!* Would you not think a man were shouting and running after a thief to catch him?   *Stop thief! stop thief! stop thief!*

Madelon. I must admit the turn is witty and sprightly.

Mascarille. I will sing you the tune I made to it.

Cathos. Have you learned music?

Mascarille. I? Not at all.

Cathos. How can you make a tune then?

Mascarille. People of rank know everything without ever having learned anything.

Madelon. His lordship is quite in the right, my dear.

Mascarille. Listen if you like the tune: *hem, hem, la, la.* The inclemency of the season has greatly injured the delicacy of my voice; but no matter, it is in a free and easy way. (*He sings: Oh! oh! quite without heed was I,* etc.)

Cathos. What a passion there breathes in this music. It is enough to make one expire with delight!

Madelon. There is something plaintive in it.

Mascarille. Do you not think that the air perfectly well expresses the sentiment, *Stop thief, stop thief!*? And then as if some one cried out very loud, *Stop, stop, stop, stop, stop, stop thief!* Then all at once like a person out of breath, *Stop thief!*

Madelon. This is to understand the perfection of things, the grand perfection, the perfection of perfections. I declare it is altogether a wonderful performance. I am quite enchanted with the air and the words.

Cathos. I never yet met with anything so excellent.

Mascarille. All that I do comes naturally to me; it is without study.

Madelon. Nature has treated you like a very fond mother; you are her spoiled child.   •

Mascarille. How do you pass away the time, ladies?

Cathos. With nothing at all.

Madelon. Until now we have lived in a terrible dearth of amusements.

Mascarille. I am at your service to attend you to the play, one of these days, if you will permit me. Indeed, a new comedy is to be acted which I should be very glad we might see together.

Madelon. There is no refusing you anything.

Mascarille. But I beg of you to applaud it well, when we are there; for I have promised to give a helping hand to the piece. The author called upon me this very morning to beg me so to do. It is the custom for authors to come and read their new plays to people of rank, that they may induce us to approve of them and give them a reputation. I leave you to imagine if, when we say anything, the pit dares contradict us. As for me, I am very punctual in these things, and when I have made a promise to a poet, I always cry out "Bravo" before the candles are lighted.

Madelon. Do not say another word; Paris is an admirable place. A hundred things happen every day which people in the country, however clever they may be, have no idea of.

Cathos. Since you have told us, we shall consider it our duty to cry up lustily every word that is said.

Mascarille. I do not know whether I am deceived, but you look as if you had written some play yourself.

Madelon. Eh! there may be something in what you say.

Mascarille. Ah! upon my word, we must see it. Between ourselves, I have written one which I intend to have brought out.

Cathos. Ay! to what company do you mean to give it?

Mascarille. That is a very nice question, indeed. To the actors of the hôtel de Bourgogne; they alone can bring things into good repute; the rest are ignorant creatures who recite their parts just as people speak in every-day life; they do not understand how to declaim the verses, or to pause at a beautiful passage; how can it be known where the fine lines are, if an actor does not stop at them, and thereby tell you to applaud heartily?

Cathos. Indeed! that is one way of making an audience feel the beauties of any work; things are only prized when they are well set off.

Mascarille. What do you think of my top-knot, sword-knot, and rosettes? Do you find them harmonize with my coat?

Cathos. Perfectly.

Mascarille. Do you think the ribbon well chosen?

Madelon. Furiously well. It is real Perdrigeon.

Mascarille. What do you say to my rolls?

Madelon. They look very fashionable.

Mascarille. I may at least boast that they are a quarter of a yard wider than any that have been made.

Madelon. I must own I never saw the elegance of dress carried farther.

Mascarille. Please to fasten the reflection of your smelling faculty upon these gloves.

Madelon. They smell awfully fine.

Cathos. I never inhaled a more delicious perfume.

Mascarille. And this? (*He gives them his powdered wig to smell*).

Madelon. It has the true quality odour; it titillates the nerves of the upper region most deliciously.

Mascarille. You say nothing of my feathers. How do you like them?

Cathos. Frightfully beautiful.

Mascarille. Do you know that every single one of them cost me a Louis-d'or? But it is my hobby to have generally everything of the very best.

Madelon. I assure you that you and I sympathize. I am furiously particular in everything I wear; I cannot endure even stockings, unless they are bought at a fashionable shop.

Mascarille (*crying out suddenly*). Oh! oh! oh! gently.

Damme, ladies, you use me very ill; I have reason to complain of your behaviour; it is not fair.

Cathos. What is the matter with you?

Mascarille. What! two at once against my heart! to attack me thus right and left! Ha! This is contrary to the law of nations, the combat is too unequal, and I must cry out, "Murder!"

Cathos. Well, he does say things in a peculiar way.

Madelon. He is a consummate wit.

Cathos. You are more afraid than hurt, and your heart cries out before it is even wounded.

Mascarille. The devil it does! it is wounded all over from head to foot.

SCENE X.—CATHOS, MADELON, MASCARILLE, MAROTTE.

Marotte. Madam, somebody asks to see you.

Madelon. Who!

Marotte. The Viscount de Jodelet.

Mascarille. The Viscount de Jodelet?

Marotte. Yes, sir.

Cathos. Do you know him?

Mascarille. He is my most intimate friend.

Madelon. Shew him in immediately.

Mascarille. We have not seen each other for some time; I am delighted to meet him.

Cathos. Here he comes.

SCENE XI.—CATHOS, MADELON, JODELET, MASCARILLE, MAROTTE, ALMANZOR.

Mascarille. Ah, Viscount!

Jodelet. Ah, Marquis!

   (*Embracing each other.*)

Mascarille. How glad I am to meet you!

Jodelet. How happy I am to see you here.

Mascarille. Embrace me once more, I pray you.

Madelon (*to* CATHOS). My dearest, we begin to be known; people of fashion find the way to our house.

Mascarille. Ladies, allow me to introduce this gentleman to you. Upon my word, he deserves the honour of your acquaintance.

Jodelet. It is but just we should come and pay you what we owe; your charms demand their lordly rights from all sorts of people.

Madelon. You carry your civilities to the utmost confines of flattery.

Cathos. This day ought to be marked in our diary as a red-letter day.

Madelon (*to* ALMANZOR). Come, boy, must you always be told things over and over again? Do you not observe there must be an additional chair?

Mascarille. You must not be astonished to see the Viscount thus; he has but just recovered from an illness, which, as you perceive, has made him so pale.

Jodelet. The consequence of continual attendance at court and the fatigues of war.

Mascarille. Do you know, ladies, that in the Viscount you behold one of the heroes of the age. He is a very valiant man.

Jodelet. Marquis, you are not inferior to me; we also know what you can do.

Mascarille. It is true we have seen one another at work when there was need for it.

Jodelet. And in places where it was hot.

Mascarille (*looking at* CATHOS *and* MADELON). Ay, but not so hot as here. Ha, ha, ha!

Jodelet. We became acquainted in the army; the first time we saw each other he commanded a regiment of horse aboard the galleys of Malta.

Mascarille. True, but for all that you were in the service before me; I remember that I was but a young officer when you commanded two thousand horse.

Jodelet.   War is a fine thing; but, upon my word, the court does not properly reward men of merit like us.

Mascarille.   That is the reason I intend to hang up my sword.

Cathos.   As for me, I have a tremendous liking for gentlemen of the army.

Madelon.   I love them, too; but I like bravery seasoned with wit.

Mascarille.   Do you remember, Viscount, our taking that half-moon from the enemy at the siege of Arras?

Jodelet.   What do you mean by a half-moon? It was a complete full moon.

Mascarille.   I believe you are right.

Jodelet.   Upon my word, I ought to remember it very well. I was wounded in the leg by a hand-grenade, of which I still carry the marks. Pray, feel it, you can perceive what sort of a wound it was.

Cathos (putting her hand to the place).   The scar is really large.

Mascarille.   Give me your hand for a moment, and feel this; there, just at the back of my head. Do you feel it?

Madelon.   Ay, I feel something.

Mascarille.   A musket shot which I received the last campaign I served in.

Jodelet (unbuttoning his breast).   Here is a wound which went quite through me at the attack of Gravelines.

Mascarille (putting his hand upon the button of his breeches).   I am going to show you a tremendous wound.

Madelon.   There is no occasion for it, we believe it without seeing it.

Mascarille.   They are honour's marks, that show what a man is made of.

Cathos.   We have not the least doubt of the valour of you both.

Mascarille. Viscount, is your coach in waiting?

Jodelet. Why?

Mascarille. We shall give these ladies an airing, and offer them a collation.

Madelon. We cannot go out to-day.

Mascarille. Let us send for musicians then, and have a dance.

Jodelet. Upon my word, that is a happy thought.

Madelon. With all our hearts, but we must have some additional company.

Mascarille. So ho! Champagne, Picard, Bourguignon, Cascaret, Basque, La Verdure, Lorrain, Provençal, La Violette. I wish the deuce took all these footmen! I do not think there is a gentleman in France worse served than I am! These rascals are always out of the way.

Madelon. Almanzor, tell the servants of my lord marquis to go and fetch the musicians, and ask some of the gentlemen and ladies hereabouts to come and people the solitude of our ball.

(*Exit* ALMANZOR.)

Mascarille. Viscount, what do you say of those eyes?

Jodelet. Why, Marquis, what do you think of them yourself?

Mascarille. I? I say that our liberty will have much difficulty to get away from here scot free. At least mine has suffered most violent attacks; my heart hangs by a single thread.

Madelon. How natural is all he says! He gives to things a most agreeable turn.

Cathos. He must really spend a tremendous deal of wit.

Mascarille. To show you that I am in earnest, I shall make some extempore verses upon my passion. (*Seems to think.*)

Cathos. Oh! I beseech you by all that I hold sacred, let us hear something made upon us.

Jodelet. I should be glad to do so too, but the quantity of blood that has been taken from me lately, has greatly exhausted my poetic vein.

Mascarille. Deuce take it! I always make the first verse well, but I find the others more difficult. Upon my word, this is too short a time; but I will make you some extempore verses at my leisure, which you shall think the finest in the world.

Jodelet. He is devilish witty.

Madelon. He—his wit is so gallant and well expressed.

Mascarille. Viscount, tell me, when did you see the Countess last?

Jodelet. I have not paid her a visit these three weeks.

Mascarille. Do you know that the duke came to see me this morning; he would fain have taken me into the country to hunt a stag with him?

Madelon. Here come our friends.

Scene XII.—Lucile, Célimène, Cathos, Madelon, Mascarille, Jodelet, Marotte, Almanzor, and Musicians.

Madelon. Lawk! my dears, we beg your pardon. These gentlemen had a fancy to put life into our heels; we sent for you to fill up the void of our assembly.

Lucile. We are certainly much obliged to you for doing so.

Mascarille. This is a kind of extempore ball, ladies, but one of these days we shall give you one in form. Have the musicians come?

Almanzor. Yes, sir, they are here.

Cathos. Come then, my dears, take your places.

Mascarille (*dancing by himself and singing*). La, la, la, la, la, la, la, la.

Madelon. What a very elegant shape he has.

Cathos. He looks as if he were a first-rate dancer.

Mascarille (*taking out* MADELON *to dance*). My free-dom will dance a Couranto as well as my feet. Play in time, musicians, in time. Oh, what ignorant wretches! There is no dancing with them. The devil take you all, can you not play in time? La, la, la, la, la, la, la, la? Steady, you country-scrapers!

Jodelet (*dancing also*). Hold, do not play so fast. I have but just recovered from an illness.

SCENE XIII.—DU CROISY, LA GRANGE, CATHOS, MADE-LON, LUCILE, CÉLIMÈNE, JODELET, MASCARILLE, MAROTTE. AND MUSICIANS.

La Grange (*with a stick in his hand*). Ah! ah! scoun-drels, what are you doing here? We have been looking for you these three hours. (*He beats* MASCARILLE.)

Mascarille. Oh! oh! oh! you did not tell me that blows should be dealt about.

Jodelet (*who is also beaten*). Oh! oh! oh!

La Grange. It becomes you well, you rascal, to pre-tend to be a man of rank.

Du Croisy. This will teach you to know yourself.

SCENE XIV.—CATHOS, MADELON, LUCILE, CÉLIMÈNE MASCARILLE, JODELET, MAROTTE, AND MUSICIANS

Madelon. What is the meaning of this?

Jodelet. It is a wager.

Cathos. What, allow yourselves to be beaten thus?

Mascarille. Good Heavens! I did not wish to appear to take any notice of it; because I am naturally very violent, and should have flown into a passion.

Madelon. To suffer an insult like this in our pres-ence!

Mascarille. It is nothing. Let us not leave off. We have known one another for a long time, and among friends one ought not to be so quickly offended for such a trifle.

SCENE XV.—DU CROISY, LA GRANGE, MADELON, CATHOS, LUCILE, CÉLIMÈNE, MASCARILLE, JODELET, MAROTTE, AND MUSICIANS.

La Grange. Upon my word, rascals, you shall not laugh at us, I promise you. Come in, you there. (*Three or four men enter.*)

Madelon. What means this impudence to come and disturb us in our own house?

Du Croisy. What, ladies, shall we allow our footmen to be received better than ourselves? Shall they come to make love to you at our expense, and even give a ball in your honour?

Madelon. Your footmen?

La Grange. Yes, our footmen; and you must give me leave to say that it is not acting either handsome or honest to spoil them for us, as you do.

Madelon. O Heaven! what insolence!

La Grange. But they shall not have the advantage of our clothes to dazzle your eyes. Upon my word, if you are resolved to like them, it shall be for their handsome looks only. Quick, let them be stripped immediately.

Jodelet. Farewell, a long farewell to all our fine clothes.

Mascarille. The marquisate and viscountship are at an end.

Du Croisy. Ah! ah! you knaves, you have the impudence to become our rivals. I assure you, you must go somewhere else to borrow finery to make yourselves agreeable to your mistresses.

La Grange. It is too much to supplant us, and that with our own clothes.

Mascarille. O fortune, how fickle you are!

Du Croisy. Quick, pull everything off them.

La Grange. Make haste and take away all these clothes. Now, ladies, in their present condition you may continue your amours with them as long as you please; we leave you perfectly free; this gentleman and I declare solemnly that we shall not be in the least degree jealous.

SCENE XVI.—MADELON, CATHOS, JODELET, MASCA-
RILLE, AND MUSICIANS.

Cathos. What a confusion!

Madelon. I am nearly bursting with vexation.

First Musician (*to* MASCARILLE). What is the meaning of this? Who is to pay us?

Mascarille. Ask my lord the viscount.

First Musician (*to* JODELET). Who is to give us our money?

Jodelet. Ask my lord the marquis.

SCENE XVII.—GORGIBUS, MADELON, CATHOS, JODELET
MASCARILLE, AND MUSICIANS.

Gorgibus. Ah! you hussies, you have put us in a nice pickle, by what I can see; I have heard about your fine goings on from those two gentlemen who just left.

Madelon. Ah, father! they have played us a cruel trick.

Gorgibus. Yes, it is a cruel trick, but you may thank your own impertinence for it, you jades. They have revenged themselves for the way you treated them; and yet, unhappy man that I am, I must put up with the affront.

Madelon. Ah! I swear we will be revenged, or I shall die in the attempt. And you, rascals, dare you remain here after your insolence?

Mascarille. Do you treat a marquis in this manner? This is the way of the world; the least misfortune causes us to be slighted by those who before caressed us. Come along, brother, let us go and seek our fortune somewhere else; I preceive they love nothing here but outward show, and have no regard for worth unadorned. (*They both leave.*)

SCENE XVIII.—GORGIBUS, MADELON, CATHOS, AND MUSICIANS.

First Musician. Sir, as they have not paid us, we expect you to do so, for it was in this house we played.

Gorgibus (*beating them*). Yes, yes, I shall satisfy you; this is the coin I will pay you in. As for you, you sluts, I do not know why I should not serve you in the same way; we shall become the common talk and laughing-stock of everybody; this is what you have brought upon yourselves by your fooleries. Out of my sight and hide yourselves, you jades; go and hide yourselves forever. (*Alone.*) And you, that are the cause of their folly, you stupid trash, mischievous amusements for idle minds, you novels, verses, songs, sonnets, and sonatas, the devil take you all.

THE SCHOOL FOR WIVES

THE SCHOOL FOR WIVES

(L'ÉCOLE DES FEMMES)

DRAMATIS PERSONÆ

ARNOLPHE, *alias* M. DE LA SOUCHE.
CHRYSALDE, *friend to Arnolphe.*
HORACE, *in love with Agnès.*
ENRIQUE, *brother-in-law of Chrysalde.*
ORONTE, *father to Horace and a great friend of Arnolphe.*
ALAIN, *a country fellow, servant to Arnolphe.*
A NOTARY.
AGNÈS, *a young innocent girl, brought up by Arnolphe.*
GEORGETTE, *a country-woman, servant to Arnolphe.*

Scene.—A SQUARE IN A TOWN

ACT I

SCENE I.—CHRYSALDE, ARNOLPHE.

Chrysalde. You have come to marry her, you say?

Arnolphe. Yes, I mean to settle the business to-morrow.

Chrysalde. We are here alone, and I think we can speak together without fear of being overheard. Do you wish me to open my heart to you like a friend? Your plan makes me tremble with fear for you. To take a wife is a rash step for you, whichever way you consider the matter.

Arnolphe. True, my friend. Possibly you find in your own home reasons why you should fear for me. I fancy that your own forehead shows that horns are everywhere the infallible accompaniment of marriage.

Chrysalde. These are accidents against which we cannot insure ourselves; it seems to me that the trouble people take about this is very ridiculous. But when I fear for you, it is on account of this raillery of which a hundred poor husbands have felt the sting. For you know that neither great nor small have been safe from your criticism; that your greatest pleasure, wherever you are, is to make a mighty outcry about secret intrigues . . .

Arnolphe. Exactly. Is there another city in the world where husbands are so patient as here? Do we not meet with them in every variety, and well provided with everything? One heaps up wealth, which his wife shares with those who are eager to make him a dupe; another, slightly more fortunate, but not less infamous, sees his wife receive presents day after day, and is not troubled in mind by any jealous twinge when she tells him that they are the rewards of virtue. One makes a great noise, which does him not the slightest good; another lets matters take their course in all meekness, and, seeing the gallant arrive at his house, very politely takes up his gloves and his cloak. One married woman cunningly pretends to make a confidant of her confiding husband, who slumbers securely under such a delusion, and pities the gallant for his pains, which, however, the latter does not throw away. Another married woman, to account for her extravagance, says that the money she spends has been won at play; and the silly husband, without considering at what play, thanks Heaven for her winnings. In short, we find subjects for satire everywhere, and may I, as a spectator, not laugh at them? Are not these fools . . .

Chrysalde. Yes; but he who laughs at another must beware, lest he in turn be laughed at himself. I hear what is said, and how some folks delight in retailing what goes on; but no one has seen me exult at reports, which are bruited about in the places I frequent. I am rather reserved in this respect; and, though I might condemn a certain toleration of these matters, and am resolved by no means to suffer quietly what some husbands endure, yet I have never affected to say so; for, after all, satire may fall upon ourselves, and we should never vow in such cases what we should or should not do. Thus, if by an overruling fate, some natural disgrace should ever happen to my brow, I am almost sure, after the way in which I have acted, that people would be content to laugh at it in their sleeve; and possibly, in addition, I may reap this advantage, that a few good fellows will say "What a pity!" But with you, my dear friend, it is otherwise. I tell you again you are running a plaguy risk. As your tongue has always persistently bantered husbands accused of being tolerant; as you have shown yourself like a demon let loose upon them, you must walk straight for fear of being made a laughing-stock; and, if it happens that they get the least pretext, take care they do not publish your disgrace at the public market-cross, and . . .

Arnolphe. Good Heaven, friend, do not trouble yourself. He will be a clever man who catches me in this way. I know all the cunning tricks and subtle devices which women use to deceive us, and how one is fooled by their dexterity, and I have taken precautions against this mischance. She whom I am marrying possesses all the innocence which may protect my forehead from evil influence.

Chrysalde. Why, what do you imagine? That a silly girl, to be brief . . .

Arnolphe. To marry a silly girl is not to become silly myself. I believe, as a good Christian, that your better half is very wise; but a clever wife is ominous, and I know what some people have to pay for choosing theirs with too much talent. What, I go and saddle myself with an intellectual woman, who talks of nothing but of her assembly and *ruelle;* who writes tender things in prose and in verse, and is visited by Marquises and wits, whilst, as "Mrs. So-and-so's husband," I should be like a saint, whom no one calls upon! No, no, I will have none of your lofty minds. A woman who writes knows more than she ought to do. I intend that my wife shall not even be clever enough to know what a rhyme is. If one plays at *corbillon* with her, and asks her in her turn "What is put into the basket," I will have her answer, "A cream tart." In a word, let her be very ignorant; and to tell you the plain truth, it is enough for her that she can say her prayers, love me, sew and spin.

Chrysalde. A stupid wife, then, is your fancy?

Arnolphe. So much so that I should prefer a very stupid and ugly woman to a very beautiful one with a great deal of wit.

Chrysalde. Wit and beauty . . .

Arnolphe. Virtue is quite enough.

Chrysalde. But how can you expect, after all, that a mere simpleton can ever know what it is to be virtuous? Besides, to my mind, it must be very wearisome for a man to have a stupid creature perpetually with him. Do you think you act rightly, and that, by reliance on your plan, a man's brow is saved from danger? A woman of sense may fail in her duty; but she must at least do so knowingly; a stupid woman may at any time fail in hers, without desiring or thinking of it.

Arnolphe. To this fine argument, this deep discourse, I reply as Pantagruel did to Panurge: Urge me to marry any other woman than a stupid one; preach and lecture till Whitsuntide, you shall be amazed to find, when you have done, that you have not persuaded me in the very slightest.

Chrysalde. I do not want to say another word.

Arnolphe. Every man has his own way. With my wife, as in everything, I mean to follow my fashion. I think I am rich enough to take a partner who shall owe all to me, and whose humble station and complete dependence cannot reproach me either with her poverty or her birth. A sweet and staid look made me love Agnès, amongst other children, when she was only four. It came into my mind to ask her from her mother, who was very poor; the good country-woman, learning my wish, was delighted to rid herself of the charge. I had her brought up, according to my own notions, in a little solitary convent; that is to say, directing them what means to adopt in order to make her as idiotic as possible. Thank Heaven, success has crowned my efforts; and I am very thankful to say, I have found her so innocent that I have blessed Heaven for having done what I wished, in giving me a wife according to my desire. Then I brought her away; and as my house is continually open to a hundred different people, and as we must be on our guard against everything, I have kept her in another house where no one comes to see me; and where her good disposition cannot be spoiled, as she meets none but people as simple as herself. You will say, "Wherefore this long story?" It is to let you see the care I have taken. To crown all, and as you are a trusty friend, I ask you to sup with her to-night. I wish you would examine her a little, and see if I am to be condemned for my choice.

Chrysalde. With all my heart.

Arnolphe. You can judge of her looks and her innocence when you converse with her.

Chrysalde. As to that, what you have told me cannot . . .

Arnolphe. What I have told you falls even short of the truth: I admire her simplicity on all occasions; sometimes she says things at which I split my sides with laughing. The other day—would you believe it?—she was uneasy, and came to ask me, with unexampled innocence, if children came through the ears.

Chrysalde. I greatly rejoice, M. Arnolphe . . .

Arnolphe. What! will you always call me by that name?

Chrysalde. Ah, it comes to my lips in spite of me; I never remember M. de la Souche. Who on earth has put it into your head to change your name at forty-two years of age, and give yourself a title from a rotten old tree on your farm?

Arnolphe. Besides the fact that the house is known by that name, la Souche pleases my ear better than Arnolphe.

Chrysalde. What a pity to give up the genuine name of one's fathers, and take one based on chimeras! Most people have an itching that way, and, without including you in the comparison, I knew a country-fellow called Gros-Pierre, who, having no other property but a rood of land, had a muddy ditch made all around it, and took the high-sounding name of M. de l'Isle.

Arnolphe. You might dispense with such examples. But, at all events, de la Souche is the name I bear. I have a reason for it, I like it; and to call me otherwise is to annoy me.

Chrysalde. Most people find it hard to fall in with it; I even yet see letters addressed . . .

Arnolphe. I endure it easily from those who are not informed; but you . . .

Chrysalde. Be it so; we will make no difficulty about that; I will take care to accustom my lips to call you nothing else than M. de la Souche.

Arnolphe. Farewell. I am going to knock here, to wish them good morning, and simply to say that I have come back.

Chrysalde (*aside*). Upon my word, I think he is a perfect fool.

Arnolphe (*alone*). He is a little touched on certain points. Strange, to see how each man is passionately fond of his own opinion. (*Knocks at his door.*) Hulloa!

SCENE II.—ARNOLPHE, ALAIN, GEORGETTE, *within*.

Alain.—Who knocks?

Arnolphe. Open the door! (*Aside.*) I think they will be very glad to see me after ten days' absence.

Alain. Who is there?

Arnolphe. I.

Alain. Georgette!

Georgette. Well!

Alain. Open the door there!

Georgette. Go, and do it yourself!

Alain. You go and do it!

Georgette. Indeed, I shall not go.

Alain. No more shall I.

Arnolphe. Fine compliments, while I am left without. Hulloa! Here, please.

Georgette. Who knocks?

Arnolphe. Your master.

Georgette. Alain!

Alain. What!

Georgette. It is the master. Open the door quickly.

Alain. Open it yourself.

Georgette. I am blowing the fire.

Alain. I am taking care that the sparrow does not go out, for fear of the cat.

Arnolphe. Whoever of you two does not open the door shall have no food for four days. Ah!

Georgette. Why do you come when I was running?

Alain. Why should you more than I? A pretty trick indeed!

Georgette. Stand out of the way.

Alain. Stand out of the way yourself.

Georgette. I wish to open the door.

Alain. And so do I.

Georgette. You shall not.

Alain. No more shall you.

Georgette. Nor you.

Arnolphe. I need have patience here.

Alain (entering). There; it is I, master.

Georgette (entering). Your servant; it is I.

Alain. If it were not out of respect for master here, I . . .

Arnolphe (receiving a push from ALAIN). Hang it!

Alain. Pardon me.

Arnolphe. Look at the lout!

Alain. It was she also, master . . .

Arnolphe. Hold your tongues, both of you. Just answer me and let us have no more fooling. Well, Alain, how is every one here?

Alain. Master, we . . . (ARNOLPHE *takes off* ALAIN'S *hat.*) Master, we . . . (ARNOLPHE *takes it off again.*) Thank Heaven, we . . .

Arnolphe (taking off the hat a third time and flinging it on the ground). Who taught you, impertinent fool, to speak to me with your hat on your head?

Alain. You are right; I am wrong.

Arnolphe (to ALAIN). Ask Agnès to come down.

SCENE III.—ARNOLPHE, GEORGETTE.

Arnolphe. Was she sad after I went away?

Georgette. Sad? No.

Arnolphe. No?

Georgette. Yes, yes.

Arnolphe. Why, then?

Georgette. May I die on the spot, but she expected to see you return every minute; and we never heard a horse, an ass, or a mule pass by without her thinking it was you.

SCENE IV.—ARNOLPHE, AGNÈS, ALAIN, GEORGETTE.

Arnolphe. Work in hand? That is a good sign. Well, Agnès, I have returned. Are you glad of it?

Agnès. Yes, sir, Heaven be thanked.

Arnolphe. I too am glad to see you again. You have always been well? I see you have.

Agnès. Except for the fleas, which troubled me in the night.

Arnolphe. Ah, you shall soon have some one to drive them away.

Agnès. I shall be pleased with that.

Arnolphe. I can easily imagine it. What are you doing there?

Agnès. I am making myself some caps. Your night-shirts and caps are finished.

Arnolphe. Ah, that is all right. Well, go up stairs. Do not tire yourself. I will soon return, and talk to you of important matters.

SCENE V.—ARNOLPHE, *alone.*

Heroines of the day, learned ladies, who spout tender and fine sentiments, I defy in a breath all your verses, your novels, your letters, your love-letters, your entire science, to be worth as much as this virtuous and modest ignorance. We must not be dazzled by riches; and so long as honour is . . .

SCENE VI.—HORACE, ARNOLPHE.

Arnolphe. What do I see? Is it . . . Yes. I am mistaken. But no. No; it is himself. Hor . . .

Horace. Mr. Arn . . .

Arnolphe. Horace.

Horace. Arnolphe.

Arnolphe. Ah! what joy indeed! And how long have you been here?

Horace. Nine days.

Arnolphe. Really.

Horace. I went straight to your house, but in vain.

Arnolphe. I was in the country.

Horace. Yes, you had been gone ten days.

Arnolphe. Oh, how these children spring up in a few years! I am amazed to see him so tall, after having known him no higher than that.

Horace. You see how it is.

Arnolphe. But tell me how is Oronte, your father, my good and dear friend, whom I esteem and revere? What is he doing? What is he saying? Is he still hearty? He knows I am interested in all that affects him; we have not seen one another these four years, nor, what is more, written to each other, I think.

Horace. M. Arnolphe, he is even more cheerful than we; I had a letter from him for you. But he has since informed me in another letter, that he is coming here, though as yet I do not know the reason for it. Can you tell me which of your townsmen has returned with abundance of wealth earned during a fourteen years' residence in America?

Arnolphe. No. Have you not heard his name?

Horace. Enrique.

Arnolphe. No.

Horace. My father speaks of him and his return, as though he should be well known to me; he writes that they are about to set out together, on an affair of consequence, of which his letter says nothing. (*Gives* ORONTE'S *letter to* ARNOLPHE.)

Arnolphe. I shall assuredly be very glad to see him, and shall do my best to entertain him. (*After reading the letter.*) Friends do not need to send such polite letters, and all these compliments are unnecessary. Even if he had not taken the trouble to write one word, you might have freely disposed of all I have.

Horace. I am a man who takes people at their word; and I have present need of a hundred pistoles.

Arnolphe. Upon my word, you oblige me by using

me thus. I rejoice that I have them with me. Keep the purse too.

Horace. I must . . .

Arnolphe. Drop this ceremony. Well, how do you like this town so far?

Horace. Its inhabitants are numerous, its buildings splendid, and I should think that its amusements are wonderful.

Arnolphe. Everyone has his own pleasures, after his own fashion; but for those whom we christen our gallants, they have in this town just what pleases them, for the women are born flirts. Dark and fair are amiably disposed, and the husbands also are the most kind in the world. It is a pleasure fit for a King; to me it is a mere comedy to see the pranks I do. Perhaps you have already smitten some one. Have you had no adventure yet? Men of your figure can do more than men who have money, and you are cut out to make a cuckold.

Horace. Not to deceive you as to the simple truth, I have had a certain love-passage in these parts, and friendship compels me to tell you of it.

Arnolphe (*aside*). Good. Here is another queer story to set down in my pocket-book.

Horace. But pray, let these things be secret.

Arnolphe. Oh!

Horace. You know that in these matters a secret divulged destroys our expectations. I will then frankly confess to you that my heart has been smitten in this place by a certain fair maid. My little attentions were at once so successful that I obtained a pleasant introduction to her; not to boast too much, nor to do her an injustice, affairs go very well with me.

Arnolphe (*laughing*). Ha! ha! And she is . . .

Horace (*pointing to the house of* Agnès). A young creature living in yonder house, of which you can see the red walls from this. Simple, of a truth, through the

matchless folly of a man who hides her from all the world;
but who, amidst the ignorance in which he would enslave
her, discloses charms that throw one into raptures, as
well as a thoroughly engaging manner, and something
indescribably tender, against which no heart is proof.
But perhaps you have seen this young star of love,
adorned by so many charms. Agnès is her name.

Arnolphe (*aside*). Oh, I shall burst with rage!

Horace. As for the man, I think his name is De la
Zousse, or Souche; I did not much concern myself about
the name. He is rich, by what they told me, but not
one of the wisest of men; they say he is a ridiculous
fellow. Do you not know him?

Arnolphe (*aside*). It is a bitter pill I have to swallow!

Horace. Why, you do not speak a word.

Arnolphe. Oh, yes . . . I know him

Horace. He is a fool, is he not?

Arnolphe. Ugh!

Horace. What do you say? Ugh!—that means yes?
Jealous, I suppose, ridiculously so? Stupid? I see he
is just as they told me. To be brief, the lovely Agnès
has succeeded in enslaving me. She is a pretty jewel, to
tell you honestly; it would be a sin if such a rare beauty
were left in the power of this eccentric fellow. For me,
all my efforts, all my dearest wishes, are to make her
mine in spite of this jealous wretch; and the money
which I so freely borrow of you. was only to bring this
laudable enterprise to a conclusion. You know better
than I, that, whatever we undertake, money is the master-
key to all great plans, and that this sweet metal, which
distracts so many, promotes our triumphs, in love as
in war. You seem vexed? Can it be that you dis-
approve of my design?

Arnolphe. No; but I was thinking . . .

Horace. This conversation wearies you? Farewell.
I will soon pay you a visit to return thanks.

Arnolphe (*thinking himself alone*). What! must it . . .

Horace (*returning*). Once again, pray be discreet; do not go and spread my secret abroad.

Arnolphe (*thinking himself alone*). I feel within my soul . . .

Horace (*returning again*). And above all to my father, who would perhaps get enraged, if he knew of it.

Arnolphe (*expecting* HORACE *to return again*). Oh! . . .

SCENE VII.—ARNOLPHE, *alone.*

Oh, what I have endured during this conversation! Never was trouble of mind equal to mine! With what rashness and extreme haste did he come to tell me of this affair! Though my second name keeps him at fault, did ever any blunderer run on so furiously? But, having endured so much, I ought to have refrained until I had learned that which I have reason to fear, to have drawn out his foolish chattering to the end, and ascertained their secret understanding completely. Let me try to overtake him; I fancy he is not far off. Let me worm from him the whole mystery. I tremble for the misfortune which may befall me; for we often seek more than we wish to find.

ACT II

SCENE I.—ARNOLPHE, *alone.*

It is no doubt well, when I think of it, that I have lost my way, and failed to find him; for after all, I should not have been able entirely to conceal from his eyes the overwhelming pang of my heart. The grief that preys upon me would have broken forth, and I do not wish him to know what he is at present ignorant of. But I am not the man to put up with this, and leave a free field for this young spark to pursue his design. I am resolved to check his progress, and learn, without delay, how far they understand each other. My honour is specially involved in this. I regard her already as my wife. She cannot have made a slip without covering me with shame; and whatever she does will be placed to my account. Fatal absence! Unfortunate voyage! (*Knocks at his door.*)

SCENE II.—ARNOLPHE, ALAIN, GEORGETTE.

Alain. Ah, master, this time . . .

Arnolphe. Peace. Come here, both of you. That way, that way. Come along, come, I tell you.

Georgette. Ah, you frighten me; all my blood runs cold.

Arnolphe. Is it thus you have obeyed me in my absence? You have both combined to betray me!

Georgette (falling at ARNOLPHE's *feet*). Oh, master, do not eat me, I implore you.

Alain (aside). I am sure some mad dog has bitten him.

Arnolphe (aside). Ugh, I cannot speak, I am so filled with rage. I am choking, and should like to throw off

58

my clothes . . . (*to* ALAIN *and* GEORGETTE). You cursed
scoundrels, you have permitted a man to come . . . (*to*
ALAIN, *who tries to escape*). You would run away,
would you! You must this instant . . . (*to* GEORGETTE).
If you move. . . . Now I wish you to tell me . . . (*to*
ALAIN). Hi! . . . Yes, I wish you both . . . (ALAIN
and GEORGETTE *rise, and again try to escape*) . . .
Whoever of you moves, upon my word, I shall knock
him down. How came that man into my house? Now
speak. Make haste, quick, directly, instantly, no thinking! Will you speak?

Both. Oh, oh!

Georgette (*falling at his knees*). My heart fails me!

Alain (*falling at his knees*). I am dying.

Arnolphe (*aside*). I perspire all over. Let me take
a breath. I must fan myself, and walk about. Could I
believe, when I saw Horace as a little boy, that he would
grow up for this? Heaven, how I suffer! I think it
would be better that I should gently draw from Agnès'
own mouth an account of what touches me so. Let me
try to moderate my anger. Patience, my heart; softly,
softly. (*To* ALAIN *and* GEORGETTE.) Rise, go in, and
bid Agnès come to me. . . . Stay, her surprise would be
less. They will go and tell her how uneasy I am. I will
go myself and bring her out. (*To* ALAIN *and* GEOR-
GETTE.) Wait for me here.

SCENE III.—ALAIN, GEORGETTE.

Georgette. Heavens, how terrible he is! His looks
made me afraid—horribly afraid. Never did I see a
more hideous Christian.

Alain. This gentleman has vexed him; I told you so.

Georgette. But what on earth is the reason that he
so strictly makes us keep our mistress in the house?
Why does he wish to hide her from all the world, and
cannot bear to see any one approach her?

Alain. Because that makes him jealous.

Georgette. But how has he got such a fancy in his head?

Alain. Because . . . because he is jealous.

Georgette. Yes; but wherefore is he so? and why this anger?

Alain. Because jealousy . . . understand me, Georgette, jealousy is a thing . . . a thing . . . which makes people uneasy . . . and which drives folk all round the house. I am going to give you an example, so that you may understand the thing better. Tell me, is it not true that, when you have your broth in your hand, and some hungry person comes up to eat it, you would be in a rage, and be ready to beat him?

Georgette. Yes, I understand that.

Alain. It is just the same. Woman is in fact the broth of man; and when a man sees other folks sometimes, trying to dip their fingers in his broth, he soon displays extreme anger at it.

Georgette. Yes; but why does not every one do the same? Why do we see some who appear to be pleased when their wives are with handsome fine gentlemen?

Alain. Because every one has not the greedy love which will give nothing away.

Georgette. If I am not blind, I see him returning.

Alain. Your eyes are good; it is he.

Georgette. See how vexed he is.

Alain. That is because he is in trouble.

SCENE IV.—ARNOLPHE, ALAIN, GEORGETTE.

Arnolphe (*aside*). A certain Greek told the Emperor Augustus, as an axiom as useful as it was true, that when any accident puts us in a rage, we should, first of all, repeat the alphabet; so that in the interval our anger may abate, and we may do nothing that we ought not to do. I have followed his advice in the matter of Agnès; and I have brought her here designedly, under pretence of taking a walk, so that the suspicions of my disordered mind may cunningly lead her to the topic, and, by sounding her heart, gently find out the truth.

SCENE V.—ARNOLPHE, AGNÈS, ALAIN, GEORGETTE.

Arnolphe. Come, Agnès. (*To* ALAIN *and* GEORGETTE.) Get you in.

SCENE VI.—ARNOLPHE, AGNÈS.

Arnolphe. This is a nice walk.

Agnès. Very nice.

Arnolphe. What a fine day.

Agnès. Very fine.

Arnolphe. What news?

Agnès. The kitten is dead.

Arnolphe. Pity! But what then? We are all mortal, and every one is for himself. Did it rain when I was in the country?

Agnès. No.

Arnolphe. Were you not wearied?

Agnès. I am never wearied.

Arnolphe. What did you do then, these nine or ten days?

Agnès. Six shirts, I think, and six nightcaps also.

Arnolphe (*after musing*). The world, dear Agnès, is a strange place. Observe the scandal, and how everybody gossips. Some of the neighbours have told me that an unknown young man came to the house in my absence; that you permitted him to see and talk to you. But I did not believe these slandering tongues, and I offered to bet that it was false . . .

Agnès. Oh, Heaven, do not bet; you would assuredly lose.

Arnolphe. What! It is true that a man . . .

Agnès. Quite true. I declare to you that he was scarcely ever out of the house.

Arnolphe (*aside*). This confession, so candidly made, at least assures me of her simplicity. (*Aloud.*) But I think, Agnès, if my memory is clear, that I forbade you to see any one.

Agnès. Yes; but you do not know why I saw him; you would doubtless have done as much.

Arnolphe. Possibly; but tell me then how it was.

Agnès. It is very wonderful, and hard to believe. I was on the balcony, working in the open air, when I saw a handsome young man passing close to me under the trees, who, seeing me look at him, immediately bowed very respectfully. I, not to be rude, made him a curtsey. Suddenly he made another bow; I quickly made another curtsey; and when he repeated it for the third time, I answered it directly with a third curtsey. He went on, returned, went past again, and each time made me another bow. And I, who was looking earnestly at all these acts of politeness, returned him as many curtseys; so that if night had not fallen just then, I should have kept on continually in that way; not wishing to yield, and have the vexation of his thinking me less civil than himself.

Arnolphe. Very good.

Agnès. Next day, being at the door, an old woman accosted me, and said to me something like this: "My child, may good Heaven bless you, and keep you long in all your beauty. It did not make you such a lovely creature to abuse its gifts; you must know that you have wounded a heart which to-day is driven to complain."

Arnolphe (*aside*). Oh, tool of Satan! damnable wretch!

Agnès. "Have I wounded any one?" I answered, quite astonished. "Yes," she said, "wounded; you have indeed wounded a gentleman. It is him you saw yesterday from the balcony." "Alas!" said I, "what could have been the cause? Did I, without thinking,

let anything fall on him?" "No," replied she; "it was
your eyes which gave the fatal blow; from their glances
came all his injury." "Alas! good Heaven," said I, "I
am more than ever surprised. Do my eyes contain
something bad, that they can give it to other people?"
"Yes," cried she, "your eyes, my girl, have a poison to
hurt withal, of which you know nothing. In a word, the
poor fellow pines away; and if," continued the charitable
old woman, "your cruelty refuses him assistance, it is
likely he shall be carried to his grave in a couple of
days." "Bless me!" said I, "I would be very sorry for
that; but what assistance does he require of me?" "My
child," said she, "he requests only the happiness of seeing and conversing with you. Your eyes alone can prevent his ruin, and cure the disease they have caused."
"Oh! gladly," said I; "and, since it is so, he may come
to see me here as often as he likes."

Arnolphe (*aside*). O cursed witch! poisoner of souls!
may hell reward your charitable tricks!

Agnès. That is how he came to see me, and got
cured. Now tell me, frankly, if I was not right? And
could I, after all, have the conscience to let him die for
lack of aid?—I, who feel so much pity for suffering
people, and cannot see a chicken die without weeping!

Arnolphe (*aside*). All this comes only from an innocent soul; I blame my imprudent absence for it, which
left this kindliness of heart without a protector, exposed
to the wiles of artful seducers. I fear that the rascal,
in his bold passion, has carried the matter somewhat
beyond a joke.

Agnès. What ails you? I think you are a little angry.
Was there anything wrong in what I have told you?

Arnolphe. No. But tell me what followed, and how
the young man behaved during his visits.

Agnès. Alas! if you but knew how delightful he was;
how he got rid of his illness as soon as I saw him, the

present he made me of a lovely casket, and the money which Alain and Georgette have had from him, you would no doubt love him, and say, as we say . . .

Arnolphe. Yes. But what did he do when he was alone with you?

Agnès. He swore that he loved me with an unequalled passion, and said the prettiest words possible, things that nothing ever can equal, the sweetness of which charms me whenever I hear him speak, and moves I know not what within me.

Arnolphe (aside). Oh! sad inquiry into a fatal mystery, in which the inquirer alone suffers all the pain. *(Aloud.)* Besides all these speeches, all these pretty compliments, did he not also bestow a few caresses on you?

Agnès. Oh, so many! He took my hands and my arms, and was never tired of kissing them.

Arnolphe. Agnès, did he take nothing else from you? *(Seeing her confused.)* Ugh!

Agnès. Why, he . . .

Arnolphe. What?

Agnès. Took . . .

Arnolphe. Ugh!

Agnès. The . . .

Arnolphe. Well?

Agnès. I dare not tell you; you will perhaps be angry with me.

Arnolphe. No.

Agnès. Yes, but you will.

Arnolphe. Good Heavens! no.

Agnès. Swear on your word.

Arnolphe. On my word, then.

Agnès. He took my . . . You will be in a passion.

Arnolphe. No.

Agnès. Yes.

Arnolphe. No, no, no, no! What the devil is this mystery? What did he take from you?

Agnès. He . . .

Arnolphe (aside). I am suffering the torments of the damned.

Agnès. He took away from me the ribbon you gave me. To tell you the truth, I could not prevent him.

Arnolphe (drawing his breath). Oh! let the ribbon go. But I want to know if he did nothing to you but kiss your arms.

Agnès. Why! do people do other things?

Arnolphe. Not at all. But, to cure the disorder which he said had seized him, did he not ask you for any other remedy?

Agnès. No. You may judge that I would have granted him anything to do him good, if he had asked for it.

Arnolphe (aside). By the kindness of Heaven, I am cheaply out of it! May I be blessed if I fall into such a mistake again! *(Aloud).* Pooh! That is the result of your innocence, Agnès. I shall say no more about it. What is done is done. I know that, by flattering you, the gallant only wishes to deceive you, and to laugh at you afterwards.

Agnès. Oh, no! He told me so more than a score of times.

Arnolphe. Ah! you do not know that he is not to be believed. But, now, learn that to accept caskets, and to listen to the nonsense of these handsome fops, to allow them languidly to kiss your hands and charm your heart, is a mortal sin, and one of the greatest that can be committed.

Agnès. A sin, do you say? And why, pray?

Arnolphe. Why? The reason is the absolute law that Heaven is incensed by such things.

Agnès. Incensed! But why should it be incensed?

Ah, it is so sweet and agreeable! How strange is the joy one feels from all this; up to this time I was ignorant of these things.

Arnolphe. Yes, all these tender passages, these pretty speeches and sweet caresses, are a great pleasure; but they must be enjoyed in an honest manner, and their sin should be taken away by marriage.

Agnès. Is it no longer a sin when one is married?

Arnolphe. No.

Agnès. Then please marry me quickly.

Arnolphe. If you wish it, I wish it also; I have returned hither for the purpose of marrying you.

Agnès. Is that possible?

Arnolphe. Yes.

Agnès. How happy you will make me!

Arnolphe. Yes, I have no doubt that marriage will please you.

Agnès. Then we two shall . . .

Arnolphe. Nothing is more certain.

Agnès. How I shall caress you, if this comes to pass

Arnolphe. Ha! And I shall do the same to you.

Agnès. I can never tell when people are jesting. Do you speak seriously?

Arnolphe. Yes, you might see that I do.

Agnès. We are to be married?

Arnolphe. Yes.

Agnès. But when?

Arnolphe. This very evening.

Agnès (*laughing*). This very evening?

Arnolphe. This very evening. Does that make you laugh?

Agnès. Yes.

Arnolphe. To see you happy is my desire.

Agnès. Oh, how greatly I am obliged to you, and what satisfaction I shall have with him!

Arnolphe. With whom?

Agnès. With . . . him there . . .

Arnolphe. Him there! I am not speaking of him there. You are a little quick in selecting a husband. In a word, it is some one else whom I have ready for you. And as for that gentleman, I require, by your leave (though the illness of which he accuses you should be the death of him), that henceforth you break off all intercourse with him; that, when he comes to the house, you will, by way of compliment, just shut the door in his face; throw a stone out of the window at him when he knocks, and oblige him in good earnest never to appear again. Do you hear me, Agnès? I shall observe your behaviour, concealed in a recess.

Agnès. Oh dear, he is so handsome! He is . . .

Arnolphe. Ha! How you are talking!

Agnès. I shall not have the heart . . .

Arnolphe. No more chatter. Go up stairs.

Agnès. But surely! Will you . . .

Arnolphe. Enough. I am master; I command; do you go and obey.

ACT III

Scene I.—Arnolphe, Agnès, Alain, Georgette.

Arnolphe. Yes, all has gone well; my joy is extreme. You have obeyed my orders to perfection, and brought the fair seducer to utter confusion. See what it is to have a wise counsellor. Your innocence, Agnès, had been betrayed; look what you had been brought to, before you had been aware of it. You were treading, deprived of my warnings, right-down the broad path to hell and perdition. The way of all these young fops is but too well known. They have their fine rolls, plenty of ribbons and plumes, big wigs, good teeth, a smooth address; but I tell you they have the cloven foot beneath; and they are very devils, whose corrupt appetites try to prey upon the honour of women. This time, however, thanks to the care that has been taken, you have escaped with your virtue. The style in which I saw you throw that stone at him, which has dashed the hopes of all his plans, still more determines me not to delay the marriage for which I told you to prepare. But, before all, it is well I should speak a few words with you which may be salutary. (*To* Georgette *and* Alain). Bring out a chair in the open air. As for you, if you ever . . .

Georgette. We shall take care to remember all your instructions, that other gentleman imposed on us, but . . .

Alain. If he ever gets in here, may I never drink another drop. Besides he is a fool. He gave us two gold crowns the other day, which were under weight.

Arnolphe. Well, get what I ordered for supper; and as to the contract I spoke of, let one of you fetch the notary who lives at the corner of the market-place.

Scene II.—Arnolphe, Agnès.

Arnolphe (*seated*). Agnès, put your work down, and
listen to me. Raise your head a little, and turn your
face round. (*Putting his finger on his forehead.*) There,
look at me here while I speak, and take good note of
even the smallest word. I am going to wed you, Agnès;
you ought to bless your stars a hundred times a day, to
think of your former low estate, and at the same time,
to wonder at my goodness in raising you from a poor
country girl to the honourable rank of a citizen's wife;
to enjoy the bed and the embraces of a man who has
shunned all such trammels, and whose heart has refused
to a score of women, well fitted to please, the honour
which he intends to confer on you. You must always
keep in mind, I say, how insignificant you would be
without this glorious alliance, in order that the picture
may teach you the better to merit the condition in which
I shall place you, and make you always know yourself,
so that I may never repent of what I am doing. Marriage, Agnès, is no joke. The position of a wife calls
for strict duties; I do not mean to exalt you to that
condition, in order that you may be free and take your
ease. Your sex is formed for dependence. Omnipotence
goes with the beard. Though there are two halves in
the connection, yet these two halves are by no means
equal. The one half is supreme, and the other subordi-
nate: the one is all submission to the other which rules;
the obedience which the well disciplined soldier shows
to his leader, the servant to his master, a child to his
parent, the lowest monk to his superior, is far below the
docility, obedience, humility, and profound respect due
from the wife to her husband, her chief, her lord, and
her master. When he looks at her gravely, her duty
is at once to lower her eyes, never daring to look him
in the face, until he chooses to favour her with a tender

glance. Our women now-a-days do not understand this; but do not be spoiled by the example of others. Take care not to imitate those miserable flirts whose pranks are talked of all over the city; and do not let the evil one tempt you, that is, do not listen to any young cox-comb. Remember, Agnès, that, in making you part of myself, I give my honour into your hands, which honour is fragile, and easily damaged; that it will not do to trifle in such a matter, and that there are boiling caul-drons in hell, into which wives who live wickedly are thrown for evermore. I am not telling you a parcel of stories; you ought to let these lessons sink into your heart. If you practice them sincerely, and take care not to flirt, your soul will ever be white and spotless as a lily; but if you stain your honour, it will become as black as coal. You will seem hideous to all, and one day you will become the devil's own property, and boil in hell to all eternity—from which may the goodness of Heaven defend you! Make a curtsey. As a novice in a convent ought to know her duties by heart, so it ought to be on getting married: here in my pocket I have an important document which will teach you the duty of a wife. I do not know the author, but it is some good soul or other; and I desire that this shall be your only study. (*Rises.*) Stay. Let me see if you can read it fairly.

Agnès (*reads*). "*The Maxims of Marriage; or the Duties of a Wife; together with her Daily Exercise.*

"*First Maxim.*

"She who is honourably wed should remember, not-withstanding the fashion now-a-days, that the man who marries does not take a wife for anyone but himself."

Arnolphe. I shall explain what that means, but at present let us only read.

Agnès (*continues*)—

"*Second Maxim.*

"She ought not to bedeck herself more than her husband likes. The care of her beauty concerns him alone; and if others think her plain, that must go for nothing.

"*Third Maxim.*

"Far from her be the study of ogling, washes, paints, pomatums, and the thousand preparations for a good complexion. These are ever fatal poisons to honour; and the pains bestowed to look beautiful are seldom taken for a husband.

"*Fourth Maxim.*

"When she goes out, she should conceal the glances of her eyes beneath her hood, as honour requires; for in order to please her husband rightly, she should please none else.

"*Fifth Maxim.*

"It is fit that she receive none but those who visit her husband. The gallants that have no business but with the wife, are not agreeable to the husband.

"*Sixth Maxim.*

"She must firmly refuse presents from men, for in these days nothing is given for nothing.

"*Seventh Maxim.*

"Amongst her furniture, however she dislikes it, there must be neither writing-desk, ink, paper, nor pens. According to all good rules everything written in the house should be written by the husband.

"*Eighth Maxim.*

"Those disorderly meetings, called social gatherings, ever corrupt the minds of women. It is good policy to forbid them; for there they conspire against the poor husbands.

"Ninth Maxim.

"Every woman who wishes to preserve her honour should abstain from gambling as a plague; for play is very seductive, and often drives a woman to put down her last stake.

"Tenth Maxim.

"She must not venture on public promenades nor picnics; for wise men are of opinion that it is always the husband who pays for such treats.

"Eleventh Maxim . . ."

Arnolphe. You shall finish it by yourself; and, by and by, I shall explain these things to you properly, word for word. I bethink myself of an engagement. I have but one word to say, and I shall not stay long. Go in again, and take special care of this volume. If the notary comes, let him wait for me a short time.

SCENE III.—ARNOLPHE, *alone.*

I cannot do better than make her my wife. I shall be able to mould her as I please; she is like a bit of wax in my hands, and I can give her what shape I like. She was near being wiled away from me in my absence through her excess of simplicity; but, to say the truth, it is better that a wife should err on that side. The cure for these faults is easy; every simple person is docile; and if she is led out of the right way, a couple of words will instantly bring her back again. But a clever woman is quite another sort of animal. Our lot depends only on her judgment; nought can divert her from what she is set on, and our teaching in such a case is futile. Her wit avails her to ridicule our maxims, often to turn her vices into virtues, and to find means to cheat the ablest, so as to compass her own ends. We labour in vain to parry the blow; a clever woman is a devil at intrigue, and when her whim has mutely passed sentence on our honour, we must knock under. Many good fellows could tell as much. But my blundering friend shall have no cause to laugh; he has reaped the harvest of his gossip. This is the general fault of Frenchmen. When they have a love adventure, secrecy bores them, and silly vanity has so many charms for them, that they would rather hang themselves than hold their tongues. Ah! women are an easy prey to Satan when they go and choose such addle-pates! And when . . . But here he is . . . I must dissemble, and find out how he has been mortified.

SCENE IV.—HORACE, ARNOLPHE.

Horace. I am come from your house. Fate seems resolved that I shall never meet you there. But I shall go so often that some time or other . . .

Arnolphe. Bah, for goodness' sake, do not let us begin these idle compliments. Nothing vexes me like ceremony; and, if I could have my way, it should be abolished. It is a wretched custom, and most people foolishly waste two-thirds of their time on it. Let us put on our hats, without more ado. (*Puts on his hat.*) Well, how about your love affair? May I know, Mr. Horace, how it goes? I was diverted for a while by some business that came into my head; but since then I have been thinking of it. I admire the rapidity of your commencement, and am interested in the issue.

Horace. Indeed, since I confided in you, my love has been unfortunate.

Arnolphe. Ay! How so?

Horace. Cruel fate has brought her governor back from the country.

Arnolphe. What bad luck!

Horace. Moreover, to my great sorrow, he has discovered what has passed in private between us.

Arnolphe. How the deuce could he discover this affair so soon?

Horace. I do not know; but it certainly is so. I meant, at the usual hour, to pay a short visit to my young charmer, when, with altered voice and looks, her two servants barred my entrance, and somewhat rudely shut the door in my face, saying "Begone, you bring us into trouble!"

Arnolphe. The door in your face!

Horace. In my face.

Arnolphe. That was rather hard.

Horace. I wished to speak to them through the door; but to all I said their only answer was, "You shan't come in; master has forbidden it."

Arnolphe. Did they not open the door then?

Horace. No. And Agnès from the window made me more certain as to her master's return, by bidding me begone in a very angry tone, and flinging a stone at me into the bargain.

Arnolphe. What, a stone?

Horace. Not a small one either; that was how she rewarded my visit with her own hands.

Arnolphe. The devil! These are no trifles. Your affair seems to me in a bad way.

Horace. True, I am in a quandary through this unlucky return.

Arnolphe. Really I am sorry for you; I declare I am.

Horace. This fellow mars all.

Arnolphe. Yes, but that is nothing. You will find a way to recover yourself.

Horace. I must try by some device to baffle the strict watch of this jealous fellow.

Arnolphe. That will be easy: after all the girl loves
you.

Horace. Doubtless.

Arnolphe. You will compass your end.

Horace. I hope so.

Arnolphe. The stone has put you out, but you cannot
wonder at it.

Horace. True; and I understood in a moment that my
rival was there, and that he was directing all without being seen. But what surprised me, and will surprise you,
is another incident I am going to tell you of; a bold
stroke of this lovely girl, which one could not have
expected from her simplicity. Love, it must be allowed,
is an able master; he teaches us to be what we never
were before; a complete change in our manners is often
the work of a moment under his tuition. He breaks
through the impediments in our nature, and his sudden
feats have the air of miracles. In an instant he makes
the miser liberal, a coward brave, a churl polite. He
renders the dullest soul fit for anything, and gives wit
to the most simple. Yes, this last miracle is surprising
in Agnès; for, blurting out these very words: "Begone,
I am resolved never to receive your visits. I know all
you would say, and *there* is my answer!"—this stone, or
pebble, at which you are surprised, fell at my feet, with a
letter. I greatly admire this note, chiming in with the
significance of her words, and the casting of the stone.
Are you not surprised by such an action as this? Does
not love know how to sharpen the understanding? And
can it be denied that his ardent flames have marvellous
effects on the heart? What say you of the trick, and of
the letter? Ah, do you not admire her cunning con-
trivance? Is it not amusing to see what a part my
jealous rival has played in all this game? Say . . .

Arnolphe. Ay, very amusing.

Horace. Laugh at it, then. (ARNOLPHE *forces a*

laugh. This fellow, garrisoned against my passion, who shuts himself up in his house, and seems provided with stones, as though I were preparing to enter by storm, who, in his ridiculous terror, encourages all his household to drive me away, is tricked before his very eyes by her whom he would keep in the utmost ignorance! For my part, I confess that, although his return throws my love affair in disorder, I think all this so exceedingly comical, that I cannot forbear laughing at it whenever it comes into my head. It seems to me that you do not laugh at it half enough.

Arnolphe (with a forced laugh). I beg pardon; I laugh at it as much as I can.

Horace. But I must shew you her letter, for friendship's sake. Her hand knew how to set down all that her heart felt; but in such touching terms, so kind, so innocently tender, so ingenuous—in a word, just as an unaffected nature confesses its first attack of love.

Arnolphe (softly). This is the use you make of writing, you hussy. It was against my wish you ever learned it.

Horace (reads). "*I wish to write to you, but I am at a loss how to begin. I have some thoughts which I should like you to know; but I do not know how to tell them to you, and I mistrust my own words. As I begin to feel that I have been always kept in ignorance, I fear to say something which is not right, and to express more than I ought. In fact I do not know what you have done to me; but I feel that I am desperately vexed at what I am made to do against you, that it will be the hardest thing in the world for me to do without you, and that I should be very glad to be with you. Perhaps it is wrong to say that, but the truth is I cannot help saying it, and I wish it could be brought about without harm. I am assured that all young men are deceivers, that they must not be listened to, and that all you told me was but to deceive me; but I assure you I have not yet come to believe that of you, and I am so touched by your words that I could not believe them false. Tell me frankly if they be: for, to be brief, as I am without an evil thought, you would be extremely wicked to deceive me, and I think I should die of vexation at such a thing."*

Arnolphe (*aside*). Ah, the cat!

Horace. What is wrong?

Arnolphe. Wrong? Nothing! I was only coughing.

Horace. Have you ever heard a more tender expression? In spite of the cursed endeavours of unreasonable power, could you imagine a more genuine nature? Is it not beyond doubt a terrible crime villainously to mar such an admirable spirit, to try to stifle this bright soul in ignorance and stupidity? Love has begun to tear away the veil, and if, thanks to some lucky star, I can deal, as I hope, with this sheer animal, this wretch, this hang-dog, this scoundrel, this brute . . .

Arnolphe. Good-bye.

Horace. Why are you in such a hurry?

Arnolphe. It just occurs to me that I have a pressing engagement.

Horace. But do you not know anyone, for you live close by, who could get access to this house? I am open with you, and it is the usual thing for friends to help each other in these cases. I have no one there now except people who watch me; maid and man, as I just experienced, would not cease their rudeness and listen to me, do what I would. I had for some time in my interest an old woman of remarkable shrewdness; in fact more than human. She served me well in the beginning; but the poor woman died four days ago. Can you not devise some plan for me?

Arnolphe. No, really. You will easily find some one without me.

Horace. Good-by then. You see what confidence I put in you.

SCENE V.—ARNOLPHE, *alone.*

How I am obliged to suffer before him! How hard it is to conceal my gnawing pain! What! Such ready wit in a simpleton? The traitress has pretended to be so to my face, or the devil has breathed this cunning into her heart. But now that cursed letter is the death of me. I see that the rascal has corrupted her mind, and has established himself there in my stead. This is despair and deadly anguish for me. I suffer doubly by being robbed of her heart, for love as well as honour is injured by it. It drives me mad to find my place usurped, and I am enraged to see my prudence defeated. I know that to punish her guilty passion I have only to leave her to her evil fate, and that I shall be revenged on her by herself; but it is very vexatious to lose what we love. Good Heaven! after employing so much philosophy in my choice, why am I to be so terribly bewitched by her charms? She has neither relatives, friends, nor money; she abuses my care, my kindness, my tenderness; and yet I love her to distraction, even after this base trick! Fool, have you no shame? Ah, I cannot contain myself; I am mad; I could punch my head a thousand times over. I shall go in for a little; but only to see what she looks like after so vile a deed. Oh, Heaven, grant that my brow may escape dishonour; or rather, if it is decreed that I must endure it, at least grant me, under such misfortunes, that fortitude with which few are endowed.

ACT IV

Scene I.—Arnolphe, *alone.*

I declare I cannot rest anywhere; my mind is troubled by a thousand cares, thinking how to contrive, both in-doors and out, so as to frustrate the attempts of this cox-comb. With what assurance the traitress stood the sight of me! She is not a whit moved by all that she has done and though she has brought me within an inch of the grave, one could swear, to look at her, that she had no hand in it. The more composed she looked when I saw her, the more I was enraged, and those ardent transports which inflamed my heart seemed to redouble my great love for her. I was provoked, angry, incensed against her, and yet I never saw her look so lovely. Her eyes never seemed to me so bright; never before did they in-spire me with such vehement desires; I feel that it will be the death of me, if my evil destiny should bring upon me this disgrace. What! I have brought her up with so much tenderness and forethought; I have had her with me from her infancy; I have indulged in the fondest hopes about her; my heart trusted to her growing charms; I have fondled her as my own for thirteen years, as I imagined—all for a young fool, with whom she is in love, to come and carry her off before my face, and that when she is already half married to me! No, by Heaven —no, by Heaven, my foolish young friend; you will be a cunning fellow to overturn my scheme, for, upon my word, all your hopes will be in vain, and you shall find no reason for laughing at me!

SCENE II.—A NOTARY, ARNOLPHE.

Notary. Ah, there he is. Good-day. Here I am, ready to draw up the contract which you wish.

Arnolphe (*not seeing or hearing him*). How is it to be done?

Notary. It must be in the usual form.

Arnolphe (*thinking himself alone*). I shall take the greatest possible care.

Notary. I shall do nothing contrary to your interests.

Arnolphe (*not seeing him*). I must guard against all surprise.

Notary. It is enough that your affairs are placed in my hands. For fear of deception, you must not sign the contract before receiving the portion.

Arnolphe (*thinking himself alone*). I fear, if I let anything get abroad, that this business will become town talk.

Notary. Well, it is easy to avoid this publicity, and your contract can be drawn up privately.

Arnolphe (*thinking himself alone*). But how shall I manage it with her?

Notary. The jointure should be proportionate to the fortune she brings you.

Arnolphe (*not seeing him*). I love her, and that love is my great difficulty.

Notary. In that case the wife may have so much the more.

Arnolphe (*thinking himself alone*). How can I act towards her in such a case?

Notary. The regular way is that the husband that is to be settles on the wife that is to be a third of her marriage portion as a jointure; but this rules goes for nothing, and you may do a great deal more if you have a mind to it.

Arnolphe. If . . . (*seeing him*).

Notary. As for the *préciput*, that is a question for both sides. I say the husband can settle on his wife what he thinks proper.

Arnolphe. Eh?

Notary. He can benefit her, when he loves her much, and wishes to do her a favour, and that by way of jointure, or settlement as it is called, which is lost upon her death; either without reversion, going from her to her heirs, or by statute, as people have a mind, or by actual deed of gift in form, which may be made either single or mutual. Why do you shrug your shoulders? Am I talking like a fool, or do I not understand contracts? Who can teach me? No one, I imagine. Do I not know that when people are married, they have a joint right to all moveables, moneys, fixtures, and acquisitions, unless they resign it by act of renunciation? Do I not know that a third part of the portion of the wife that is to be becomes common, in order . . .

Arnolphe. Yes, verily, you know all this; but who has said one word to you about it?

Notary. You, who seem to take me for a fool, shrugging your shoulders, and making faces at me.

Arnolphe. Hang the man his beastly face! Good day: that's the way to get rid of you.

Notary. Was I not brought here to draw up a contract?

Arnolphe. Yes, I sent for you. But the business is put off; I shall send for you again when the time is fixed. What a devil of a fellow he is with his jabbering!

Notary (*alone*). I think he is mad, and I believe I am right.

SCENE III.—A NOTARY, ALAIN, GEORGETTE.

Notary. Did you not come to fetch me to your master?

Alain. Yes.

Notary. I do not know what you think; but go and tell him from me that he is a downright fool.

Georgette. We will not fail.

SCENE IV.—ARNOLPHE, ALAIN, GEORGETTE.

Georgette. Sir . . .

Arnolphe. Come here! You are my faithful, my good, my real friends; I have news for you.

Alain. The notary . . .

Arnolphe. Never mind; some other day for that. A foul plot is contrived against my honour. What a disgrace it would be for you, my children, if your master's honour were taken away! After that, you would not dare to be seen anywhere; for whoever saw you would point at you. So, since the affair concerns you as well as me, you must take care that this spark may not in any way . . .

Georgette. You have taught us our lesson just now.

Arnolphe. But take care not to listen to his fine speeches.

Alain. Oh, certainly . . .

Georgette. We know how to deny him.

Arnolphe. Suppose he should come now, wheedling: "Alain, my good fellow, cheer my drooping spirits by a little help."

Alain. You are a fool.

Arnolphe. You are right! (*To* GEORGETTE.) "Georgette, my darling, you look so sweet-tempered and so kind!"

Georgette. You are a lout.

Arnolphe. You are right. (*To* ALAIN). "What harm do you find in an honest and perfectly virtuous scheme?"

Alain. You are a rogue.

Arnolphe. Capital! (*To* GEORGETTE.) " I shall surely die if you do not take pity on my sufferings."

Georgette. You are a brazen-faced blockhead.

Arnolphe. First-rate! (*To* ALAIN.) "I am not one who expects something for nothing; I can remember those who serve me. Here, Alain, is a trifle in advance, to have a drink with; and, Georgette, here is wherewith to buy you a petticoat. (*Both hold out their hands and take the money.*) This is only an earnest of what I intend to do for you; I ask no other favour but that you will let me see your pretty mistress."

Georgette (*pushing him*). Try your games elsewhere.

Arnolphe. That was good.

Alain (*pushing him*). Get out of this.

Arnolphe. Very good!

Georgette (*pushing him*). Immediately!

Arnolphe. Good! Hulloa, that is enough.

Georgette. Am I not doing right?

Alain. Is this how you would have us act?

Arnolphe. Yes, capital; except for the money, which you must not take.

Georgette. We did not think of that.

Alain. Shall we begin again now?

Arnolphe. No. It is enough. Go in, both of you.

Alain. You need only say so.

Arnolphe. No, I tell you; go in when I desire you. You may keep the money. Go. I shall soon be with you again; keep your eyes open, and second my efforts.

SCENE V.—ARNOLPHE, *alone.*

I will get the cobbler, who lives at the corner of the street, to be my spy, and tell me everything. I mean to keep her always indoors, watch her constantly . . . and banish in particular all sellers of ribbons, tire-women, hair-dressers, kerchief-makers, glove-sellers, dealers in cast-off apparel, and all those folks who make it their business clandestinely to bring people together who are

in love. In fact, I have seen the world, and understand
its tricks. My spark must be very cunning, if a love-
letter or message gets in here.

SCENE VI.—HORACE, ARNOLPHE.

Horace. How lucky I am to meet you here! I had
a narrow escape just now, I can assure you. As I left
you, I unexpectedly saw Agnès alone on her balcony,
breathing the fresh air from the neighbouring trees.
After giving me a sign, she contrived to come down into
the garden and open the door. But we were scarcely
into her room before she heard her jealous gentleman
upon the stairs; and all she could do in such a case was
to lock me into a large wardrobe. He entered the room
at once. I did not see him, but I heard him walking
up and down at a great rate, without saying a word,
but sighing desperately at intervals, and occasionally
thumping the table, striking a little frisky dog, and madly
throwing about whatever came in his way. In his rage
he broke the very vases with which the beauty had
adorned her mantel-piece; doubtless the tricks she
played must have come to the ears of this cuckold in em-
bryo. At last, having in a score of ways vented his
passion on things that could not help themselves, my
restless jealous gentleman left the room without saying
what disturbed him, and I left my wardrobe. We
would not stay long together, for fear of my rival;
it would have been too great a risk. But late to-night
I am to enter her room without making a noise. I am
to announce myself by three hems, and then the window
is to be opened; whereby, with a ladder, and the help
of Agnès, my love will try to gain me admittance. I tell
you this as my only friend. Joy is increased by imparting
it; and should we taste perfect bliss a hundred times
over, it would not satisfy us unless it were known to

some one. I believe you will sympathize in my success. Good-bye. I am going to make the needful preparations.

SCENE VII.—ARNOLPHE, *alone*.

What, will the star which is bent on driving me to despair allow me no time to breathe? Am I to see, through their mutual understanding, my watchful care and my wisdom defeated one after another? Must I, in my mature age, become the dupe of a simple girl and a scatter-brained young fellow? For twenty years, like a discreet philosopher, I have been musing on the wretched fate of married men, and have carefully informed myself of the accidents which plunge the most prudent into misfortune. Profiting in my own mind by the disgrace of others, and having a wish to marry, I sought how to secure my forehead from attack, and prevent its being matched with those of other men. For this noble end, I thought I had put in practice all that human policy could invent; but, as though it were decreed by fate that no man here below should be exempt from it, after all my experience and the knowledge I have been able to glean of such matters, after more than twenty years of meditation, so as to guide myself with all precaution, I have avoided the tracks of so many husbands to find myself after all involved in the same disgrace! Ah, cursed fate, you shall yet be a liar! I am still possessor of the loved one; if her heart be stolen by this obnoxious fop, I shall at least take care that he does not seize anything else. This night, which they have chosen for their pretty plan, shall not be spent so agreeably as they anticipate. It is some pleasure to me, amidst all this, to know that he has warned me of the snare he is laying, and that this blunderer, who would be my ruin, makes a confidant of his own rival.

SCENE VIII.—CHRYSALDE, ARNOLPHE.

Chrysalde. Well, shall we take our supper before our walk?

Arnolphe. No, I fast to-night.

Chrysalde. Whence this fancy?

Arnolphe. Pray excuse me; there is something that hinders me.

Chrysalde. Is not your intended marriage to take place?

Arnolphe. You take too much trouble about other people's affairs.

Chrysalde. Oh ho, so snappish? What ails you? Have you encountered any little mishap in your love, my friend? By your face I could almost swear you have.

Arnolphe. Whatever happens, I shall at least have the advantage of being unlike some folks, who meekly suffer the visits of gallants.

Chrysalde. It is an odd thing that, with so much intelligence, you always get so frightened at these matters; that you set your whole happiness on this, and imagine no other kind of honour in the world. To be a miser, a brute, a rogue, wicked and cowardly, is nothing in your mind compared with this stain; and however a man may have lived, he is a man of honour if he is not a cuckold. After all, why do you imagine that our glory depends on such an accident, and that a virtuous mind must reproach itself for the evil which it cannot prevent? Tell me, why do you hold that a man in taking a wife deserves praise or blame for the choice he makes, and why do you form a frightful bugbear out of the offence caused by her want of fidelity? Be persuaded that a man of honour may have a less serious notion of cuckoldom; that as none is secure from strokes of chance, this accident ought to be a matter of indifference; and that all the evil, whatever

the world may say, is in the mode of receiving it. To
behave well under these difficulties, as in all else, a man
must shun extremes; not ape those over-simple folks who
are proud of such affairs, and are ever inviting the gallants of their wives, praising them everywhere, and crying them up, displaying their sympathy with them, coming to all their entertainments and all their meetings,
and making everyone wonder at their having the assurance to show their faces there. This way of acting is
no doubt highly culpable; but the other extreme is no
less to be condemned. If I do not approve of such as
are the friends of their wives' gallants; no more do I
approve of your violent men whose indiscreet resentment,
full of rage and fury, draws the eyes of all the world
on them by its noise, and who seem, from their outbreaks,
unwilling that any one should be ignorant of what is
wrong with them. There is a mean between these extremes, where a wise man stops in such a case. When
we know how to take it, there is no reason to blush for
the worst a woman can do to us. In short, say what you
will, cuckolding may easily be made to seem less terrible;
and, as I told you before, all your dexterity lies in being
able to turn the best side outwards.

Arnolphe. After this fine harangue, all the brother-
hood owes your worship thanks; any one who hears you
speak will be delighted to enrol himself.

Chrysalde. I do not say that; for that is what I have
found fault with. But as fortune gives us a wife, I say
that we should act as we do when we gamble with dice,
when, if you do not get what you want, you must be
shrewd and good-tempered, to amend your luck by good
management.

Arnolphe. That is, sleep and eat well, and persuade
yourself that it is all nothing.

Chrysalde. You think to make a joke of it; but, to

be candid, I know a hundred things in the world more
to be dreaded, and which I should think a much greater
misfortune, than the accident you are so grievously
afraid of. Do you think that, in choosing between the
two alternatives, I should not prefer to be what you say,
rather than see myself married to one of those good
creatures whose ill-humour makes a quarrel out of nothing—those dragons of virtue, those respectable she-
devils, ever piquing themselves on their wise conduct,
who, because they do not do us a trifling wrong, take on
themselves to behave haughtily, and, because they are
faithful to us, expect that we should bear everything
from them? Once more, my friend, know that cuckoldom
is just what we make of it, that on some accounts it is
even to be desired, and that it has its pleasures like
other things.

Arnolphe. If you are of a mind to be satisfied with
it, I am not disposed to try it myself; and rather than
submit to such a thing . . .

Chrysalde. Bless me! do not swear, lest you should
be forsworn. If fate has willed it, your precautions are
useless; and your advice will not be taken in the matter.

Arnolphe. I!—I a cuckold!

Chrysalde. You are in a bad way. A thousand folks
are so—I mean no offence—who, for bearing, courage,
fortune and family, would scorn comparison with you.

Arnolphe. And I, on my side, will not draw comparisons with them. But, let me tell you, this pleasantry
annoys me. Let us have done with it, if you please.

Chrysalde. You are in a passion. We shall know the
cause. Good-bye; but remember, whatever your honour
prompts you to do in this business, to swear you will
never be what we have talked of is half-way towards
being it.

Arnolphe. And I swear it again! I am going this
instant to find a good remedy against such an accident.

SCENE IX.—ARNOLPHE, ALAIN, GEORGETTE.

Arnolphe. My friends, now is the time that I beg your assistance. I am touched by your affection; but it must be well proved on this occasion; and if you serve me in this, as I am sure you will, you may count on your reward. The man you wot of (but not a word!) seeks, as I understand, to trick me this very night, and enter, by a ladder, into Agnès' room. But we three must lay a trap for him. I would have each of you take a good cudgel, and, when he shall be nearly on the top round of the ladder (for I shall open the window at the proper time), both of you shall fall on the rascal for me, so that his back may be sure to remember it, in order that he may learn never to come here again. Yet do it without naming me in any way, or making it appear that I am behind. Would you have the courage to execute my resentment?

Alain. If the thrashing is all, sir, rely on us. You shall see, when I beat, if I am a slow coach.

Georgette. Though my arm may not look so strong, it shall play its part in the drubbing.

Arnolphe. Get you in, then; and, above all, mind you do not chatter. (*Alone.*) This is a useful lesson for my neighbours; if all the husbands in town were to receive their wives' gallants in this fashion, the number of cuckolds would not be so great.

ACT V

Scene I.—Arnolphe, Alain, Georgette.

Arnolphe. Wretches! what have you done by your violence?

Alain. We have obeyed you, sir.

Arnolphe. It is of no use trying to defend yourselves by such an excuse. My orders were to beat him, not to murder him. I told you to discharge your blows on his back, and not on his head. Good Heavens! into what a plight my fate has now thrown me! And what course can I take, as the man is dead? Go into the house, and be sure to say nothing of the harmless order that I gave you. (*Alone.*) It will be daylight presently, and I shall go and consider how to bear myself under this misfortune. Alas! what will become of me? And what will Horace's father say when he shall suddenly hear of this affair?

Scene II.—Arnolphe, Horace

Horace (aside). I must go and make out who it is.

Arnolphe (thinking himself alone). Could one ever have foreseen . . . (*Running against* Horace.) Who is there, pray?

Horace. Is it you, M. Arnolphe?

Arnolphe. Yes; but who are you?

Horace. Horace. I was going to your house to beg a favour. You are out very early.

Arnolphe (to himself aside). Wonderful! Is it magic? Is it a vision?

Horace. To tell the truth, I was in a great difficulty;

I thank Heaven's great goodness that at the nick of time I thus meet you. Let me tell you that everything has succeeded, much better even than I could have predicted, and by an accident which might have spoiled all. I do not know how our appointment could possibly have been suspected; but just as I was reaching the window, I unluckily saw some persons, who, unceremoniously raising their hand against me, made me miss my footing, and fall to the ground, which, at the expense of a bruise, saved me from a score of blows. These people, of whom, I fancy, my jealous rival was one, attributed my fall to their blows, and as the pain compelled me to lie for some time motionless, they honestly thought they had killed me, and were greatly alarmed. I heard all their noise in profound silence. Each, accusing the other of the violence, and complaining of their ill fortune, came softly, without a light, to feel if I were dead. You may imagine that I contrived in the darkness of night, to assume the appearance of a real corpse. They went away in great terror; and as I was thinking how I should make my escape, the young Agnès, frightened by my pretended death, came to me in great concern. For the talking of those people had reached her ears from the very first, and, being unobserved during all this commotion, she easily escaped from the house. But finding me unhurt, she displayed a transport which it would be difficult to describe. What more need I say? The lovely girl obeyed the promptings of her affection, would not return to her room, and committed her fate to my honour. You may judge, from this instance of innocence, to what she is exposed by the mad intolerance of a fool, and what frightful risks she might have run, if I were a man to hold her less dear than I do. But too pure a passion fills my soul; I would rather die than wrong her. I see in her charms worthy of a better fate, and nought but death shall part us. I foresee the rage my father will be in. But we must find an opportunity to appease his anger. I cannot help being transported by charms so delightful; and, in short, we must in this life be satisfied with our lot. What I wish you to do, as a confidential friend, is to let me place this beauty under your care; and that, in the interest of my love, you will conceal her in your house for at least a day or two. For, besides that I must conceal her flight from every one, to prevent any successful pursuit of her, you know that a young girl, especially such a beautiful one, would be strongly suspected in the company of a young man; and as I have trusted the whole secret of my passion to you, being assured of your prudence, so to you only, as a generous friend, can I confide this beloved treasure.

Arnolphe. Be assured I am entirely at your service.

Horace. You will really do me so great a favour?

Arnolphe. Very willingly, I tell you; I am delighted at the opportunity of serving you. I thank Heaven for putting it in my way; I never did anything with so much pleasure.

Horace. How much I am obliged to you for all your kindness! I feared a difficulty on your part; but you know the world, and your wisdom can excuse the ardour of youth. One of my servants is with her at the corner of this street.

Arnolphe. But how shall we manage, for day begins to break? If I take her here, I may be seen; and if you come to my house the servants will talk. To take a safe course you must bring her to me in a darker place. That alley of mine is convenient; I shall wait for her there.

Horace. It is quite right to use these precautions. I shall only place her in your hands, and return at once to my lodgings, without more ado.

Arnolphe (*alone*). Ah, fortune! This propitious accident makes amends for all the mischief which your caprice has done!   (*He muffles himself up in his cloak.*)

SCENE III.—AGNÈS, HORACE, ARNOLPHE.

Arnolphe (*to* AGNÈS).   Do not be uneasy at the place I am taking you to.   I conduct you to a safe abode.   It would ruin all for you to lodge with me.   Go in at this door, and follow where you are led.   (ARNOLPHE *takes her hand, without being recognised by her.*)

Agnès (*to* HORACE).   Why do you leave me?

Horace.   Dear Agnès, it must be so.

Agnès.   Remember, then, I pray you to return soon.

Horace.   My love urges me sufficiently for that.

Agnès.   I feel no joy but when I see you.

Horace.   Away from you I also am sad.

Agnès.   Alas, if that were so, you would stay here.

Horace.   What!   Can you doubt my excessive love?

Agnès.   No; you do not love me as much as I love you!   Ah, he is pulling me too hard!   (ARNOLPHE *pulls her away*).

Horace.   It is because it is dangerous, dear Agnès, for us to be seen together here; this true friend, whose hand draws you away, acts with the prudent zeal that inspires him on our behalf.

Agnès.   But to follow a stranger . . .

Horace.   Fear nothing.   In such hands you cannot but be safe.

Agnès.   I would rather be in Horace's; and I should . . . (*To* ARNOLPHE, *who still drags her away*).   Stay a little.

Horace.   Farewell.   The day drives me away.

Agnès.   When shall I see you, then?

Horace.   Very soon, you may be sure.

Agnès.   How weary I shall be till I do!

Horace.   (*Going*).   Thank Heaven, my happiness is no longer in suspense; now I can sleep securely.

SCENE IV.—ARNOLPHE, AGNÈS.

Arnolphe. (*concealed by his cloak, and disguising his voice*). Come; it is not there you are going to lodge. I have provided a room for you elsewhere, and intend to place you where you will be safe enough. (*Discovering himself.*) Do you know me?

Agnès. Ah!

Arnolphe. My face frightens you now, hussy; it is a disappointment to you to see me here. I interrupt your love and its pretty contrivances. (AGNÈS *looks for* HORACE). Do not imagine you can call your lover to your aid with those eyes of yours; he is too far off to give you any assistance. So, so! young as you are, you can play such pranks. Your simplicity, that seemed so extraordinary, asks if infants come through the ear; yet you manage to make an assignation by night, and to slink out silently in order to follow your gallant? Gad, how coaxing your tongue was with him! You must have been at a good school. Who the deuce has taught you so much all on a sudden? You are no longer afraid, then, to meet ghosts; this gallant has given you courage in the night time. Ah, baggage, to arrive at such a pitch of deceit! To form such a plot in spite of all my kindness! Little serpent that I have warmed in my bosom, and that as soon as it feels it is alive, tries ungratefully to injure him that cherished it!

Agnès. Why do you scold me?

Arnolphe. Of a truth, I do wrong!

Agnès. I am not conscious of harm in all that I have done.

Arnolphe. To run after a gallant is not, then, an infamous thing?

Agnès. He is one who says he wishes to marry me. I followed your directions; you have taught me that we ought to marry in order to avoid sin.

Arnolphe. Yes; but I meant to take you to wife myself; I think I gave you to understand it clearly enough.

Agnès. You did. But, to be frank with you, he is more to my taste for a husband than you. With you, marriage is a trouble and a pain, and your descriptions give a terrible picture of it; but there—he makes it seem so full of joy that I long to marry.

Arnolphe. Oh, traitress, that is because you love him!

Agnès. Yes, I love him.

Arnolphe. And you have the impudence to tell me so!

Agnès. Why, if it is true, should I not say so?

Arnolphe. Ought you to love him, minx?

Agnès. Alas! can I help it? He alone is the cause of it; I was not thinking of it when it came about.

Arnolphe. But you ought to have driven away that amorous desire.

Agnès. How can we drive away what gives us pleasure?

Arnolphe. And did you not know that it would displease me?

Agnès. I? Not at all. What harm can it do you?

Arnolphe. True. I ought to rejoice at it. You do not love me then after all?

Agnès. You?

Arnolphe. Yes.

Agnès. Alack! no.

Arnolphe. How! No?

Agnès. Would you have me tell a fib?

Arnolphe. Why not love me, Madam Impudence?

Agnès. Heaven! you ought not to blame me. Why did you not make yourself loved, as he has done? I did not prevent you, I fancy.

Arnolphe. I tried all I could; but all my pains were to no purpose.

Agnès. Of a truth then he knows more about it than you; for he had no difficulty in making himself loved.

Arnolphe (*aside*). See how the jade reasons and retorts! Plague! could one of your witty ladies say more about it? Ah, I was a dolt; or else, on my honour, a fool of a girl knows more than the wisest man. (*To* AGNÈS.) Since you are so good at reasoning, Madam Chop-logic, should I have maintained you so long for his benefit?

Agnès. No. He will pay you back, even to the last farthing.

Arnolphe (*aside*). She hits on words that double my vexation. (*Aloud*). With all his ability, hussy, will he discharge me the obligations that you owe me?

Agnès. I do not owe you so much as you may think.

Arnolphe. Was the care of bringing you up nothing?

Agnès. Verily, you have been at great pains there, and have caused me to be finely taught throughout. Do you think I flatter myself so far as not to know in my own mind that I am an ignoramus? I am ashamed of myself, and at my age, I do not wish to pass any longer for a fool, if I can help it.

Arnolphe. You shrink from ignorance, and would learn something of your spark, at any cost.

Agnès. To be sure. It is from him I know what I do know; I fancy I owe him much more than you.

Arnolphe. Really, what prevents me from revenging this saucy talk with a cuff? I am enraged at the sight of her provoking coldness: and to beat her would be a satisfaction to me.

Agnès. Ah, you can do that if you choose.

Arnolphe (*aside*). That speech and that look disarm my fury, and bring back the tenderness to my heart which effaces all her guilt. How strange it is to be in love! To think that men should be subject to such weakness for these traitresses! Everyone knows their

imperfection. They are extravagant and indiscreet.
Their mind is wicked and their understanding weak.
There is nought weaker, more imbecile, more faithless;
and, in spite of all, everything in the world is done for
the sake of these bipeds. (*To* Agnès). Well, let us
make peace. Listen, little wretch, I forgive all, and
restore you to my affection. Learn thus how much I
love you; and, seeing me so good, love me in return.

Agnès. With all my heart I should like to please you,
if it were in my power.

Arnolphe. Poor little darling, you can if you will.
Just listen to this sigh of love. See this dying look,
behold my person, and forsake this young coxcomb and
the love he inspires. He must have thrown some spell
over you, and you will be a hundred times happier with
me. Your desire is to be finely dressed and frolicsome;
then I swear you shall ever be so; I will fondle you
night and day, I will hug you, kiss you, devour you; you
shall do everything you have a mind to. I do not enter
into particulars; and that is saying everything. (*Aside*).
To what length will my passion go? (*Aloud*). In
short, nothing can equal my love. What proof would
you have me give you, ungrateful girl? Would you have
me weep? Shall I beat myself? Shall I tear out one
half of my hair? Shall I kill myself? Yes, say so if
you will. I am quite ready, cruel creature, to convince
you of my love.

Agnès. Stay. All you say does not touch my heart.
Horace could do more with a couple of words.

Arnolphe. Ah, this is too great an insult, and provokes my anger too far. I will pursue my design, you
intractable brute, and will pack you out of the town
forthwith. You reject my addresses and drive me to extremities: but the innermost cell of a convent shall
avenge me of all.

Scene V.—Arnolphe, Agnès, Alain.

Alain. I do not know how it is, master, but it seems to me that Agnès and the corpse have run away together.

Arnolphe. She is here. Go and shut her up in my room. (*Aside*). Horace will not come here to see her. Besides, it is only for half an hour. (*To* Alain). Go and get a carriage, for I mean to find her a safe dwelling. Shut yourself safely in, and, above all, do not take your eyes off her. (*Alone*). Perhaps when her mind is buried in solitude, she will be disabused of this passion.

Scene VI.—Horace, Arnolphe.

Horace. Oh, I come here, plunged in grief. Heaven, Mr. Arnolphe, has decreed my ill fortune! By a fatal stroke of extreme justice, I am to be torn away from the beauty whom I love. My father arrived this very evening. I found him alighting close by. In a word the reason of his coming, with which, as I said, I was unacquainted, is, that he has made a match for me, without a word of warning; he has arrived here to celebrate the nuptials. Feel for my anxiety, and judge if a more cruel disappointment could happen to me. That Enrique, whom I asked you about yesterday, is the source of all my trouble. He has come with my father to complete my ruin; it is for his only daughter that I am destined. I thought I should have swooned when they first spoke of it; not caring to hear more, as my father spoke of paying you a visit, I hurried here before him, my mind full of consternation. I pray you be sure not to let him know anything of my engagement, which might incense him; and try, since he has confidence in you, to dissuade him from this other match.

Arnolphe. Ay, to be sure!

Horace. Advise him to delay; and thus, like a friend help me in my passion.

Arnolphe. No fear!

Horace. All my hope is in you.

Arnolphe. It could not be better placed.

Horace. I look on you as my real father. Tell him that my age . . . Ah, I see him coming. Hear the argu ments I can supply you with.

SCENE VII.—ENRIQUE, ORONTE, CHRYSALDE, HORACE, ARNOLPHE.

(HORACE *and* ARNOLPHE *retire to the back of the stage and whisper together*.)

Enrique (*to* CHRYSALDE). As soon as I saw you, before anyone could tell me, I should have known you. I recognise in your face the features of your lovely sister, whom marriage made mine in former days. Happy should I have been if cruel fate had permitted me to bring back that faithful wife, to enjoy with me the great delight of seeing once more, after our continual misfortunes, all her former friends. But since the irre-sistible power of destiny has for ever deprived us of her dear presence, let us try to submit, and to be content with the only fruit of love which remains to me. It concerns you nearly; without your consent I should do wrong in wishing to dispose of this pledge. The choice of the son of Oronte is honourable in itself; but you must be pleased with this choice as well as I.

Chrysalde. It would argue a poor opinion of my judgment to doubt my approbation of so reasonable a choice.

Arnolphe (*aside to* HORACE). Ay, I will serve you finely!

Horace. Beware, once more . . .

Arnolphe. Have no uneasiness. (*Leaves* HORACE, *and goes up to embrace* ORONTE.)

Oronte. Ah, this is indeed a tender embrace.

Arnolphe. How delighted I am to see you!

Oronte. I am come here . . .

Arnolphe. I know what brings you, without your tell-ing me.

Oronte. You have already heard?

Arnolphe. Yes.

Oronte. So much the better.

Arnolphe. Your son is opposed to this match; his heart being pre-engaged, he looks on it as a misfortune. He has even prayed me to dissuade you from it; for my part, all the advice I can give you is, to exert a father's authority, and not allow the marriage to be delayed. Young people should be managed with a high hand; we do them harm by being indulgent.

Horace (*aside*). Oh, the traitor!

Chrysalde. If it is repugnant to him, I think we ought not to force him. I think my brother will be of my mind.

Arnolphe. What? Will he let himself be ruled by his son? Would you have a father so weak as to be unable to make his son obey him? It would be fine indeed to see him at his time of life receiving orders from one who ought to receive them from him. No, no, he is my intimate friend, and his honour is my own. His word is passed, and he must keep it. Let him now dis-play his firmness, and control his son's affections.

Oronte. You speak well; in this match I will answer for my son's obedience.

Chrysalde (*to* ARNOLPHE). I am indeed surprised at the great eagerness which you shew for this marriage, and cannot guess what is your motive . . .

Arnolphe. I know what I am about, and speak sen-sibly.

Oronte. Yes, yes, M. Arnolphe; he is . . .

Chrysalde. That name annoys him.   He is Monsieur
de la Souche, as you were told before.

Oronte. It makes no difference.

Horace (aside). What do I hear?

Arnolphe (turning to HORACE*).* Ay, that is the mystery; you can judge as to what it behooved me to do.

Horace (aside). What a scrape . . .

SCENE VIII.—ENRIQUE, ORONTE, CHRYSALDE, HORACE,
    ARNOLPHE, GEORGETTE.

Georgette. Sir, if you do not come, we shall scarcely
be able to hold Agnès; she is trying all she can to get
away; I fear she will throw herself out of the window.

Arnolphe. Bring her to me, for I mean to take her
away. (*To* HORACE). Do not be disturbed. Continual
good fortune makes a man proud. Every dog has his
day, as the proverb says.

Horace (aside). Good Heaven, what misfortune
can equal mine? Was ever a man in such a mess as
this?

Arnolphe (to ORONTE). Hasten the day of the ceremony. I am bent on it, and invite myself beforehand.

Oronte. That is just my intention.

SCENE IX.—AGNÈS, ORONTE, ENRIQUE, ARNOLPHE,
    HORACE, CHRYSALDE, ALAIN, GEORGETTE.

Arnolphe (to AGNÈS). Come hither, my beauty,
whom they cannot hold, and who rebels. Here is your
gallant, to whom, to make amends, you may make a
sweet and humble curtesy. (*To* HORACE). Farewell.
The issue rather thwarts your desires; but all lovers are
not fortunate.

Agnès. Horace, will you let me be carried off in
this manner?

Horace. I scarcely know where I am, my sorrow is
so great.

Arnolphe. Come along, chatterbox.

Agnès. I shall stay here.

Oronte. Tell us the meaning of this mystery. We are all staring at each other without being able to understand it.

Arnolphe. I shall inform you at a more convenient time. Till then, good-bye.

Oronte. Where are you going? You do not speak to us as you should.

Arnolphe. I have advised you to complete the marriage, let Horace grumble as much as he likes.

Oronte. Ay; but to complete it, have you not heard —if they have told you all—that the lady concerned in this affair is in your house?—that she is the daughter of Enrique and of the lovely Angelica, who were privately married? Now, what was at the bottom of your talk just now?

Chrysalde. I too was astonished at his proceedings.

Arnolphe. What?

Chrysalde. My sister had a daughter by a secret marriage, whose existence was concealed from the whole family.

Oronte. And in order that nothing might be discovered, she was put out to nurse in the country by her husband, under a feigned name.

Chrysalde. At that time, fortune being against him, he was compelled to quit his native land.

Oronte. To encounter a thousand various dangers in far-distant countries, and beyond many seas.

Chrysalde. Where his industry has acquired what in his own land he lost through roguery and envy.

Oronte. And when he returned to France, the first thing he did was to seek out her to whom he had confided the care of his daughter.

Chrysalde. This country-woman frankly told him

that she had committed her to your keeping from the age of four.

Oronte. And that she did it because she received money from you, and was very poor.

Chrysalde. Oronte, transported with joy, has even brought this woman hither.

Oronte. In short, you shall see her here directly to clear up this mystery to every one.

Chrysalde (*to* ARNOLPHE). I can almost imagine what is the cause of your grief; but fortune is kind to you. If it seems so good to you not to be a cuckold, your only course is not to marry.

Arnolphe (*going away full of rage, and unable to speak*). Ugh! ugh! ugh!

SCENE X.—ENRIQUE, ORONTE, CHRYSALDE, AGNÈS, HORACE

Oronte. Why does he run away without saying a word?

Horace. Ah, father, you shall know the whole of this surprising mystery. Accident has done here what your wisdom intended. I had engaged myself to this beauty in the sweet bonds of mutual love; it is she, in a word, whom you come to seek, and for whose sake I was about to grieve you by my refusal.

Enrique. I was sure of it as soon as I saw her; my heart has yearned for her ever since. Ah, daughter, I am overcome by such tender transports!

Chrysalde. I could be so, brother, just as well as you. But this is hardly the place for it. Let us go inside, and clear up these mysteries. Let us shew our friend some return for his great pains, and thank Heaven, which orders all for the best.

TARTUFFE;
OR, THE IMPOSTOR

TARTUFFE;
OR, THE IMPOSTOR

(Tartuffe; ou, L'Imposteur)

DRAMATIS PERSONÆ

Orgon, *husband to* Elmire.
Damis, *his son.*
Valère, Mariane's *lover.*
Cléante, Orgon's *brother-in-law.*
Tartuffe.
M. Loyal, *a tipstaff.*
A Police Officer.
Elmire, Orgon's *wife.*
Madame Pernelle, Orgon's *mother.*
Mariane, Orgon's *daughter.*
Dorine, *her maid.*
Flipote, Madame Pernelle's *servant.*

The Scene is in Paris, *in* Orgon's House

ACT I

Scene I.—Madame Pernelle, Elmire, Mariane, Cléante, Damis, Dorine, Flipote.

Madame Pernelle. Come along, Flipote, come along; let us get away from them.

Elmire. You walk so fast, that one can hardly keep up with you.

Madame Pernelle. Do not trouble yourself, daughter

107

in-law, do not trouble yourself, do not come any farther; there is no need for all this ceremony.

Elmire. We only give you your due. But pray,
mother, why are you in such haste to leave us?

Madame Pernelle. Because I cannot bear to see such
goings on. No one cares to please me. I leave your
house very little edified: all my advice is despised;
nothing is respected, everyone has his say aloud, and it
is just like the court of King Pétaud.

Dorine. If . . .

Madame Pernelle. You are, my dear, a little too much
of a talker, and a great deal too saucy for a waiting
maid. You give your advice about everything.

Damis. But . . .

Madame Pernelle. Four letters spell your name, my
child, a "fool": I, your grandmother, tell you so; and I
have already predicted to my son, your father, a
hundred times, that you are fast becoming a good-for-
nothing, who will give him nought but trouble.

Mariane. I think . . .

Madame Pernelle. Good-lack! grand-daughter, you
play the prude, and to look at you, butter would not
melt in your mouth. But still waters run deep, as the
saying is; and I do not like your sly doings at all.

Elmire. But, mother . . .

Madame Pernelle. By your leave, daughter-in-law,
your whole conduct is altogether wrong; you ought to
set them a good example; and their late mother managed them a great deal better. You are extravagant;
and it disgusts me to see you decked out like a princess. The woman who wishes to please her husband
only, daughter-in-law, has no need of so much finery.

Cléante. But after all, Madam . . .

Madame Pernelle. As for you, Sir, who are her
brother, I esteem, love, and respect you very much; but,
nevertheless, if I were my son and her husband, I would

beg of you earnestly not to enter our house. You are always laying down maxims which respectable people ought not to follow. I speak to you rather frankly; but it is a way I have got, and I do not mince my words when I have something on my mind.

Damis. Your M. Tartuffe is an angel, no doubt. . . .

Madame Pernelle. He is a very worthy man, who ought to be listened to; and I cannot, without getting angry, suffer him to be sneered at by a fool like you.

Damis. What! am I to allow a censorious bigot to usurp an absolute authority in this house! and shall we not be permitted to amuse ourselves, unless that precious gentleman condescends to give us leave!

Dorine. If any one were to listen to him and believe in his maxims, one could not do anything without committing a sin; for he controls everything, this carping critic.

Madame Pernelle. And whatever he does control, is well controlled. He wishes to lead you on the road to Heaven: and my son ought to make you all love him.

Damis. No, look here, grandmother, neither father nor anyone else shall ever induce me to look kindly upon him. I should belie my heart to say otherwise, His manners every moment enrage me; I can foresee the consequence, and one time or other I shall have to come to an open quarrel with this low-bred fellow.

Dorine. Certainly, it is a downright scandal to see a stranger exercise such authority in this house; to see a beggar, who, when he came, had not a shoe to his foot, and whose whole dress may have been worth twopence, so far forget himself as to cavil at everything, and to assume the authority of a master.

Madame Pernelle. Eh! mercy on me! things would go on much better if everything were managed according to his pious directions.

Dorine. He passes for a saint in your opinion; but believe me, he is nothing but a hypocrite.

Madame Pernelle. What a tongue!

Dorine. I should not like to trust myself with him, nor with his man Laurent, without a good guarantee.

Madame Pernelle. I do not know what the servant may be at heart; but as for the master, I will vouch for him as a good man. You bear him ill-will, and only reject him because he tells all of you the truth. It is against sin that his heart waxes wroth, and his only motive is the interest of Heaven.

Dorine. Ay; but why, particularly for some time past, can he not bear any one to come to the house? What is there offensive to Heaven in a civil visit, that there must be a noise about it fit to split one's ears? Between ourselves, do you wish me to explain? . . . (*Pointing to* ELMIRE). Upon my word, I believe him to be jealous of my mistress.

Madame Pernelle. Hold your tongue, and mind what you say. It is not he only who blames these visits. All the bustle of these people who frequent this house, these carriages everlastingly standing at the door, and the noisy crowd of so many servants, cause a great disturbance in the whole neighbourhood. I am willing to believe that there is really no harm done; but people will talk of it, and that is not right.

Cléante. Alas, Madam, will you prevent people talking? It would be a very hard thing if, in life, for the sake of the foolish things which may be said about us, we had to renounce our best friends. And even if we could resolve to do so, do you think we could compel every one to hold his tongue? There is no protection against slander. Let us, therefore, pay no regard to all this silly tittle-tattle; let us endeavour to live honestly, and leave the gossips to say what they please.

Dorine. May not Daphné, our neighbour, and her little husband, be those who speak ill of us? They whose own conduct is the most ridiculous are always the first to slander others. They never fail to catch eagerly at the slightest rumour of a love-affair, to spread the news of it with joy, and to give it the turn which they want. They think to justify their own actions before the world by those of others, painted in colours of their choosing, either in the false expectation of glossing over their own intrigues with some semblance of innocence, or else by making to fall elsewhere some part of that public blame with which they are too heavily burdened.

Madame Pernelle. All these arguments are nothing to the purpose. Orante is known to lead an exemplary life. All her cares tend to Heaven; and I have learned from people that she strongly condemns the company who visit here.

Dorine. An admirable pattern indeed, and she is very good, this lady! It is true that she lives very austerely; but age has put this ardent zeal into her breast; people know that she is a prude against her own will. She enjoyed her advantages well enough as long as she was capable of attracting attentions; but, seeing the lustre of her eyes become somewhat dim, she renounces the world which is renouncing her, and conceals under the pompous cloak of lofty wisdom, the decay of her worn-out charms. These are the vicissitudes of coquettes in our time. They find it hard to see their admirers desert them. Thus forsaken, their gloomy anxiety sees no other resource but that of prudery; and the severity of these good women censures everything and pardons nothing. Loudly they blame everyone's life, not through charity, but through envy, which cannot bear another to enjoy those pleasures for which their age gives them no longer a relish.

Madame Pernelle (*to* ELMIRE). These are cock-and-bull stories, made to please you, daughter-in-law. One is obliged to keep silence here, for Madam keeps the ball rolling all day. But I also will have my say in my turn. I tell you that my son has never done anything more sensible than in receiving this devout personage in his house; that Heaven itself, in time of need, has sent him here to reclaim all your erring minds; that for your salvation's sake, you ought to listen to him; and that he censures nothing but what is reprehensible. These visits, these balls, these conversations, are all inventions of the evil one. One never hears a pious word uttered at any of them; nothing but tittle-tattle, nonsense, and silly gossip. Very often our neighbour comes in for his share of it, and there is back-biting going on right and left. In short, sensible people have their heads turned by the confusion of such meetings. A thousand idle stories are told in no time; and, as a certain doctor said very aptly the other day, it is a perfect tower of Babylon, for every one chatters to his heart's content; and to show you what brought this up . . . (*pointing to* CLÉANTE). But here is this gentleman giggling already! Go and look for some fools to laugh at, and without . . . (*to* ELMIRE). Good-bye, daughter-in-law; I will say no more. I make you a present of the rest, but it will be a fine day when I set my foot in your house again. (*Slapping* FLIPOTE's *face.*) Come along you, you stand dreaming and gaping here. Ods bobs! I shall warm your ears for you. March on, slut, march on.

SCENE II.—CLÉANTE, DORINE.

Cléante. I shall not go with her, for fear she should fall foul of me again; that this good lady . . .

Dorine. Ah! it is a pity that she does not hear you

say so: she would tell you that you are good, but that she is not yet old enough to be called so.

Cléante. How she fired up against us for nothing! And how infatuated she seems with her Tartuffe!

Dorine. Oh! indeed, all this is nothing compared with the son: and if you saw him, you would say it is much worse. During our troubles he acted like a man of sense, and displayed some courage in the service of his prince; but since he has grown so fond of this Tartuffe, he is become a perfect dolt. He calls him brother, and loves him in his very soul a hundred times better than either mother, son, daughter, or wife. He is the sole confidant of all his secrets, and the prudent director of all his actions; he caresses him, embraces him; and one could show no more affection, I think, to a mistress. He will have him seated at the upper end of the table, and is delighted to see him eat as much as six; the choicest morsels of everything must be given to him; and, if he happens to belch, he says to him "God preserve you." In short, he is crazy about him; he is his all, his hero; he admires everything he does, he quotes him on all occasions; he looks upon his most trifling actions as miracles, and every word he utters is considered an oracle. The other, who knows his dupe, and wishes to make the most of him, has the art of dazzling him by a hundred deceitful appearances. His pretended devotion draws money from him at every hour of the day; and assumes the right of commenting upon the conduct of every one of us. Even the jackanapes, his servant, pretends also to read us a lesson; he comes preaching to us with fierce looks, and throws away our ribbons, our paint, and our patches. Only the other day, the wretch tore a handkerchief which he had found between the leaves of *"The Flower of the Saints,"* saying that it was a dreadful sin to bring these holy things into contact with the devil's deckings.

SCENE III.—ELMIRE, MARIANE, DAMIS, CLÉANTE, DORINE.

Elmire (*to* CLÉANTE). You are very fortunate not to have assisted at the speech to which she treated us at the door. But I have just seen my husband; and as he did not see me, I shall go upstairs to await his coming.

Cléante. I will wait for him here, with small pleasure; and merely say how do ye do to him.

SCENE IV.—CLÉANTE, DAMIS, DORINE.

Damis. Just sound him about this marriage of my sister. I suspect that Tartuffe is opposed to it, because he makes my father use so many evasions; and you are not ignorant how greatly I am interested in it. . . . If the same passion fires my sister's and Valère's heart, the sister of this friend is, as you know, dear to me; and 'i it were necessary . . .

Dorine. Here he is.

SCENE V.—ORGON, CLÉANTE, DORINE.

Orgon. Ha! good morrow, brother.

Cléante. I was just going, and am glad to see you returned. The country is not very cheering at present.

Orgon. Dorine . . . (*to* CLÉANTE). Pray, one moment, brother-in-law. Allow me to inquire the news here to ease my mind. (*To* DORINE). Has everything gone on well these two days? What are they doing, and how are they all?

Dorine. The day before yesterday my mistress had an attack of fever until evening, accompanied by an extraordinary headache.

Orgon. And Tartuffe?

Dorine. Tartuffe! He is wonderfully well, stout and fat, with a fresh complexion, and a ruddy mouth.

Orgon. Poor fellow!

Dorine. In the evening she felt very sick, and could not touch a morsel of supper, so violent was still the pain in her head.

Orgon. And Tartuffe?

Dorine. He supped by himself in her presence; and very devoutly ate two partridges, and half a leg of mutton hashed.

Orgon. Poor fellow!

Dorine. The whole night she did not close her eyes for a moment. She was so feverish that she could not sleep, and we were obliged to sit up with her until morning.

Orgon. And Tartuffe?

Dorine. Pleasantly overcome with sleep, he went to his room when he left the table; and jumped into his cozy bed, where he slept undisturbed until morning.

Orgon. Poor fellow!

Dorine. We at length prevailed upon the mistress to be bled; and she was almost immediately relieved.

Orgon. And Tartuffe?

Dorine. He picked up his courage again as he ought to; and, to fortify himself against all harm, he drank four large draughts of wine at breakfast, to make up for the blood that the mistress had lost.

Orgon. Poor fellow!

Dorine. At present, they are both well; and I shall go and inform the mistress how glad you feel at her recovery.

Scene VI.—Orgon, Cléante.

Cléante. She is laughing at you to your face, brother: and, without wishing to make you angry, I must tell you candidly that it is not without reason. Was there ever such a whim heard of? Can it be possible that any man could so charm you now-a-days as to make you forget everything for him? That after having relieved his

indigence, in your own house, you should go as far
as . . .

Orgon. Stop, brother-in-law, you do not know the
man of whom you are speaking?

Cléante. I do not know him, if you like; but after all,
in order to know what sort of man he is . . .

Orgon. You would be charmed to know him, brother;
and there would be no end to your delight. He is a
man . . . who . . . ah . . . a man . . . in short, a man.
One who acts up to his own precepts, enjoys a profound
peace, and looks upon the whole world as so much dirt.
Yes; I am quite another man since I conversed with him;
he teaches me to set my heart upon nothing; he detaches
my mind from all friendship; and I could see brother,
children, mother, and wife die, without troubling myself
in the least about it.

Cléante. Humane sentiments these, brother!

Orgon. Ah! if you had seen how I first met him, you
would have conceived the same friendship for him that
I feel. Every day he came to church, and, with a gentle
mien, kneeled down opposite me. He attracted the notice of the whole congregation by the fervency with which
he sent up his prayers to heaven. He uttered sighs, was
enraptured, and humbly kissed the ground every moment:
and when I went out, he swiftly ran before me to offer
me holy water at the door. Informed by his servant,
who imitates him in everything, of his poverty, and who
he was, I made him some presents: but, with great modesty, he always wished to return some part of them.
"It is too much," he would say; "too much by half; I
do not deserve your pity." And when I refused to take
them back again, he would go and give them to the poor
before my face. At length Heaven moved me to take
him to my house, and since then, everything seems to
prosper here. I perceive that he reproves everything,
and that he takes a great interest, even in my wife, for

my sake. He warns me of the people who look too lov-
ingly at her, and he is six times more jealous of her than
I am. But you cannot believe how far his zeal goes: the
slightest trifle in himself he calls a sin; a mere nothing is
sufficient to shock him; so much so that he accused himself, the other day, of having caught a flea whilst he was
at his devotions, and of having killed it with too much
anger.

Cléante. Zounds! I believe you are mad, brother.
Are you making game of me with such a speech? and do
you pretend that all this fooling . . .

Orgon. Brother, this discourse savours of free-think-
ing. You are somewhat tainted with it; and, as I have
often told you, you will get yourself into some unpleasant scrape.

Cléante. The usual clap-trap of your set; they wish
everyone to be blind like themselves. To keep one's
eyes open is to be a free-thinker; and whosoever does not
worship empty mummeries has neither respect for, nor
faith in, holy things. Go along; all your speeches do not
frighten me; I know what I am saying, and Heaven sees
my heart. We are not the slaves of your formalists.
There are hypocrites in religion as well as pretenders to
courage; and as we never find the truly brave man make
much noise where honour leads him, no more are the
good and truly pious, whom we ought to follow, those
who make so many grimaces. What! would you make
no distinction between hypocrisy and true devotion?
Would you treat them both alike, and give the same
honour to the mask as to the face; put artifice on a level
with sincerity, confound appearance with reality, value
the shadow as much as the substance; and false coin the
same as real? Men, for the most part, are strange creatures, and never keep the right mean; reason's boundaries
are too narrow for them; in every character they overact
their parts; and they often spoil the noblest designs, be-

cause they exaggerate, and carry them too far. This
by the way, brother.

Orgon. Yes, you are no doubt a doctor to be looked
up to; you possess all the world's wisdom; you are the
only sage, and the only enlightened man, an oracle, a
Cato of the present age; and all men, compared with
you, are fools.

Cléante. I am not, brother, a doctor to be looked up
to; nor do I possess all the world's wisdom. But, in
one word, I know enough to distinguish truth from falsehood. And as I know no character more worthy of
esteem than the truly devout, nor anything in the world
more noble or beautiful than the holy fervour of sincere
piety, so I know nothing more odious than the whited
sepulchre of a pretended zealot, than those downright
impostors, those devotees, for public show, whose sacri-
legious and deceitful grimaces abuse with impunity, and
make a jest, according to their fancy, of what men hold
most holy and sacred; those men who, from motives of
self-interest, make a trade of piety, and would purchase
honour and reputation at the cost of a hypocritical turning up of the eyes and pretended raptures; those men,
I say, whom we see possessed with such an uncommon
ardour for the next world, in order to make their fortunes in this; who, with great unction and many
prayers, daily recommend and preach solitude in the
midst of the court; who know how to reconcile their
zeal with their vices; who are passionate, vindictive,
without belief, full of artifice, and would, in order to
destroy a man, insolently cover their fierce resentment
under the cloak of Heaven's interests. They are the
more dangerous in their bitter wrath because they use
against us weapons which men reverence, and because
their passion, for which they are commended, prompts
them to assassinate us with a consecrated blade. One
sees too many of those vile characters, but the really de-

vout at heart are easily recognized. Our age has shown
us some, brother, who may serve us as glorious exam
ples. Look at Ariston, look at Périandre, Oronte, Al
cidamas, Polydore, Clitandre—no one disputes their title.
But they do not boast of their virtue. One does not
see this unbearable ostentation in them; and their piety
is human, is tractable; they do not censure all our doings,
they think that these corrections would show too much
pride on their part; and, leaving big words to others,
they reprove our actions by their own. They do not
think anything evil, because it seems so, and their mind
is inclined to judge well of others. They have no cabals,
no intrigues; all their anxiety is to live well themselves.
They never persecute a sinner; they hate sin only, and
do not vindicate the interest of Heaven with greater zeal
than Heaven itself. These are my people, that is the true
way to act; that is, in short, an example to be followed.
Your man, to speak plainly, is not of that stamp; you
vaunt his zeal with the utmost good faith; but I believe
that you are dazzled by a false glare.

Orgon. My dear brother-in-law, have you had your
say?

Cléante. Yes.

Orgon (*going*). I am your humble servant.

Cléante. Pray, one word more, brother. Let us drop
this conversation. You know that Valère has your promise to be your son-in-law.

Orgon. Yes.

Cléante. And that you would appoint a day for the
wedding.

Orgon. True.

Cléante. Why then defer the ceremony?

Orgon. I do not know.

Cléante. Have you another design in your mind?

Orgon. Perhaps so.

Cléante. Will you break your word?

Orgon. I do not say that.

Cléante. There is no obstacle, I think, to prevent you from fulfilling your promise?

Orgon. That is as it may be.

Cléante. Why so much ado about a single word? Valère sent me to you about it.

Orgon. Heaven be praised for that!

Cléante. But what answer shall I give him?

Orgon. Whatever you please.

Cléante. But it is necessary to know your intentions. What are they?

Orgon. To do just what Heaven ordains.

Cléante. But to the point. Valère has your promise: will you keep it or not?

Orgon. Farewell.

Cléante (alone). I fear some misfortune for his love, and I ought to inform him of what is going on.

ACT II

Scene I.—Orgon, Mariane.

Orgon. Mariane.

Mariane. Father?

Orgon. Come here; I have something to say to you privately.

Mariane (*to* Orgon, *who is looking into a closet*) What are you looking for?

Orgon. I am looking whether there is anyone there who might overhear us; for it is a most likely little place for such a purpose. Now we are all right. Mariane, I have always found you of a sweet disposition, and you have always been very dear to me.

Mariane. I am much obliged to you for this fatherly affection.

Orgon. That is very well said, daughter; and to deserve it, your only care should be to please me.

Mariane. That is my greatest ambition.

Orgon. Very well. What say you of our guest Tartuffe?

Mariane. Who? I?

Orgon. You. Be careful how you answer.

Mariane. Alas! I will say whatever you like of him.

Scene II.—Orgon, Mariane, Dorine (*entering softly and keeping behind* Orgon, *without being seen*).

Orgon. That is sensibly spoken. . . . Tell me then, my child, that he is a man of the highest worth; that he has touched your heart; and that it would be pleasant to you to see him, with my approbation, become your husband. Eh? (Mariane *draws away with surprise.*)

Mariane. He!

Orgon. What is the matter?

Mariane. What did you say?

Orgon. What?

Mariane. Did I mistake?

Orgon. How?

Mariane. What would you have me say has touched my heart, father, and whom would it be pleasant to have for a husband, with your approbation?

Orgon. Tartuffe.

Mariane. But it is nothing of the kind, father, I assure you. Why would you have me tell such a falsehood?

Orgon. But I wish it to be a truth; and it is sufficient for you that I have resolved it so.

Mariane. What, father would you . . .

Orgon. Yes, daughter, I intend by your marriage to unite Tartuffe to my family. He shall be your husband; I have decided that; and as on your duty I . . . (*perceiving* DORINE). What are you doing here? Your anxious curiosity is very great, my dear, to induce you to listen to us in this manner.

Dorine. In truth, I do not know whether this is a mere report, arising from conjecture or from chance; but they have just told me the news of this marriage, and I treated it as a pure hoax.

Orgon. Why so! Is the thing incredible?

Dorine. So much so, that even from you, Sir, I do not believe it.

Orgon. I know how to make you believe it, though.

Dorine. Yes, yes, you are telling us a funny story.

Orgon. I am telling you exactly what you will see shortly.

Dorine. Nonsense!

Orgon. What I say is not in jest, daughter.

Dorine. Come, do not believe your father; he is joking.

Orgon. I tell you . . .

Dorine. No, you may say what you like; nobody will believe you.

Orgon. My anger will at last . . .

Dorine. Very well! we will believe you then; and so much the worse for you. What! is it possible, Sir, that, with that air of common sense, and this great beard in the very midst of your face, you would be foolish enough to be willing to . . .

Orgon. Now listen: you have taken certain liberties in this house, which I do not like; I tell you so, my dear.

Dorine. Let us speak without getting angry, Sir, I beg. Is it to laugh at people that you have planned this scheme? Your daughter is not suitable for a bigot: he has other things to think about. And, besides, what will such an alliance bring you? Why, with all your wealth, go and choose a beggar for your son-in-law . . .

Orgon. Hold your tongue. If he has nothing, know that it is just for that that we ought to esteem him. His poverty is no doubt an honest poverty; it ought to raise him above all grandeur, because he has allowed himself to be deprived of his wealth by his little care for worldly affairs, and his strong attachment to things eternal. But my assistance may give him the means of getting out of his troubles, and of recovering his property. His estates are well known in his country; and, such as you see him, he is quite the nobleman.

Dorine. Yes, so he says; and this vanity, Sir, does not accord well with piety. Whosoever embraces the innocence of a holy life should not boast so much about his name and his lineage; and the humble ways of piety do but ill agree with this outburst of ambition. What is the good of this pride. . . . But this discourse offends you: let us speak of himself, and leave his nobility alone. Would you, without some compunction, give a girl like her to a man like him? And ought you not to have some regard for propriety, and foresee the consequences of such a union? Be sure that a girl's virtue is in danger when her choice is thwarted in her marriage; that her living virtuously depends upon the qualities of the husband whom they have chosen for her, and that those whose foreheads are pointed at everywhere often make of their wives what we see that they are. It is, in short, no easy task to be faithful to husbands cut out after a certain model; and he who gives to his daughter a man whom she hates, is responsible to Heaven for the faults she commits. Consider to what perils your design exposes you.

Orgon. I tell you I must learn from her what to do!

Dorine. You cannot do better than follow my advice.

Orgon. Do not let us waste any more time with this silly prattle, daughter; I am your father, and know what is best for you. I had promised you to Valère; but besides his being inclined to gamble, as I am told, I also suspect him to be somewhat of a free-thinker; I never notice him coming to church.

Dorine. Would you like him to run there at your stated hours, like those who go there only to be seen?

Orgon. I am not asking your advice upon that. The other candidate for your hand is, in short, on the best of terms with Heaven, and that is a treasure second to none. This union will crown your wishes with every kind of blessings, it will be replete with sweetness and delight. You shall live together in faithful love, really like two children, like two turtle-doves; there will be no annoying disputes between you; and you will make anything you like of him.

Dorine. She? she will never make anything but a fool of him, I assure you.

Orgon. Heyday! what language!

Dorine. I say that he has the appearance of one, and

that his destiny, Sir, will be stronger than all your daughter's virtue.

Orgon. Leave off interrupting me, and try to hold your tongue, without poking your nose into what does not concern you.

Dorine (*she continually interrupts him as he turns round to speak to his daughter*). I speak only for your interest, Sir.

Orgon. You interest yourself too much; hold your tongue, if you please.

Dorine. If one did not care for you . . .

Orgon. I do not wish you to care for me.

Dorine. And I will care for you, Sir, in spite of yourself.

Orgon. Ah!

Dorine. Your honour is dear to me, and I cannot bear to see you the byeword of everyone.

Orgon. You will not hold your tongue?

Dorine. It is a matter of conscience to allow you to form such an alliance.

Orgon. Will you hold your tongue, you serpent, whose brazen face . . .

Dorine. What! you are religious, and fly in a rage?

Orgon. Yes, all your nonsense has excited my choler, and once for all, you shall hold your tongue.

Dorine. Be it so. But, though I do not say a word I will think none the less.

Orgon. Think, if you like; but take care not to say a word, or . . . (*turning to his daughter*). That will do. As a sensible man, I have carefully weighed everything.

Dorine (*aside*). It drives me mad that I must not speak.

Orgon. Without being a fop, Tartuffe's mien is such . . .

Dorine. Yes, his is a very pretty phiz!

Orgon. That even if you have no sympathy with his other gifts . . .

Dorine (*aside*). She has got a bargain! (ORGON *turns to* DORINE, *and, with crossed arms, listens and looks her in the face.*) If I were in her place, assuredly no man should marry me against my will with impunity; and I would show him, and that soon after the ceremony, that a woman has always a revenge at hand.

Orgon (*to* DORINE). Then you do not heed what I say?

Dorine. What are you grumbling at? I did not speak to you.

Orgon. What did you do then?

Dorine. I was speaking to myself.

Orgon (*aside*). Very well! I must give her a back-hander to pay her out for her extreme insolence. (*He puts himself into a position to slap* DORINE'S *face; and, at every word which he says to his daughter, he turns round to look at* DORINE, *who stands bolt upright without speaking.*) You ought to approve of my plan, daughter . . . and believe that the husband whom I have selected for you . . . (*to* DORINE). Why do you not speak to yourself?

Dorine. I have nothing to say to myself.

Orgon. Just another little word.

Dorine. It does not suit me.

Orgon. I was looking out for you, be sure.

Dorine. I am not such a fool as you think me!

Orgon. In short, daughter, you must obey, and show a complete deference to my choice.

Dorine (*running away*). I would not care a straw for such a husband.

Orgon (*failing to slap* DORINE'S *face*). You have a pestilent hussy with you, daughter, with whom I cannot put up any longer without forgetting myself. I do not feel equal to continue our conversation now; her insolent remarks have set my brain on fire, and I must have a breath of air to compose myself.

Scene III.—Mariane, Dorine.

Dorine. Tell me have you lost your speech? And must I act your part in this affair? To allow such a senseless proposal to be made to you, without saying the least word against it!

Mariane. What would you have me do against a tyrannical father?

Dorine. That which is necessary to ward off such a threat.

Mariane. What?

Dorine. Tell him that you cannot love by proxy, that you marry for yourself, and not for him; that, you being the only one concerned in this matter, it is you, and not he, who must like the husband, and that since Tartuffe is so charming in his eyes, he may marry him himself without let or hindrance.

Mariane. Ah! a father, I confess, has so much authority over us, that I have never had the courage to answer him.

Dorine. But let us argue this affair. Valère has proposed for you: do you love him, pray, or do you not?

Mariane. Ah! you do my feelings great injustice, Dorine, to ask me such a question. Have I not a hundred times opened my heart to you? and do not you know the warmth of my affection for him?

Dorine. How do I know whether your lips have spoken what your heart felt? and whether you have any real regard for this lover?

Mariane. You wrong me greatly in doubting it, Dorine; for my true sentiments have been but too clearly shown.

Dorine. You really love him, then?

Mariane. Yes, very passionately.

Dorine. And, to all appearance, he loves you as well?

Mariane. I believe so.

Dorine. And you are both equally eager to marry each other?

Mariane. Assuredly.

Dorine. What do you expect from this other match then?

Mariane. To kill myself, if they force me to it.

Dorine. Very well. That is a resource I did not think of; you have only to die to get out of trouble. The remedy is doubtless admirable. It drives me mad to hear this sort of talk.

Mariane. Good gracious! Dorine, what a temper you get into! You do not sympathize in the least with people's troubles.

Dorine. I do not sympathize with people who talk stupidly, and, when an opportunity presents itself, give way as you do!

Mariane. But what would you have me do? If I am timid . . .

Dorine. Love requires firmness.

Mariane. But have I wavered in my affection towards Valère? and is it not his duty to obtain a father's consent?

Dorine. But what! if your father is a downright churl, who is completely taken up with Tartuffe, and will break off a match he had agreed on, is your lover to be blamed for that?

Mariane. But am I, by a flat refusal and a scornful disdain, to let everyone know how much I am smitten? However brilliant Valère may be, am I to forget the modesty of my sex, and my filial duty? And would you have me display my passion to the whole world . . .

Dorine. No, I would have you do nothing of the sort. I perceive that you would like to be M. Tartuffe's; and I should be wrong, now that I come to think of it, to

turn you from such a union. What right have I to oppose your wishes? The match in itself is very advan-
tageous. Monsieur Tartuffe! oh, oh! That is not a proposal to be despised. Certainly Monsieur Tartuffe, all
things considered, is no fool; no, not at all, and it is no
small honour to be his better half. Already everyone
crowns him with glory. He is a noble in his own country,
handsome in appearance; he has red ears and a florid
complexion. You will live only too happily with such
a husband.

Mariane. Good gracious! . . .

Dorine. How joyful you will be to see yourself the
wife of such a handsome husband!

Mariane. Ah! leave off such talk, I pray, and rather
assist me to free myself from this match. It is finished:
I yield, and am ready to do anything.

Dorine. No, a daughter ought to obey her father,
even if he wishes her to marry an ape. Yours is an
enviable fate: of what do you complain? You will drive
down in the stage-coach to his native town, where you
will find plenty of uncles and cousins, whom it will be
your great delight to entertain. You will be introduced
directly into the best society. You will go and pay the
first visits to the wife of the bailie, and of the assessor,
who will do you the honour of giving you a folding-chair.
There, at carnival time, you may expect a ball, with the
grand band of musicians, to wit, two bagpipes, and sometimes Fagotin and the marionettes. If your husband,
however . . .

Mariane. Oh! you kill me. Try rather to assist me
with your counsels.

Dorine. I am your servant.

Mariane. Ah! for pity's sake, Dorine . . .

Dorine. This affair ought to go on, to punish you.

Mariane. There's a good girl!

Dorine. No.

Mariane. If I declare to you that . . .

Dorine. Not at all. Tartuffe is the man for you, and you shall have a taste of him.

Mariane. You know that I have always confided in you: do . . .

Dorine. No, it is of no use, you shall be Tartuffed.

Mariane. Very well, since my misfortunes cannot move you, leave me henceforth entirely to my despair. My heart shall seek help from that; and I know an infallible remedy for my sufferings. (*She wishes to go.*)

Dorine. Stop, stop, come back. I give in. In spite of all, I must take compassion on you.

Mariane. Look here, Dorine, if they inflict this cruel martyrdom upon me, I shall die of it, I tell you.

Dorine. Do not fret yourself. We will cleverly prevent. . . . But here comes Valère, your lover.

SCENE IV.—VALÈRE, MARIANE, DORINE.

Valère. I have just been told a piece of news, Madam, which I did not know, and which is certainly very pretty.

Mariane. What is it?

Valère. That you are going to be married to Tartuffe.

Mariane. My father has taken this idea into his head, certainly.

Valère. Your father, Madam . . .

Mariane. Has altered his mind: he has just proposed this affair to me.

Valère. What! seriously?

Mariane. Yes, seriously, he has openly declared himself for this match.

Valère. And what have you decided, in your own mind, Madam?

Mariane. I know not.

Valère. The answer is polite. **You know not?**

Mariane. No.

Valère. No?

Mariane. What do you advise me?

Valère. I, I advise you to take this husband.

Mariane. Is that your advice?

Valère. Yes.

Mariane. Seriously?

Valère. Doubtless. The choice is glorious, and well worth consideration.

Mariane. Very well, Sir, I shall act upon the advice.

Valère. That will not be very painful, I think.

Mariane. Not more painful than for you to give it.

Valère. I gave it to please you, Madam.

Mariane. And I shall follow it to please you.

Dorine. (*Retiring to the further part of the stage*). Let us see what this will come to.

Valère. This then is your affection? And it was all deceit when you . . .

Mariane. Do not let us speak of that, I pray. You have told me quite candidly that I ought to accept the husband selected for me; and I declare that I intend to do so, since you give me this wholesome advice.

Valère. Do not make my advise your excuse. Your resolution was taken beforehand; and you catch at a frivolous pretext to justify the breaking of your word.

Mariane. Very true, and well put.

Valère. No doubt; and you never had any real affection for me.

Mariane. Alas! think so, if you like.

Valère. Yes, yes, if I like; but my offended feelings may perhaps forestall you in such a design; and I know where to offer both my heart and my hand.

Mariane. Ah! I have no doubt of it; and the love which merit can command . . .

Valère. For Heaven's sake, let us drop merit. I have but little, no doubt; and you have given proof of it. But I hope much from the kindness of some one whose heart is open to me, and who will not be ashamed to consent to repair my loss.

Mariane. The loss is not great: and you will easily enough console yourself for this change.

Valère. I shall do my utmost, you may depend. A heart that forgets us wounds our self-love; we must do our best to forget it also; if we do not succeed, we must at least pretend to do so: for the meanness is unpardonable of still loving when we are forsaken.

Mariane. This is, no doubt, an elevated and noble sentiment.

Valère. It is so; and every one must approve of it. What! would you have me forever to nourish my ardent affection for you, and not elsewhere bestow that heart which you reject, whilst I see you, before my face, pass into the arms of another?

Mariane. On the contrary; as for me, that is what I would have you do, and I wish it were done already.

Valère. You wish it?

Mariane. Yes.

Valère. That is a sufficient insult, Madam; and I shall satisfy you this very moment. (*He pretends to go*).

Mariane. Very well.

Valère (*coming back*). Remember at least, that you yourself drive me to this extremity.

Mariane. Yes.

Valère (*coming back once more*). And that I am only following your example.

Mariane. Very well, my example.

Valère (*going*). That will do: you shall be obeyed on the spot.

Mariane. So much the better.

Valère (*coming back again*). This is the last time that you will ever see me.

Mariane. That is right.

Valère (*goes, and turns round at the door*). He?

Mariane. What is the matter?

Valère. Did you call me?

Mariane. I! You are dreaming.

Valère. Well! then I will be gone. Farewell, Madam. (*He goes slowly.*)

Mariane. Farewell, Sir.

Dorine (*to* MARIANE). I think that you are losing your senses with all this folly. I have all along allowed you to quarrel, to see what it would lead to at last. Hullo, M. Valère. (*She takes hold of* VALÈRE'S *arm.*)

Valère (*pretending to resist*). Well! what do you want, Dorine?

Dorine. Come here.

Valère. No, no, I feel too indignant. Do not hinder me from doing as she wishes me.

Dorine. Stop.

Valère. No; look here, I have made up my mind.

Dorine. Ah!

Mariane (*aside*). He cannot bear to see me, my presence drives him away; and I had therefore much better leave the place.

Dorine (*quitting* VALÈRE *and running after* MARIANE). Now for the other! Where are you running to?

Mariane. Let me alone.

Dorine. You must come back.

Mariane. No, no, Dorine; it is of no use detaining me.

Valère (*aside*). I see, but too well, that the sight of me annoys her; and I had, no doubt, better free her from it.

Dorine (*leaving* MARIANE *and running after* VALÈRE). What, again! The devil take you! Yes. I will have it so. Cease this fooling, and come here, both of you. (*She holds them both.*)

Valère (*to* DORINE). But what are you about?

Mariane (*to* DORINE). What would you do?

Dorine. I would have you make it up together, and get out of this scrape. (*To* VALÈRE.) Are you made to wrangle in this way?

Valère. Did you not hear how she spoke to me?

Dorine (*to* MARIANE). Aren't you silly to have got into such a passion?

Mariane. Did you not see the thing, and how he has treated me?

Dorine. Folly on both sides (*to* VALÈRE). She has no other wish than to remain yours, I can vouch for it. (*To* MARIANE.) He loves none but you, and desires nothing more than to be your husband. I will answer for it with my life.

Mariane (*to* VALÈRE). Why then did you give me such advice?

Valère (*to* MARIANE). Why did you ask me for it on such a subject?

Dorine. You are a pair of fools. Come, your hands, both of you. (*To* VALÈRE.) Come, yours.

Valère (*giving his hand to* DORINE). What is the good of my hand?

Dorine (*to* MARIANE). Come now! yours.

Mariane (*giving hers*). What is the use of all this?

Dorine. Good Heavens! quick, come on. You love each other better than you think. (VALÈRE *and* MARIANE *hold each other's hands for some time without speaking*.)

Valère (*turning towards* MARIANE). Do not do things with such bad grace; look at one a little without any hatred. (MARIANE *turns to* VALÈRE, *and gives him a little smile*).

Dorine. Truth to tell, lovers are great fools!

Valère (*to* MARIANE). Now really! have I no reason to complain of you; and, without an untruth, are you not a naughty girl to delight in saying disagreeable things?

Mariane. And you, are you not the most ungrateful fellow . . .

Dorine. Leave all this debate till another time, and let us think about averting this confounded marriage.

Mariane. Tell us, then, what we are to do.

Dorine. We must do many things (*to* MARIANE). Your father does but jest (*to* VALÈRE); and it is all talk. (*To* MARIANE.) But as for you, you had better appear to comply quietly with his nonsense, so that, in case of need, it may be easier for you to put off this proposed marriage. In gaining time, we gain everything. Sometimes you can pretend a sudden illness, that will necessitate a delay; then you can pretend some evil omens, that you unluckily met a corpse, broke a looking-glass, or dreamed of muddy water. In short, the best of it is that they cannot unite you to any one else but him, unless you please to say yes. But, the better to succeed, I think it advisable that you should not be seen talking together. (*To* VALÈRE.) Now go; and without delay, employ your friends to make Orgon keep his promise to you. We will interest her brother, and enlist her mother-in-law on our side. Good-bye.

Valère (*to* MARIANE). Whatever efforts we may make together, my greatest hope, to tell the truth, is in you.

Mariane (*to* VALÈRE). I cannot answer for the will of a father; but I shall be no one but Valère's.

Valère. Oh, how happy you make me! And, whatever they may attempt . . .

Dorine. Ah! lovers are never weary of prattling. Be off, I tell you.

Valère (*goes a step, and returns*). After all . . .

Dorine. What a cackle! Go you this way; and you, the other. (DORINE *pushes each of them by the shoulder, and compels them to separate.*)

ACT III

Scene I.—Damis, Dorine.

Damis. May lightning strike me dead on the spot, may everyone treat me as the greatest of scoundrels, if any respect or authority shall stop me from doing something rash!

Dorine. Curb this temper for Heaven's sake: your father did but mention it. People do not carry out all their proposals; and the road between the saying and the doing is a long one.

Damis. I must put a stop to this fellow's plots, and whisper a word or two in his ear.

Dorine. Gently, pray! leave him, and your father as well, to your mother-in-law's management. She has some influence with Tartuffe: he agrees to all that she says, and I should not wonder if he had some sneaking regard for her. Would to Heaven that it were true! A pretty thing that would be. In short, your interest obliges her to send for him: she wishes to sound him about this marriage that troubles you, to know his intentions, and to acquaint him with the sad contentions which he may cause, if he entertains any hope on this subject. His servant told me he was at prayers, and that I could not get sight of him; but said that he was coming down. Go, therefore, I pray you, and let me wait for him.

Damis. I may be present at this interview.

Dorine. Not at all. They must be alone.

Damis. I shall not say a word to him.

Dorine. You deceive yourself: we know your usual outbursts; and that is just the way to spoil all. Go.

Damis. No; I will see, without getting angry.

Dorine. How tiresome you are! Here he comes. Go away. (DAMIS *hides himself in a closet at the farther end of the stage.*)

SCENE II.—TARTUFFE, DORINE.

Tartuffe. (*The moment he perceives* DORINE, *he begins to speak loudly to his servant, who is behind*). Laurent, put away my hair shirt and my scourge, and pray that Heaven may ever enlighten you. If any one calls to see me, say that I have gone to the prisoners to distribute the alms which I have received.

Dorine (*aside*). What affectation and boasting!

Tartuffe. What do you want?

Dorine. To tell you . . .

Tartuffe (*pulling a handkerchief from his pocket*). For Heaven's sake! before you go any farther, take this handkerchief, I pray.

Dorine. For what?

Tartuffe. Cover this bosom, which I cannot bear to see. The spirit is offended by such sights, and they evoke sinful thoughts.

Dorine. You are, then, mighty susceptible to temptation; and the flesh seems to make a great impression on your senses! I cannot tell, of course, what heat inflames you: but my desires are not so easily aroused; and I could see you naked from top to toe, without being in the least tempted by the whole of your skin.

Tartuffe. Be a little more modest in your expressions, or I shall leave you on the spot.

Dorine. No, no, it is I who am going to leave you to yourself; and I have only two words to say to you. My mistress is coming down into this parlour, and wishes the favour of a minute's conversation with you.

Tartuffe. Alas! with all my heart.

Dorine (*aside*). How he softens down! Upon my
word, I stick to what I have said of him.

Tartuffe. Will she be long?

Dorine. Methinks I hear her. Yes, it is herself, and
I leave you together.

SCENE III.—ELMIRE, TARTUFFE.

Tartuffe. May Heaven, in its mighty goodness, for
ever bestow upon you health, both of soul and body, and
bless your days as much as the humblest of its votaries
desires.

Elmire. I am much obliged for this pious wish. But
let us take a seat, to be more at ease.

Tartuffe (*seated*). Are you quite recovered from your
indisposition?

Elmire (*seated*). Quite; the fever soon left me.

Tartuffe. My prayers are not deserving enough to
have drawn this grace from above; but not one of them
ascended to Heaven that had not your recovery for its
object.

Elmire. You are too anxious in your zeal for me.

Tartuffe. We cannot cherish your dear health too
much; and to re-establish yours, I would have given
mine.

Elmire. That is pushing Christian charity very far;
and I feel much indebted to you for all this kindness.

Tartuffe. I do much less for you than you deserve.

Elmire. I wished to speak to you in private about a
certain matter, and am glad that no one is here to observe us.

Tartuffe. I am equally delighted; and, indeed, it is
very pleasant to me, Madam, to find myself alone with
you. I have often asked Heaven for this opportunity,
but, till now, in vain.

Elmire. What I wish is a few words with you, upon
a small matter, in which you must open your heart and

conceal nothing from me. (Damis, *without showing himself, half opens the door of the closet into which he had retired to listen to the conversation.*)

Tartuffe. And I will also, in return for this rare favour, unbosom myself entirely to you, and swear to you that the reports which I have spread about the visits which you receive in homage of your charms, do not spring from any hatred towards you, but rather from a passionate zeal which carries me away, and out of a pure motive . . .

Elmire. That is how I take it. I think it is for my good that you trouble yourself so much.

Tartuffe (*taking* Elmire's *hand and pressing her fingers*). Yes, Madam, no doubt; and my fervour is such . . .

Elmire. Oh! you squeeze me too hard.

Tartuffe. It is through excess of zeal. I never had any intention of hurting you, and would sooner . . . (*He places his hand on* Elmire's *knee*).

Elmire. What does your hand there?

Tartuffe. I am only feeling your dress: the stuff is very soft.

Elmire. Oh! please leave off, I am very ticklish. (Elmire *pushes her chair back, and* Tartuffe *draws near with his*).

Tartuffe (*handling* Elmire's *collar*). Bless me! how wonderful is the workmanship of this lace! They work in a miraculous manner now-a-days; never was anything so beautifully made.

Elmire. It is true. But let us have some talk about our affair. I have been told that my husband wishes to retract his promise, and give you his daughter. Is it true? Tell me.

Tartuffe. He has hinted something to me; but to tell you the truth, Madam, that is not the happiness for which I am sighing: I behold elsewhere the marvellous attractions of that bliss which forms the height of my wishes.

Elmire.   That is because you have no love for earthly things.

Tartuffe.   My breast does not contain a heart of flint.

Elmire.   I believe that all your sighs tend towards Heaven, and that nothing here below rouses your desires.

Tartuffe.   The love which attaches us to eternal beauties does not stifle in us the love of earthly things; our senses may easily be charmed by the perfect works which Heaven has created.   Its reflected loveliness shines forth in such as you; but in you alone it displays its choicest wonders.   It has diffused on your face such beauty, that it dazzles the eyes and transports the heart; nor could I behold you, perfect creature, without admiring in you nature's author, and feeling my heart smitten with an ardent love for the most beautiful of portraits, wherein he has reproduced himself.   At first I feared that this secret ardour might be nothing but a cunning snare of the foul fiend; and my heart even resolved to fly your presence, thinking that you might be an obstacle to my salvation.   But at last I found, O most lovely beauty, that my passion could not be blameable; that I could reconcile it with modesty; and this made me freely indulge it.   It is, I confess, a great presumption in me to dare to offer you this heart; but I expect, in my affections, everything from your kindness, and nothing from the vain efforts of my own weakness.   In you is my hope, my happiness, my peace; on you depends my torment or my bliss; and it is by your decision solely that I shall be happy if you wish it; or miserable, if it pleases you.

Elmire.   The declaration is exceedingly gallant; but it is, to speak truly, rather a little surprising.   Methinks you ought to arm your heart better, and to reflect a little upon such a design.   A pious man like you, and who is everywhere spoken of . . .

Tartuffe. Ah! although I am a pious man, I am not the less a man; and, when one beholds your heavenly charms, the heart surrenders and reasons no longer. I know that such discourse from me must appear strange; but, after all, Madam, I am not an angel; and if my confession be condemned by you, you must blame your own attractions for it. As soon as I beheld their more than human loveliness, you became the queen of my soul. The ineffable sweetness of your divine glances broke down the resistance of my obstinate heart; it overcame everything—fastings, prayers, tears—and led all my desires to your charms. My looks and my sighs have told you so a thousand times; and, the better to explain myself, I now make use of words. If you should graciously contemplate the tribulations of your unworthy slave; if your kindness would console me, and will condescend to stoop to my insignificant self, I shall ever entertain for you, O miracle of sweetness, an unexampled devotion. Your honour runs not the slightest risk with me, and need not fear the least disgrace on my part. All these court gallants, of whom women are so fond, are noisy in their doings and vain in their talk; they are incessantly pluming themselves on their successes, and they receive no favours which they do not divulge. Their indiscreet tongues, in which people confide, desecrate the altar on which their hearts sacrifice. But men of our stamp love discreetly, and with them a secret is always surely kept. The care which we take of our own reputation is a sufficient guarantee for the object of our love; and it is only with us, when they accept our hearts, that they find love without scandal, and pleasure without fear.

Elmire. I have listened to what you say, and your rhetoric explains itself in sufficiently strong terms to me. But are you not afraid that the fancy may take me to tell my husband of this gallant ardour; and that the prompt knowledge of such an amour might well change the friendship which he bears you.

Tartuffe. I know that you are too gracious, and that you will pardon my boldness; that you will excuse, on the score of human frailty, the violent transports of a passion which offends you, and consider, by looking at yourself, that people are not blind, and men are made of flesh and blood.

Elmire. Others would perhaps take it in a different fashion; but I shall show my discretion. I shall not tell the matter to my husband: but in return, I require something of you: that is, to forward, honestly and without quibbling, the union of Valère with Mariane, to renounce the unjust power which would enrich you with what belongs to another; and . . .

SCENE IV.—ELMIRE, DAMIS, TARTUFFE.

Damis (*coming out of the closet in which he was hidden*). No, Madam, no; this shall be made public. I was in there when I overheard it all; and Providence seems to have conducted me thither to abash the pride of a wretch who wrongs me; to point me out a way to take vengeance on his hypocrisy and insolence; to undeceive my father, and to show him plainly the heart of a villain who talks to you of love.

Elmire. No, Damis; it suffices that he reforms, and endeavours to deserve my indulgence. Since I have promised him, do not make me break my word. I have no wish to provoke a scandal; a woman laughs at such follies, and never troubles her husband's ears with them.

Damis. You have your reasons for acting in that way, and I also have mine for behaving differently. It is a farce to wish to spare him; and the insolent pride of his bigotry has already triumphed too much over my just anger, and caused too much disorder amongst us. The scoundrel has governed my father too long, and plotted against my affections as well as Valère's. My father must be undeceived about this perfidious wretch; and Heaven offers me an easy means. I am indebted to it for this opportunity, and it is too favourable to be neglected. I should deserve to have it snatched away from me, did I not make use of it, now that I have it in hand.

Elmire. Damis . . .

Damis. No, by your leave, I will use my own judgment. I am highly delighted: and all you can say will be in vain to make me forego the pleasure of revenge. I shall settle this affair without delay; and here is just the opportunity.

SCENE V.—ORGON, ELMIRE, DAMIS, TARTUFFE.

Damis. We will enliven your arrival, father, with an altogether fresh incident, that will surprise you much. You are well repaid for all your caresses, and this gentleman rewards your tenderness handsomely. His great zeal for you has just shown itself; he aims at nothing less than at dishonouring you; and I have just surprised him making to your wife an insulting avowal of a guilty passion. Her sweet disposition, and her too discreet feelings would by all means have kept the secret from you; but I cannot encourage such insolence, and think that to have been silent about it would have been to do you an injury.

Elmire. Yes, I am of opinion that we ought never to trouble a husband's peace with all those silly stories; that our honour does not depend upon that; and that it is enough for us to be able to defend ourselves. These are my sentiments; and you would have said nothing, Damis, if I had had any influence with you.

SCENE VI.—ORGON, DAMIS, TARTUFFE.

Orgon. What have I heard! Oh, Heavens! Is it credible?

Tartuffe. Yes, brother, I am a wicked, guilty, wretched sinner, full of iniquity, the greatest villain that ever existed. Each moment of my life is replete with pollutions; it is but a mass of crime and corruption; and I see that Heaven, to chastise me, intends to mortify me on this occasion. Whatever great crime may be laid to my charge, I have neither the wish nor the pride to deny it. Believe what you are told, arm your anger, and drive me like a criminal from your house. Whatever shame you may heap upon me, I deserve still more.

Orgon (*to his* SON). What, wretch! dare you, by this falsehood, tarnish the purity of his virtue?

Damis. What, shall the pretended gentleness of this hypocrite make you belie . . .

Orgon. Peace, cursed plague!

Tartuffe. Ah! let him speak; you accuse him wrongly, and you had much better believe in his story. Why will you be so favourable to me after hearing such a fact? Are you, after all, aware of what I am capable? Why trust to my exterior, brother, and why, for all that is seen, believe me to be better than I am? No, no, you allow yourself to be deceived by appearances, and I am, alas! nothing less than what they think me. Everyone takes me to be a godly man, but the real truth is that I am very worthless. (*Addressing himself to* DAMIS.) Yes, my dear child, say on; call me a perfidious, infamous, lost wretch, a thief, a murderer; load me with still more detestable names: I shall not contradict you, I have deserved them; and I am willing on my knees to suffer ignominy, as a disgrace due to the crimes of my life.

Orgon (*to* TARTUFFE). This is too much, brother. (*To his* SON). Does not your heart relent, wretch?

Damis. What! shall his words deceive you so far as to . . .

Orgon. Hold your tongue, you hangdog. (*Raising*

TARTUFFE.) Rise, brother, I beseech you. (*To his* SON.) Infamous wretch!

Damis. He can . . .

Orgon. Hold your tongue.

Damis. I burst with rage. What! I am looked upon as . . .

Orgon. Say another word, and I will break your bones.

Tartuffe. In Heaven's name, brother, do not forget yourself! I would rather suffer the greatest hardship, than that he should receive the slightest hurt for my sake.

Orgon (*to his* SON). Ungrateful monster!

Tartuffe. Leave him in peace. If I must on both knees, ask you to pardon him . . .

Orgon (*throwing himself on his knees also, and embracing* TARTUFFE). Alas! are you in jest? (*To his* SON.) Behold his goodness, scoundrel!

Damis. Thus . . .

Orgon. Cease.

Damis. What! I . . .

Orgon. Peace, I tell you: I know too well the motive of your attack. You all hate him, and I now perceive wife, children, and servants all let loose against him. Every trick is impudently resorted to, to remove this pious person from my house; but the more efforts they put forth to banish him, the more shall I employ to keep him here, and I shall hasten to give him my daughter, to abash the pride of my whole family.

Damis. Do you mean to compel her to accept him?

Orgon. Yes, wretch! and to enrage you, this very evening. Yes! I defy you all, and shall let you know that I am the master, and that I will be obeyed. Come, retract; throw yourself at his feet immediately, you scoundrel, and ask his pardon.

Damis. What! I at the feet of this rascal who, by his impostures . . .

Orgon. What, you resist, you beggar, and insult him besides! (*To* TARTUFFE). A cudgel! a cudgel! do not hold me back. (*To his* SON). Out of my house, this minute, and never dare to come back to it.

Damis. Yes, I shall go; but . . .

Orgon. Quick, leave the place. I disinherit you, you hangdog, and give you my curse besides.

SCENE VII.—ORGON, TARTUFFE.

Orgon. To offend a saintly person in that way!

Tartuffe. Forgive him, O Heaven! the pang he causes me. (*To* ORGON). Could you but know my grief at seeing myself blackened in my brother's sight . . .

Orgon. Alas!

Tartuffe. The very thought of this ingratitude tortures my soul to that extent. . . . The horror I conceive of it. . . . My heart is so oppressed that I cannot speak, and I believe it will be my death.

Orgon (*running, all in tears, towards the door, by which his son has disappeared*). Scoundrel! I am sorry my hand has spared you, and not knocked you down on the spot. (*To* TARTUFFE.) Compose yourself, brother, and do not grieve.

Tartuffe. Let us put an end to these sad disputes. I perceive what troubles I cause in this house, and think it necessary, brother, to leave it.

Orgon. What! you are jesting surely?

Tartuffe. They hate me, and I find that they are trying to make you suspect my integrity.

Orgon. What does it matter? Do you think that, in my heart, I listen to them?

Tartuffe. They will not fail to continue, you may be sure; and these self-same stories which you now reject, may, perhaps, be listened to at another time.

Orgon. No, brother, never.

Tartuffe. Ah, brother! a wife may easily impose upon a husband.

Orgon. No, no.

Tartuffe. Allow me, by removing hence promptly, to deprive them of all subject of attack.

Orgon. No, you shall remain; my life depends upon it.

Tartuffe. Well! I must then mortify myself. If, however, you would . . .

Orgon. Ah!

Tartuffe. Be it so: let us say no more about it. But I know how to manage in this. Honour is a tender thing, and friendship enjoins me to prevent reports and causes for suspicion. I shall shun your wife, and you shall not see me . . .

Orgon. No, in spite of all, you shall frequently be with her. To annoy the world is my greatest delight; and I wish you to be seen with her at all times. Nor is this all: the better to defy them all, I will have no other heir but you, and I am going forthwith to execute a formal deed of gift of all my property to you. A faithful and honest friend, whom I take for son-in-law, is dearer to me than son, wife, and parents. Will you not accept what I propose?

Tartuffe. The will of Heaven be done in all things.

Orgon. Poor fellow. Quick! let us get the draft drawn up: and then let envy itself burst with spite!

ACT IV

Scene I.—Cléante, Tartuffe.

Cléante. Yes, everyone talks about it, and you may believe me. The stir which this rumour makes is not at all to your credit; and I have just met you, Sir, opportunely, to tell you my opinion in two words. I will not sift these reports to the bottom; I refrain, and take the thing at its worst. Let us suppose that Damis has not acted well, and that you have been wrongly accused; would it not be like a Christian to pardon the offence, and to smother all desire of vengeance in your heart? And ought you, on account of a dispute with you, to allow a son to be driven from his father's home? I tell you once more, and candidly, that great and small are scandalized at it; and, if you will take my advice, you will try to make peace, and not push matters to extremes. Make a sacrifice to God of your resentment, and restore a son to his father's favour.

Tartuffe. Alas! for my own part, I would do so with all my heart. I do not bear him, Sir, the slightest ill-will; I forgive him everything; I blame him for nothing; and would serve him to the best of my power. But Heaven's interest is opposed to it; and if he comes back, I must leave the house. After his unparalleled behaviour, communication with him would give rise to scandal: Heaven knows what all the world would immediately think of it! They would impute it to sheer policy on my part; and they would say everywhere, that knowing myself to be guilty, I pretend a charitable zeal for my accuser; that I am afraid, and wish to conciliate him, in order to bribe him, in an underhand manner, into silence.

148

Cléante. You try to put forward pretended excuses, and all your reasons, Sir, are too far-fetched. Why do you charge yourself with Heaven's interests? Has it any need of us to punish the guilty? Allow it to take its own course; think only of the pardon which it enjoins for offences, and do not trouble yourself about men's judgments, when you are following the sovereign edicts of Heaven. What! shall the trivial regard for what men may think prevent the glory of a good action? No, no; let us always do what Heaven prescribes, and not trouble our heads with other cares.

Tartuffe. I have already told you that from my heart I forgive him; and that, Sir, is doing what Heaven commands us to do: but after the scandal and the insult of to-day, Heaven does not require me to live with him.

Cléante. And does it require you, Sir, to lend your ear to what a mere whim dictates to his father, and to accept the gift of a property to which in justice you have no claim whatever?

Tartuffe. Those who know me will not think that this proceeds from self-interest. All the world's goods have but few charms for me; I am not dazzled by their deceptive glare: and should I determine to accept from his father that donation which he wishes to make to me, it is only, in truth, because I fear that all that property might fall into wicked hands; lest it might be divided amongst those who would make a bad use of it in this world, and would not employ it, as I intend, for the glory of Heaven and the well-being of my fellow men.

Cléante. Oh, Sir, you need not entertain those delicate scruples, which may give cause for the rightful heir to complain. Allow him at his peril to enjoy his own, without troubling yourself in any way; and consider that it is better even that he should make a bad use of it, than that you should be accused of defrauding him of it. My only wonder is, that you could have received such a proposal unblushingly. For after all, has true piety any maxim showing how a legitimate heir may be stripped of his property? And if Heaven has put into your head an invincible obstacle to your living with Damis, would it not be better that as a prudent man you should make a civil retreat from this, than to allow that, contrary to all reason, the son should be turned out of the house for you. Believe me, Sir, this would be giving a proof of your probity . . .

Tartuffe. Sir, it is half past three: certain religious duties call me upstairs, and you will excuse my leaving you so soon.

Cléante (*alone*). Ah!

SCENE II.—ELMIRE, MARIANE, CLÉANTE, DORINE.

Dorine (*to* CLÉANTE). For Heaven's sake, Sir, bestir yourself with us for her: she is in mortal grief; and the marriage contract which her father has resolved upon being signed this evening, drives her every moment to despair. Here he comes! Pray, let us unite our efforts, and try, by force or art, to shake this unfortunate design that causes us all this trouble.

SCENE III.—ORGON, ELMIRE, MARIANE, CLÉANTE, DORINE.

Orgon. Ah! I am glad to see you all assembled. (*To* MARIANE.) There is something in this document to please you, and you know already what it means.

Mariane (*at* ORGON's *feet*). Father, in the name of Heaven which knows my grief, and by all that can move your heart, relax somewhat of your paternal rights, and absolve me from obedience in this case. Do not compel me, by this harsh command, to reproach Heaven with my duty to you; and alas! do not make wretched the life which you have given me, father. If, contrary to the sweet expectations which I have formed, you forbid me to belong to him whom I have dared to love, kindly save me at least, I implore you on my knees, from the torment of belonging to one whom I abhor; and do not drive me to despair by exerting your full power over me.

Orgon (*somewhat moved*).   Firm, my heart; none of this human weakness!

Mariane. Your tenderness for him causes me no grief; indulge it to its fullest extent, give him your wealth, and if that be not enough, add mine to it; I consent to it with all my heart, and I leave you to dispose of it. But, at least, stop short of my own self; and allow me to end in the austerities of a convent, the sad days which Heaven has allotted to me.

Orgon. Ah, that is it! When a father crosses a girl's love-sick inclination, she wishes to become a nun. Get up. The more repugnance you feel in accepting him, the greater will be your merit. Mortify your senses by this marriage, and do not trouble me any longer.

Dorine. But what . . .

Orgon. Hold your tongue. Meddle only with what concerns you. I flatly forbid you to say another word.

Cléante. If you will permit me to answer you, and advise . . .

Orgon. Your advice is the best in the world, brother; it is well argued, and I set great store by it: but you must allow me not to avail myself of it.

Elmire (*to her husband*).   I am at a loss what to say, after all I have seen; and I quite admire your blindness. You must be mightily bewitched and prepossessed in his favour, to deny to us the incidents of this day.

Orgon. I am your servant, and judge by appearances. I know your indulgence for my rascal of a son, and you were afraid of disowning the trick which he wished to play on the poor fellow. But, after all, you took it too quietly to be believed; and you ought to have appeared somewhat more upset.

Elmire. Is our honour to bridle up so strongly at the simple avowal of an amorous transport, and can there be no reply to aught that touches it, without fury in our eyes and invectives in our mouth? As for me, I simply laugh at such talk; and the noise made about it by no means pleases me. I love to show my discreetness quietly, and am not at all like those savage prudes, whose honour is armed with claws and teeth, and who at the least word would scratch people's faces. Heaven preserve me from such good behaviour! I prefer a virtue that is not diabolical, and believe that a discreet and cold denial is no less effective in repelling a lover.

Orgon. In short, I know the whole affair, and will not be imposed upon.

Elmire. Once more, I wonder at your strange weakness; but what would your unbelief answer if I were to show you that you had been told the truth.

Orgon. Show!

Elmire. Aye.

Orgon. Stuff.

Elmire. But if I found the means to show you plainly? . . .

Orgon. Idle stories.

Elmire. What a strange man! Answer me, at least. I am not speaking of believing us; but suppose that we found a place where you could plainly see and hear everything, what would you say then of your good man?

Orgon. In that case, I should say that . . . I should say nothing, for the thing cannot be.

Elmire. Your delusion has lasted too long, and I have been too much taxed with imposture. I must, for my gratification, without going any farther, make you a witness of all that I have told you.

Orgon. Be it so. I take you at your word. We shall

see your dexterity, and how you will make good this
promise.

Elmire (*to* Dorine). Bid him come to me.

Dorine (*to* Elmire). He is crafty, and it will be difficult, perhaps, to catch him.

Elmire (*to* Dorine). No; people are easily duped by
those whom they love, and conceit is apt to deceive itself.
Bid him come down. (*To* Cléante *and* Mariane.)
And do you retire.

Scene IV.—Elmire, Orgon.

Elmire. Come, and get under this table.

Orgon. Why so?

Elmire. It is necessary that you should conceal yourself well.

Orgon. But why under this table?

Elmire. Good Heavens! do as you are told; I have
thought about my plan, and you shall judge. Get under
there, I tell you, and, when you are there, take care not
to be seen or heard.

Orgon. I confess that my complaisance is great; but
I must needs see the end of your enterprise.

Elmire. You will have nothing, I believe, to reply to
me. (*To* Orgon *under the table.*) Mind! I am going
to meddle with a strange matter, do not be shocked in
any way. I must be permitted to say what I like; and
it is to convince you, as I have promised. Since I am
compelled to it, I am going to make this hypocrite drop
his mask by addressing soft speeches to him, flatter the
shameful desires of his passion, and give him full scope
for his audacity. As it is for your sake alone, and the
better to confound him, that I pretend to yield to his
wishes, I shall cease as soon as you show yourself, and
things need not go farther than you wish. It is for you
to stop his mad passion, when you think matters are
carried far enough, to spare your wife, and not to expose

me any more than is necessary to disabuse you. This is
your business, it remains entirely with you, and . . .
But he comes. Keep close, and be careful not to show
yourself.

SCENE V.—TARTUFFE, ELMIRE, ORGON (*under the table*).

Tartuffe. I have been told that you wished to speak
to me here.

Elmire. Yes. Some secrets will be revealed to you.
But close this door before they are told to you, and look
about everywhere, for fear of a surprise. (TARTUFFE
closes the door, and comes back). We assuredly do not
want here a scene like the one we just passed through:
I never was so startled in my life. Damis put me in a
terrible fright for you; and you saw, indeed, that I did
my utmost to frustrate his intentions and calm his excitement. My confusion, it is true, was so great, that
I had not a thought of contradicting him: but, thanks
to Heaven, everything has turned out the better for that,
and is upon a much surer footing. The esteem in which
you are held has allayed the storm, and my husband
will not take any umbrage at you. The better to brave
people's ill-natured comments, he wishes us to be together at all times; and it is through this that, without
fear of incurring blame, I can be closeted here alone with
you; and this justifies me in opening to you my heart,
a little too ready perhaps, to listen to your passion.

Tartuffe. This language is somewhat difficult to understand, Madam; and you just now spoke in quite a
different strain.

Elmire. Ah! how little you know the heart of a
woman, if such a refusal makes you angry! and how
little you understand what it means to convey, when it
defends itself so feebly! In those moments, our modesty always combats the tender sentiments with which
we may be inspired. Whatever reason we may find for

the passion that subdues us, we always feel some shame in owning it. We deny it at first: but in such a way as to give you sufficiently to understand that our heart surrenders; that, for honour's sake, words oppose our wishes, and that such refusals promise everything. This is, no doubt, making a somewhat plain confession to you, and showing little regard for our modesty. But, since these words have at last escaped me, would I have been so anxious to restrain Damis, would I, pray, have so complacently listened, for such a long time, to the offer of your heart, would I have taken the matter as I have done, if the offer of that heart had had nothing in it to please me? And, when I myself would have compelled you to refuse the match that had just been proposed, what ought this entreaty to have given you to understand, but the interest I was disposed to take in you, and the vexation it would have caused me, that this marriage would have at least divided a heart that I wished all to myself?

Tartuffe. It is very sweet, no doubt, Madam, to hear these words from the lips we love; their honey plentifully diffuses a suavity throughout my senses, such as was never yet tasted. The happiness of pleasing you is my highest study, and my heart reposes all its bliss in your affection; but, by your leave, this heart presumes still to have some doubt in its own felicity. I may look upon these words as a decent stratagem to compel me to break off the match that is on the point of being concluded; and, if I must needs speak candidly to you, I shall not trust to such tender words, until some of those favours, for which I sigh, have assured me of all which they intend to express, and fixed in my heart a firm belief of the charming kindness which you intend for me.

Elmire (*after having coughed to warn her husband*) What! would you proceed so fast, and exhaust the tenderness of one's heart at once? One takes the greatest pains to make you the sweetest declarations; meanwhile is not that enough for you? and will nothing content you, but pushing things to the utmost extremity?

Tartuffe. The less a blessing is deserved, the less one presumes to expect it. Our love dares hardly rely upon words. A lot full of happiness is difficult to realize, and we wish to enjoy it before believing in it. As for me, who think myself so little deserving of your favours, I doubt the success of my boldness; and shall believe nothing, Madam, until you have convinced my passion by real proofs.

Elmire. Good Heavens! how very tyrannically your love acts! And into what a strange confusion it throws me! What a fierce sway it exercises over our hearts! and how violently it clamours for what it desires! What! can I find no shelter from your pursuit? and will you scarcely give me time to breathe? Is it decent to be so very exacting, and to insist upon your demands being satisfied immediately; and thus, by your pressing efforts, to take advantage of the weakness which you see one has for you?

Tartuffe. But if you look upon my addresses with a favourable eye, why refuse me convincing proofs?

Elmire. But how can I comply with what you wish, without offending that Heaven of which you are always speaking?

Tartuffe. If it be nothing but Heaven that opposes itself to my wishes, it is a trifle for me to remove such an obstacle; and that need be no restraint upon your love.

Elmire. But they frighten us so much with the judgments of Heaven!

Tartuffe. I can dispel these ridiculous fears for you, Madam, and I possess the art of allaying scruples. Heaven, it is true, forbids certain gratifications, but there are ways and means of compounding such matters. According to our different wants, there is a science which loosens that which binds our conscience, and which rectifies the evil of the act with the purity of our intentions. We shall be able to initiate you into these secrets, Madam; you have only to be led by me. Satisfy my desires, and have no fear; I shall be answerable for everything, and shall take the sin upon myself. (ELMIRE *coughs louder*.) You cough very much, Madam?

Elmire. Yes, I am much tormented.

Tartuffe. Would you like a piece of this liquorice?

Elmire. It is an obstinate cold, no doubt; and I know that all the liquorice in the world will do it no good.

Tartuffe. That, certainly, is very sad.

Elmire. Yes, more than I can say.

Tartuffe. In short, your scruples, Madam, are easily overcome. You may be sure of the secret being kept, and there is no harm done unless the thing is bruited about. The scandal which it causes constitutes the offence, and sinning in secret is no sinning at all.

Elmire (*after having coughed once more*). In short, I see that I must make up my mind to yield; that I must consent to grant you everything; and that with less than that, I ought not to pretend to satisfy you, or to be believed. It is no doubt very hard to go to that length, and it is greatly in spite of myself that I venture thus far; but, since people persist in driving me to this; since they will not credit aught I may say, and wish for more convincing proofs, I can but resolve to act thus, and satisfy them. If this gratification offends, so much the worse for those who force me to it: the fault ought surely not to be mine.

Tartuffe. Yes, Madam, I take it upon myself; and the thing in itself . . .

Elmire. Open this door a little, and see, pray, if my husband be not in that gallery.

Tartuffe. What need is there to take so much thought

about him? Between ourselves, he is easily led by the nose. He is likely to glory in all our interviews, and I have brought him so far that he will see everything, and without believing anything.

Elmire. It matters not. Go, pray, for a moment and look carefully everywhere outside.

SCENE VI.—ORGON, ELMIRE.

Orgon (coming from under the table). This is, I admit to you, an abominable wretch! I cannot recover myself, and all this perfectly stuns me.

Elmire. What, you come out so soon! You are surely jesting. Get under the table-cloth again; it is not time yet. Stay to the end, to be quite sure of the thing, and do not trust at all to mere conjectures.

Orgon. No, nothing more wicked ever came out of hell.

Elmire. Good Heavens! you ought not to believe things so lightly. Be fully convinced before you give in; and do not hurry for fear of being mistaken. (ELMIRE *pushes* ORGON *behind her.*)

SCENE VII.—TARTUFFE, ELMIRE, ORGON.

Tartuffe (without seeing ORGON*).* Everything conspires, Madam, to my satisfaction. I have surveyed the whole apartment; there is no one there; and my delighted soul . . . (*At the moment that* TARTUFFE *advances with open arms to embrace* ELMIRE, *she draws back, and* TARTUFFE *perceives* ORGON).

Orgon (stopping TARTUFFE*).* Gently! you are too eager in your amorous transports, and you ought not to be so impetuous. Ha! ha! good man, you wished to victimize me! How you are led away by temptations! You would marry my daughter, and covet my wife! I have been a long while in doubt whether you were in earnest, and I always expected you would change your tone; but this is pushing the proof far enough: I am satisfied, and wish for no more.

Elmire (*to* TARTUFFE). It is much against my inclinations that I have done this: but I have been driven to the necessity of treating you thus.

Tartuffe (*to* ORGON). What! do you believe . . .

Orgon. Come, pray, no more. Be off! and without ceremony.

Tartuffe. My design . . .

Orgon. These speeches are no longer of any use; you must get out of this house, and forthwith.

Tartuffe. It is for you to get out, you who assume the mastership: the house belongs to me, I will make you know it, and show you plainly enough that it is useless to resort to these cowardly tricks to pick a quarrel with me; that one cannot safely, as one thinks, insult me; that I have the means of confounding and of punishing imposture, of avenging offended Heaven, and of making those repent who talk of turning me out hence.

SCENE VIII.—ELMIRE, ORGON.

Elmire. What language is this? and what does he mean?

Orgon. I am, in truth, all confusion, and this is no laughing matter.

Elmire. How so?

Orgon. I perceive my mistake by what he says; and the deed of gift troubles my mind.

Elmire. The deed of gift?

Orgon. Yes. The thing is done. But something else disturbs me too.

Elmire. And what?

Orgon. You shall know all. But first let us go and see if a certain box is still upstairs.

ACT V

Scene I.—Orgon, Cléante.

Cléante. Where would you run to?

Orgon. Indeed! how can I tell?

Cléante. It seems to me that we should begin by consulting together what had best be done in this emergency.

Orgon. This box troubles me sorely. It makes me despair more than all the rest.

Cléante. This box then contains an important secret?

Orgon. It is a deposit that Argas himself, the friend whom I pity, entrusted secretly to my own hands. He selected me for this in his flight; and from what he told me, it contains documents upon which his life and fortune depend.

Cléante. Why then did you confide it into other hands?

Orgon. It was from a conscientious motive. I straightway confided the secret to the wretch; and his arguing persuaded me to give this box into his keeping, so that, in case of any inquiry, I might be able to deny it by a ready subterfuge, by which my conscience might have full absolution for swearing against the truth.

Cléante. This is critical, at least, to judge from appearances; and the deed of gift, and his confidence, have been, to tell you my mind, steps too inconsiderately taken. You may be driven far with such pledges; and since the fellow has these advantages over you, it is a great imprudence on your part to drive him to extremities; and you ought to seek some gentler method.

Orgon. What! to hide such a double-dealing heart, so wicked a soul, under so fair an appearance of touching fervour! And I who received him in my house a beggar and penniless. . . . It is all over; I renounce all pious people. Henceforth I shall hold them in utter abhorrence, and be worse to them than the very devil.

Cléante. Just so! you exaggerate again! You never preserve moderation in anything. You never keep within reason's bounds; and always rush from one extreme to another. You see your mistake, and find out that you have been imposed upon by a pretended zeal. But is there any reason why, in order to correct yourself, you should fall into a greater error still, and say that all pious people have the same feelings as that perfidious rascal? What! because a scoundrel has audaciously deceived you, under the pompous show of outward austerity, you will needs have it that every one is like him, and that there is no really pious man to be found now-a-days? Leave those foolish deductions to free-thinkers: distinguish between real virtue and its counterfeit; never bestow your esteem too hastily, and keep in this the necessary middle course. Beware, if possible, of honouring imposture; but do not attack true piety also; and if you must fall into an extreme, rather offend again on the other side.

Scene II.—Orgon, Cléante, Damis.

Damis. What! father, is it true that this scoundrel threatens you? that he forgets all that you have done for him, and that his cowardly and too contemptible pride turns your kindness for him against yourself?

Orgon. Even so, my son; and it causes me unutterable grief.

Damis. Leave him to me, I will slice his ears off. Such insolence must not be tolerated: it is my duty to deliver you from him at once; and, to put an end to this matter, I must knock him down.

Cléante. Spoken just like a regular youth. Moderate, if you please, these violent transports. We live under a government, and in an age, in which violence only makes matters worse.

SCENE III.—MADAM PERNELLE, ORGON, ELMIRE, CLÉANTE, MARIANE, DAMIS, DORINE.

Madame Pernelle. What is all this? What dreadful things do I hear!

Orgon. Some novelties which my own eyes have witnessed, and you see how I am repaid for my kindness. I affectionately harbour a fellow creature in his misery, I shelter him and treat him as my own brother; I heap favours upon him every day; I give him my daughter, and everything I possess: and, at that very moment, the perfidious, infamous wretch forms the wicked design of seducing my wife; and, not content even with these vile attempts, he dares to threaten me with my own favours; and, to encompass my ruin, wishes to take advantage of my indiscreet good nature, drive me from my property which I have transferred to him, and reduce me to that condition from which I rescued him!

Dorine. Poor fellow!

Madame Pernelle. I can never believe, my son, that he would commit so black a deed.

Orgon. What do you mean?

Madame Pernelle. Good people are always envied.

Orgon. What do you mean by all this talk, mother?

Madame Pernelle. That there are strange goings-on in your house, and that we know but too well the hatred they bear him.

Orgon. What has this hatred to do with what I have told you?

Madame Pernelle. I have told you a hundred times, when a boy,

> "That virtue here is persecuted ever;
> That envious men may die, but envy never."

Orgon. But in what way does this bear upon to-day's doings?

Madame Pernelle. They may have concocted a hundred idle stories against him.

Orgon. I have already told you that I have seen everything myself.

Madame Pernelle. The malice of slanderers is very great.

Orgon. You will make me swear, mother. I tell you that with my own eyes I have witnessed this daring crime.

Madame Pernelle. Evil tongues have always venom to scatter abroad, and nothing here below can guard against it.

Orgon. That is a very senseless remark. I have seen it, I say, seen with my own eyes, seen, what you call seen. Am I to din it a hundred times in your ears, and shout like four people?

Madame Pernelle. Goodness me! appearances most frequently deceive: you must not always judge by what you see.

Orgon. I am boiling with rage!

Madame Pernelle. Human nature is liable to false suspicions, and good is often construed into evil.

Orgon. I must construe the desire to embrace my wife into a charitable design!

Madame Pernelle. It is necessary to have good reasons for accusing people; and you ought to have waited until you were quite certain of the thing.

Orgon. How the deuce could I be more certain? Ought I to have waited, mother, until to my very eyes he had . . . You will make me say some foolish thing.

Madame Pernelle. In short, his soul is too full of pure zeal; and I cannot at all conceive that he would have attempted the things laid to his charge.

Orgon. Go, my passion is so great that, if you were not my mother, I do not know what I might say to you

Dorine (*to* Orgon).   A just reward of things here below, Sir; you would not believe anyone, and now they
will not believe you.

Cléante.   We are wasting in mere trifling the time
that should be employed in devising some measures.
We must not remain inactive when a knave threatens.

Damis.   What! would his effrontery go to that extent?

Elmire.   As for me, I hardly think it possible, and his
ingratitude here shows itself too plainly.

Cléante (*to* Orgon).   Do not trust to that; he will
find some means to justify his doings against you; and
for less than this, a powerful party has involved people
in a vexatious maze.   I tell you once more, that, armed
with what he has, you should never have pushed him
thus far.

Orgon.   True enough; but what could I do?   I was
unable to master my resentment at the presumption of
the wretch.

Cléante.   I wish, with all my heart, that we could
patch up even a shadow of peace between you two.

Elmire.   Had I but known how he was armed against
us, I would have avoided bringing things to such a crisis;
and my . . .

Orgon (*to* Dorine, *seeing* M. Loyal *come in*).   What
does this man want?   Go and see quickly.   I am in a
fine state for people to come to see me!

Scene IV.—Orgon, Madame Pernelle, Elmire,
Mariane, Cléante, Damis, Dorine, M. Loyal.

M. Loyal (*to* Dorine *at the farther part of the stage*).
Good morning, dear sister; pray, let me speak to your
master.

Dorine.   He is engaged; and I doubt whether he can
see anyone at present.

M. Loyal.   I do not intend to be intrusive in his own
house.   I believe that my visit will have nothing to dis-

please him. I have come upon a matter of which he will be very glad.

Dorine. Your name?

M. Loyal. Only tell him that I am come from Monsieur Tartuffe, for his good.

Dorine (to ORGON). This is a man who comes, in a gentle way, from Monsieur Tartuffe, upon some business, of which, he says, you will be very glad.

Cléante (to ORGON). You must see who this man is, and what he wants.

Orgon (to CLÉANTE). Perhaps he comes to reconcile us: How shall I receive him?

Cléante. You must not allow your anger to get the upper hand, and if he speaks of an arrangement, you should listen to him.

M. Loyal (to ORGON). Your servant, Sir! May Heaven punish those who would harm you, and may it favour you as much as I wish!

Orgon (softly to CLÉANTE). This mild beginning confirms my opinion, and augurs already some reconciliation.

M. Loyal. Your whole family has always been dear to me, and I served your father.

Orgon. I am ashamed, Sir, and crave your pardon for not knowing you or your name.

M. Loyal. My name is Loyal, a native of Normandy, and I am a tipstaff to the court in spite of envy. For the last forty years, I have had the happiness, thanking Heaven, of exercising the functions thereof with much honour; and I have come, with your leave, Sir, to serve you with a writ of a certain decree . . .

Orgon. What! you are here . . .

M. Loyal. Let us proceed without anger, Sir. It is nothing but a summons; a notice to quit this house, you and yours, to remove your chattels, and to make room for others, without delay or remissness, as required hereby.

Orgon. I! leave this house!

M. Loyal. Yes, Sir, if you please. The house at present, as you well know, belongs incontestably to good Monsieur Tartuffe. Of all your property, he is henceforth lord and master, by virtue of a contract of which I am the bearer. It is in due form, and nothing can be said against it.

Damis (*to* M. LOYAL). Certainly this impudence is immense, and I admire it!

M. Loyal (*to* DAMIS). Sir, my business lies not with you (*pointing to* ORGON); it is with this gentleman. He is both reasonable and mild, and knows too well the duty of an honest man to oppose the law in any way.

Orgon. But . . .

M. Loyal. Yes, Sir, I know that you would not rebel for a million of money, and that, like a gentleman, you will allow me to execute here the orders which I have received.

Damis. M. Tipstaff, you may chance to get your black gown well dusted here.

M. Loyal (*to* ORGON). Order your son to hold his tongue or to retire, Sir. I should be very loth to have recourse to writing, and to see your name figure in my official report.

Dorine (*aside*). This M. Loyal has a very disloyal air.

M. Loyal. Having a great deal of sympathy with all honest people, I charged myself with these documents, Sir, as much to oblige and please you, as to avoid the choice of those who, not having the same consideration for you that inspires me, might have proceeded in a less gentle way.

Orgon. And what can be worse than to order people to quit their own house?

M. Loyal. You are allowed time, and I shall suspend until to-morrow the execution of the writ, Sir. I shall come only to pass the night here with ten of my people without noise or without scandal. For form's sake, you must, if you please, before going to bed, bring me the keys of your door. I shall take care not to disturb your rest, and to permit nothing which is not right. But to-morrow, you must be ready in the morning, to clear the house of even the smallest utensil; my people shall assist you, and I have selected strong ones, so that they can help you to remove everything. One cannot act better than I do, I think; and as I am treating you with great indulgence, I entreat you also, Sir, to profit by it, so that I may not be annoyed in the execution of my duty.

Orgon (*aside*). I would willingly give just now the best hundred gold pieces of what remains to me for the pleasure of striking on this snout the soundest blow that ever was dealt.

Cléante (*softly to* ORGON). Leave well enough alone. Do not let us make things worse.

Damis. I can hardly restrain myself at this strange impertinence, and my fingers are itching.

Dorine. Upon my word, M. Loyal, with such a broad back, a few cudgel blows would do you no harm.

M. Loyal. We might easily punish these infamous words, sweetheart; and there is a law against women too.

Cléante (*to* M. LOYAL). Pray let us put an end to all this, Sir. Hand over this paper quickly, and leave us.

M. Loyal. Till by-and-by. May Heaven bless you all!

Orgon. And may it confound you, and him who sends you!

SCENE V.—ORGON, MADAME PERNELLE, ELMIRE, CLÉANTE, MARIANE, DAMIS, DORINE.

Orgon. Well! mother, do you see now whether I am right; and you may judge of the rest from the writ. Do you at last perceive his treacheries?

Madame Pernelle. I stand aghast, and feel as if
dropped from the clouds!

Dorine (*to* ORGON). You are wrong to complain, you
are wrong to blame him, and his pious designs are con-
firmed by this. His virtue is perfected in the love for his
neighbour. He knows that worldly goods often corrupt
people, and he wishes, from pure charity, to take everything away from you which might become an obstacle to
your salvation.

Orgon. Hold your tongue. I must always be saying
that to you.

Cléante (*to* ORGON). Let us decide what had best be
done.

Elmire. Go and expose the audacity of the ungrateful
wretch. This proceeding destroys the validity of the
contract; and his treachery will appear too black to allow
him to meet with the success which we surmise.

SCENE VI.—VALÈRE, ORGON, MADAME PERNELLE,
ELMIRE, CLÉANTE, MARIANE, DAMIS, DORINE.

Valère. It is with great regret, Sir, that I come to
afflict you; but I see myself compelled to it by pressing
danger. A most intimate and faithful friend, who knows
the interest which I take in you, has, for my sake, by a
most hazardous step, violated the secrecy due to the
affairs of the State, and has just sent me an intimation,
in consequence of which you will be obliged to flee immediately. The scoundrel who has long imposed upon you
has an hour since accused you to the King, and amongst
other charges which he brings against you, has lodged in
his hands important documents of a state-criminal, of
which, he says, contrary to the duty of a subject, you
have kept the guilty secret. I am ignorant of the details
of the crime laid to your charge; but a warrant is out
against you; and the better to execute it, he himself is
to accompany the person who is to arrest you.

Cléante. These are his armed rights; and by this the traitor seeks to make himself master of your property.

Orgon. The man is, I own to you, a wicked brute!

Valère. The least delay may be fatal to you. I have my coach at the door to carry you off, with a thousand louis which I bring you. Let us lose no time; the blow is terrible, and is one of those which are best parried by flight. I offer myself to conduct you to a place of safety, and will accompany you to the end of your flight.

Orgon. Alas, what do I not owe to your considerate efforts! I must await another opportunity to thank you; and I implore Heaven to be propitious enough to enable me one day to acknowledge this generous service. Farewell: be careful, the rest of you . . .

Cléante. Go quickly. We will endeavour, brother, to do what is necessary.

SCENE VII.—TARTUFFE, A POLICE OFFICER, MADAME PERNELLE, ORGON, ELMIRE, CLÉANTE, MARIANE, VALÈRE, DAMIS, DORINE.

Tartuffe (*stopping* ORGON). Gently, Sir, gently, do not run so fast. You will not have to go far to find a lodging; we take you a prisoner in the King's name.

Orgon. Wretch! you have reserved this blow for the last: this is the stroke, villain, by which you dispatch me; and which crowns all your perfidies.

Tartuffe. Your abuse cannot incense me; Heaven has taught me to suffer everything.

Cléante. Your moderation is great, I confess.

Damis. How impudently the villain sports with Heaven!

Tartuffe. All your outrages cannot move me in the least; and I think of nothing but my duty.

Mariane. You may glorify yourself very much upon this; and this task is very honourable for you to undertake.

Tartuffe. A task cannot but be glorious when it proceeds from the power that sends me hither.

Orgon. But do you remember, ungrateful wretch,
that my charitable hand raised you from a miserable condition?

Tartuffe. Yes, I know what help I received from you;
but the King's interest is my first duty. The just obligation of this sacred duty stifles all gratitude of my heart;
and to such a powerful consideration, I would sacrifice
friend, wife, kindred, and myself with them.

Elmire. The impostor!

Dorine. How artfully he makes himself a lovely cloak
of all that is sacred.

Cléante. But if this zeal which guides you, and upon
which you plume yourself so much, be so perfect as you
say, why has it not shown itself until Orgon caught you
trying to seduce his wife; and why did you not think of
denouncing him until his honour obliged him to drive
you from his house? I do not say that the gift of all his
property, which he has made over to you, ought to have
turned you from your duty; but why, wishing to treat
him as a criminal to-day, did you consent to take aught
from him?

Tartuffe (*to the* OFFICER). Pray, Sir, deliver me from
this clamour, and be good enough to execute your orders.

Officer. Yes, we have no doubt, delayed too long
to discharge them; your words remind me of this just in
time; and to execute them, follow me directly to the
prison which is destined for your abode.

Tartuffe. Who? I, Sir?

Officer. Yes, you.

Tartuffe. Why to prison?

Officer. I have no account to give to you. (*To*
ORGON.) Compose yourself, Sir, after so great an alarm.
We live under a monarch, an enemy of fraud, a monarch
whose eyes penetrate into the heart, and whom all the

art of impostors cannot deceive. Blessed with great discernment, his lofty soul looks clearly at things; it is never betrayed by exaggeration, and his sound reason falls into no excess. He bestows lasting glory on men of worth; but he shows this zeal without blindness, and his love for sincerity does not close his heart to the horror which falsehood must inspire. Even this person could not hoodwink him, and he has guarded himself against more artful snares. He soon perceived, by his subtle penetration, all the vileness concealed in his inmost heart. In coming to accuse you, he has betrayed himself, and, by a just stroke of supreme justice, discovered himself to the King as a notorious rogue, against whom information had been laid under another name. His life is a long series of wicked actions, of which whole volumes might be written. Our monarch, in short, has detested his vile ingratitude and disloyalty towards you; has joined this affair to his other misdeeds, and has placed me under his orders, only to see his impertinence carried out to the end, and to make him by himself give you satisfaction for everything. Yes, he wishes me to strip the wretch of all your documents which he professes to possess, and to give them into your hands. By his sovereign power he annuls the obligations of the contract which gave him all your property, and lastly, pardons you this secret offence, in which the flight of a friend has involved you; and it is the reward of your former zeal in upholding his rights, to show that he knows how to recompense a good action when least thought of; that merit never loses aught with him; and that he remembers good much better than evil.

Dorine. Heaven be praised!

Madame Pernelle. I breathe again.

Elmire. Favourable success!

Mariane. Who dared foretell this?

Orgon (to TARTUFFE, *whom the* OFFICER *leads off).* Well, wretch, there you are . . .

SCENE VIII.—MADAME PERNELLE, ORGON, ELMIRE, MARIANE, CLÉANTE, VALÈRE, DAMIS, DORINE.

Cléante. Ah! brother, stop; and do not descend to indignities. Leave the wretch to his fate, and do not add to the remorse that overwhelms him. Rather wish that his heart, from this day, may be converted to virtue; that, through detestation of his crimes, he may reform his life, and soften the justice of our great prince; while you throw yourself at his knees to render thanks for his goodness, which has treated you so leniently.

Orgon. Yes, it is well said. Let us throw ourselves joyfully at his feet, to laud the kindness which his heart displays to us. Then, having acquitted ourselves of this first duty, we must apply ourselves to the just cares of another, and by a sweet union crown in Valère the flame of a generous and sincere lover.

THE MISANTHROPE

THE MISANTHROPE

(Le Misanthrope)

DRAMATIS PERSONÆ

ALCESTE, *in love with Célimène.*
PHILINTE, *his friend.*
ORONTE, *in love with Célimène.*
CÉLIMÈNE, *beloved by Alceste.*
ÉLIANTE, *her cousin.*
ARSINOÉ, *Célimène's friend.*
ACASTE,⎫ *marquises.*
CLITANDRE,⎭
BASQUE, *servant to Célimène.*
DUBOIS, *servant to Alceste.*
AN OFFICER OF THE MARÉCHAUSSÉE.

Scene.—AT PARIS, IN CÉLIMÈNE'S HOUSE

ACT I

SCENE I.—PHILINTE, ALCESTE.

Philinte. What is the matter? What ails you?
Alceste (*seated*). Leave me, I pray.
Philinte. But, once more, tell me what strange whim . . .
Alceste. Leave me, I tell you, and get out of my sight.
Philinte. But you might at least listen to people, without getting angry.
Alceste. I choose to get angry, and I do not choose to listen.

Philinte. I do not understand you in these abrupt moods, and although we are friends, I am the first . . .

Alceste (*rising quickly*). I, your friend? Lay not that flattering unction to your soul. I have until now professed to be so; but after what I have just seen of you, I tell you candidly that I am such no longer; I have no wish to occupy a place in a corrupt heart.

Philinte. I am then very much to be blamed from your point of view, Alceste?

Alceste. To be blamed? You ought to die from very shame; there is no excuse for such behaviour, and every man of honour must be disgusted at it. I see you almost stifle a man with caresses, show him the most ardent affection, and overwhelm him with protestations, offers, and vows of friendship. Your ebullitions of tenderness know no bounds; and when I ask you who that man is, you can scarcely tell me his name; your feelings for him, the moment you have turned your back, suddenly cool; you speak of him most indifferently to me. Zounds! I call it unworthy, base, and infamous, so far to lower one's self as to act contrary to one's own feelings, and if, by some mischance, I had done such a thing, I should hang myself at once out of sheer vexation.

Philinte. I do not see that it is a hanging matter at all; and I beg of you not to think it amiss if I ask you to show me some mercy, for I shall not hang myself, if it be all the same to you.

Alceste. That is a sorry joke.

Philinte. But, seriously, what would you have people do?

Alceste. I would have people be sincere, and that, like men of honour, no word be spoken that comes not from the heart.

Philinte. When a man comes and embraces you warmly, you must pay him back in his own coin, respond

as best you can to his show of feeling, and return offer
for offer, and vow for vow.

Alceste. Not so. I cannot bear so base a method,
which your fashionable people generally affect; there is
nothing I detest so much as the contortions of these great
time-and-lip servers, these affable dispensers of meaning-
less embraces, these obliging utterers of empty words,
who view every one in civilities, and treat the man of
worth and the fop alike. What good does it do if a man
heaps endearments on you, vows that he is your friend,
that he believes in you, is full of zeal for you, esteems
and loves you, and lauds you to the skies, when he
rushes to do the same to the first rapscallion he meets?
No, no, no heart with the least self-respect cares for
esteem so prostituted; he will hardly relish it, even when
openly expressed, when he finds that he shares it with
the whole universe. Preference must be based on esteem,
and to esteem every one is to esteem no one. Since you
abandon yourself to the vices of the times, zounds! you
are not the man for me. I decline this over-complaisant
kindness, which uses no discrimination. I like to be distinguished; and, to cut the matter short, the friend of
all mankind is no friend of mine.

Philinte. But when we are of the world, we must
conform to the outward civilities which custom demands.

Alceste. I deny it. We ought to punish pitilessly
that shameful pretence of friendly intercourse. I like
a man to be a man, and to show on all occasions the
bottom of his heart in his discourse. Let that be the
thing to speak, and never let our feelings be hidden
beneath vain compliments.

Philinte. There are many cases in which plain speaking would become ridiculous, and could hardly be tolerated. And, with all due allowance for your unbending
honesty, it is as well to conceal your feelings sometimes.
Would it be right or decent to tell thousands of people

what we think of them? And when we meet with some one whom we hate or who displeases us, must we tell him so openly?

Alceste. Yes.

Philinte. What! Would you tell old Emilia, that it ill becomes her to set up for a beauty at her age, and that the paint she uses disgusts everyone?

Alceste. Undoubtedly.

Philinte. Or Dorilas, that he is a bore, and that there is no one at court who is not sick of hearing him boast of his courage, and the lustre of his house?

Alceste. Decidedly so.

Philinte. You are jesting.

Alceste. I am not jesting at all; and I would not spare any one in that respect. It offends my eyes too much; and whether at Court or in town, I behold nothing but what provokes my spleen. I become quite melancholy and deeply grieved to see men behave to each other as they do. Everywhere I find nothing but base flattery, injustice, self-interest, deceit, roguery. I cannot bear it any longer; I am furious; and my intention is to break with all mankind.

Philinte. This philosophical spleen is somewhat too savage. I cannot but laugh to see you in these gloomy fits, and fancy that I perceive in us two, brought up together, the two brothers described in *The School for Husbands*, who . . .

Alceste. Good Heavens! drop your insipid comparisons.

Philinte. Nay, seriously, leave off these vagaries. The world will not alter for all your meddling. And as plain speaking has such charms for you, I shall tell you frankly that this complaint of yours is as good as a play, wherever you go, and that all those invectives against the manners of the age, make you a laughing stock to many people.

Alceste. So much the better, Zounds! so much the better. That is just what I want. It is a very good sign. and I rejoice at it. All men are so odious to me, that I should be sorry to appear rational in their eyes.

Philinte. But do you wish harm to all mankind?

Alceste. Yes; I have conceived a terrible hatred for them.

Philinte. Shall all poor mortals, without exception, be included in this aversion? There are some, even in the age in which we live . . .

Alceste. No, they are all alike; and I hate all men: some, because they are wicked and mischievous; others because they lend themselves to the wicked, and have not that healthy contempt with which vice ought to inspire all virtuous minds. You can see how unjustly and excessively complacent people are to that bare-faced scoundrel with whom I am at law. You may plainly perceive the traitor through his mask; he is well known everywhere in his true colours; his rolling eyes and his honeyed tones impose only on those who do not know him. People are aware that this low-bred fellow, who deserves to be pilloried, has, by the dirtiest jobs, made his way in the world; and that the splendid position he has acquired makes merit repine and virtue blush. Yet whatever dishonourable epithets may be launched against him everywhere, nobody defends his wretched honour. Call him a rogue, an infamous wretch, a confounded scoundrel if you like, all the world will say "yea," and no one contradicts you. But for all that, his bowing and scraping are welcome everywhere; he is received, smiled upon, and wriggles himself into all kinds of society; and, if any appointment is to be secured by intriguing, he will carry the day over a man of the greatest worth. Zounds! these are mortal stabs to me, to see vice parleyed with; and sometimes I feel suddenly in-

clined to fly into a wilderness far from the approach
of men.

Philinte. Great Heaven? let us torment ourselves a
little less about the vices of our age, and be a little more
lenient to human nature. Let us not scrutinize it with
the utmost severity, but look with some indulgence at its
failings. In society, we need virtue to be more pliable.
If we are too wise, we may be equally to blame. Good
sense avoids all extremes, and requires us to be soberly
rational. This unbending and virtuous stiffness of ancient times shocks too much the ordinary customs of our
own; it requires too great perfection from us mortals;
we must yield to the times without being too stubborn;
it is the height of folly to busy ourselves in correcting
the world. I, as well as yourself, notice a hundred things
every day which might be better managed, differently
enacted; but whatever I may discover at any moment,
people do not see me in a rage like you. I take men
quietly just as they are; I accustom my mind to bear
with what they do; and I believe that at Court, as well
as in the city, my phlegm is as philosophical as your bile.

Alceste. But this phlegm, good sir, you who reason
so well, could it not be disturbed by anything? And if
perchance a friend should betray you; if he forms a
subtle plot to get hold of what is yours; if people should
try to spread evil reports about you, would you tamely
submit to all this without flying into a rage?

Philinte. Ay, I look upon all these faults of which
you complain as vices inseparably connected with human
nature; in short, my mind is no more shocked at seeing
a man a rogue, unjust, or selfish, than at seeing vultures,
eager for prey, mischievous apes, or fury-lashed wolves.

Alceste. What! I should see myself deceived, torn to
pieces, robbed, without being . . . Zounds! I shall say
no more about it; all this reasoning is beside the point!

Philinte. Upon my word, you would do well to keep

silence. Rail a little less at your opponent, and attend a little more to your suit.

Alceste. That I shall not do; that is settled long ago.

Philinte. But whom then do you expect to solicit for you?

Alceste. Whom? Reason, my just right, equity.

Philinte. Shall you not pay a visit to any of the judges?

Alceste. No. Is my cause unjust or dubious?

Philinte. I am agreed on that; but you know what harm intrigues do, and . . .

Alceste. No. I am resolved not to stir a step. I am either right or wrong.

Philinte. Do not trust to that.

Alceste. I shall not budge an inch.

Philinte. Your opponent is powerful, and by his underhand work, may induce . . .

Alceste. It does not matter.

Philinte. You will make a mistake.

Alceste. Be it so. I wish to see the end of it.

Philinte. But . . .

Alceste. I shall have the satisfaction of losing my suit.

Philinte. But after all . . .

Alceste. I shall see by this trial whether men have sufficient impudence, are wicked, villainous, and perverse enough to do me this injustice in the face of the whole world.

Philinte. What a strange fellow!

Alceste. I could wish, were it to cost me ever so much, that, for the fun of the thing, I lost my case.

Philinte. But people will really laugh at you, Alceste, if they hear you go on in this fashion.

Alceste. So much the worse for those who will.

Philinte. But this rectitude, which you exact so carefully in every case, this absolute integrity in which you intrench yourself, do you perceive it in the lady you love? As for me, I am astonished that, appearing to be at war with the whole human race, you yet, notwithstanding everything that can render it odious to you, have found aught to charm your eyes. And what surprises me still more, is the strange choice your heart has made. The sincere Éliante has a liking for you, the prude Arsinoé looks with favour upon you, yet your heart does not respond to their passion; whilst you wear the chains of Célimène, who sports with you, and whose coquettish humour and malicious wit seems to accord so well with the manner of the times. How comes it that, hating these things as mortally as you do, you endure so much of them in that lady? Are they no longer faults in so sweet a charmer? Do not you perceive them, or if you do, do you excuse them?

Alceste. Not so. The love I feel for this young widow does not make me blind to her faults, and, notwithstanding the great passion with which she has inspired me, I am the first to see, as well as to condemn, them. But for all this, do what I will, I confess my weakness, she has the art of pleasing me. In vain I see her faults; I may even blame them; in spite of all, she makes me love her. Her charms conquer everything, and, no doubt, my sincere love will purify her heart from the vices of our times.

Philinte. If you accomplish this, it will be no small task. Do you believe yourself beloved by her?

Alceste. Yes, certainly! I should not love her at all, did I not think so.

Philinte. But if her love for you is so apparent, how comes it that your rivals cause you so much uneasiness?

Alceste. It is because a heart, deeply smitten, claims all to itself; I come here only with the intention of telling her what, on this subject, my feelings dictate.

Philinte. Had I but to choose, her cousin Éliante

would have all my love. Her heart, which values yours, is stable and sincere; and this more compatible choice would have suited you better.

Alceste. It is true; my good sense tells me so every day; but good sense does not always rule love.

Philinte. Well, I fear much for your affections; and the hope which you cherish may perhaps . . .

Scene II.—Oronte, Alceste, Philinte.

Oronte (*to* Alceste). I have been informed yonder, that Éliante and Célimène have gone out to make some purchases. But as I heard that you were here, I came to tell you, most sincerely, that I have conceived the greatest regard for you, and that, for a long time, this regard has inspired me with the most ardent wish to be reckoned among your friends. Yes; I like to do homage to merit; and I am most anxious that a bond of friendship should unite us. I suppose that a zealous friend, and of my standing, is not altogether to be rejected. (*All this time* Alceste *has been musing, and seems not to be aware that* Oronte *is addressing him. He looks up only when* Oronte *says to him*)—It is to you, if you please, that this speech is addressed.

Alceste. To me, sir?

Oronte. To you. Is it in any way offensive to you?

Alceste. Not in the least. But my surprise is very great; and I did not expect that honour.

Oronte. The regard in which I hold you ought not to astonish you, and you can claim it from the whole world.

Alceste. Sir . . .

Oronte. Our whole kingdom contains nothing above the dazzling merit which people discover in you.

Alceste. Sir . . .

Oronte. Yes; for my part, I prefer you to the most important in it.

Alceste. Sir . . .

Oronte. May Heaven strike me dead, if I lie! And, to convince you, on this very spot, of my feelings, allow me, sir, to embrace you with all my heart, and to solicit a place in your friendship. Your hand, if you please. Will you promise me your friendship?

Alceste. Sir . . .

Oronte. What! you refuse me?

Alceste. Sir, you do me too much honour; but friendship is a sacred thing, and to lavish it on every occasion is surely to profane it. Judgment and choice should preside at such a compact; we ought to know more of each other before engaging ourselves; and it may happen that our dispositions are such that we may both of us repent of our bargain.

Oronte. Upon my word! that is wisely said; and I esteem you all the more for it. Let us therefore leave it to time to form such a pleasing bond; but, meanwhile I am entirely at your disposal. If you have any business at Court, every one knows how well I stand with the King; I have his private ear; and, upon my word, he treats me in everything with the utmost intimacy. In short, I am yours in every emergency; and, as you are a man of brilliant parts, and to inaugurate our charming amity, I come to read you a sonnet which I made a little while ago, and to find out whether it be good enough for publicity.

Alceste. I am not fit, sir, to decide such a matter. You will therefore excuse me.

Oronte. Why so?

Alceste. I have the failing of being a little more sincere in those things than is necessary.

Oronte. The very thing I ask; and I should have reason to complain, if, in laying myself open to you that you might give me your frank opinion, you should deceive me, and disguise anything from me.

Alceste. If that be the case, sir, I am perfectly willing.

Oronte. *Sonnet* . . . It is a sonnet . . . *Hope* . . . It is to a lady who flattered my passion with some hope. *Hope* . . . They are not long, pompous verses, but mild, tender and melting little lines. (*At every one of these interruptions he looks at* ALCESTE).

Alceste. We shall see.

Oronte. Hope . . . I do not know whether the style will strike you as sufficiently clear and easy, and whether you will approve of my choice of words.

Alceste. We shall soon see, sir.

Oronte. Besides, you must know that I was only a quarter of an hour in composing it.

Alceste. Let us hear, sir; the time signifies nothing.

Oronte (*reads*). *Hope, it is true, oft gives relief,*
> *Rocks for a while our tedious pain,*
> *But what a poor advantage, Phillis,*
> *When nought remains, and all is gone!*

Philinte. I am already charmed with this little bit.

Alceste (*softly to* PHILINTE). What! do you mean to tell me that you like this stuff?

Oronte. *You once showed some complaisance,*
> *But less would have sufficed,*
> *You should not take that trouble*
> *To give me nought but hope.*

Philinte. In what pretty terms these thoughts are put!

Alceste. How now! you vile flatterer, you praise this rubbish!

Oronte. *If I must wait eternally,*
> *My passion, driven to extremes,*
> *Will fly to death.*
> *Your tender cares cannot prevent this,*
> *Fair Phillis, aye we're in despair,*
> *When we must hope for ever.*

Philinte. The conclusion is pretty, amorous, admirable.

Alceste (*softly, and aside to* PHILINTE). A plague on the conclusion! I wish you had concluded to break your nose, you poisoner to the devil!

Philinte. I never heard verses more skilfully turned.

Alceste (*softly, and aside*). Zounds! . . .

Oronte (*to* PHILINTE). You flatter me; and you are under the impression perhaps . . .

Philinte. No, I am not flattering at all.

Alceste (*softly, and aside*). What else are you doing, you wretch?

Oronte (*to* ALCESTE). But for you, you know our agreement. Speak to me, I pray, in all sincerity.

Alceste. These matters, Sir, are always more or less delicate, and every one is fond of being praised for his wit. But I was saying one day to a certain person, who shall be nameless, when he showed me some of his verses, that a gentleman ought at all times to exercise a great control over that itch for writing which sometimes attacks us, and should keep a tight rein over the strong propensity which one has to display such amusements; and that, in the frequent anxiety to show their productions, people are frequently exposed to act a very foolish part.

Oronte. Do you wish to convey to me by this that I am wrong in desiring . . .

Alceste. I do not say that exactly. But I told him that writing without warmth becomes a bore; that there needs no other weakness to disgrace a man; that, even if people, on the other hand, had a hundred good qualities, we view them from their worst sides.

Oronte. Do you find anything to object to in my sonnet?

Alceste. I do not say that. But, to keep him from writing, I set before his eyes how, in our days, that desire had spoiled a great many very worthy people.

Oronte. Do I write badly? Am I like them in any way?

Alceste. I do not say that. But, in short, I said to him, What pressing need is there for you to rhyme, and what the deuce drives you into print? If we can pardon the sending into the world of a badly-written book, it will only be in those unfortunate men who write for their livelihood. Believe me, resist your temptations, keep these effusions from the public, and do not, how much soever you may be asked, forfeit the reputation which you enjoy at Court of being a man of sense and a gentle-man, to take, from the hands of a greedy printer, that of a ridiculous and wretched author. That is what I tried to make him understand.

Oronte. This is all well and good, and I seem to understand you. But I should like to know what there is in my sonnet to . . .

Alceste. Candidly, you had better put it in your closet. You have been following bad models, and your expressions are not at all natural. Pray what is—*Rocks for a while our tedious pain?* And what, *When nought remains, and all is gone?* What, *You should not take that trouble to give me nought but hope?* And what, *Phillis, aye we're in despair when we must hope for ever?* This figurative style, that people are so vain of, is beside all good taste and truth; it is only a play upon words, sheer affectation, and it is not thus that nature speaks. The wretched taste of the age is what I dislike in this. Our forefathers, unpolished as they were, had a much better one; and I value all that is admired now-a-days far less than an old song which I am going to repeat to you:

> "Had our great monarch granted me
> His Paris large and fair;
> And I straightway must quit for aye
> The love of my true dear;

> *Then would I say, King Hal, I pray,*
> *Take back your Paris fair,*
> *I love much mo my dear, I trow,*
> *I love much mo my dear."*

This versification is not rich, and the style is antiquated; but do you not see that it is far better than all those trumpery trifles against which good sense revolts, and that in this, passion speaks from the heart?

> *"Had our great monarch granted me*
> *His Paris large and fair;*
> *And I straightway must quit for aye*
> *The love of my true dear;*
> *Then would I say, King Hal, I pray,*
> *Take back your Paris fair,*
> *I love much mo my dear, I trow,*
> *I love much mo my dear."*

This is what a really loving heart would say. (*To* PHILINTE, *who is laughing*). Yes, master wag, in spite of all your wit, I care more for this than for all the florid pomp and the tinsel which everybody is admiring now-a-days.

Oronte. And I, I maintain that my verses are very good.

Alceste. Doubtless you have your reasons for thinking them so; but you will allow me to have mine, which, with your permission, will remain independent.

Oronte. It is enough for me that others prize them.

Alceste. That is because they know how to dissemble, which I do not.

Oronte. Do you really believe that you have such a great share of wit?

Alceste. If I praised your verses, I should have more.

Oronte. I shall do very well without your approbation.

Alceste. You will have to do without it, if it be all the same.

Oronte. I should like much to see you compose some on the same subject, just to have a sample of your style.

Alceste. I might, perchance, make some as bad; but I should take good care not to show them to any one.

Oronte. You are mighty positive; and this great sufficiency . . .

Alceste. Pray, seek some one else to flatter you, and not me.

Oronte. But, my little Sir, drop this haughty tone.

Alceste. In truth, my big Sir, I shall do as I like.

Philinte (*coming between them*). Stop, gentlemen! that is carrying the matter too far. Cease, I pray.

Oronte. Ah! I am wrong, I confess; and I leave the field to you. I am your servant, Sir, most heartily.

Alceste. And I, Sir, am your most humble servant.

SCENE III.—PHILINTE, ALCESTE.

Philinte. Well! you see. By being too sincere, you have got a nice affair on your hands; I saw that Oronte, in order to be flattered . . .

Alceste. Do not talk to me.

Philinte. But . . .

Alceste. No more society for me.

Philinte. Is it too much . . .

Alceste. Leave me alone.

Philinte. If I . . .

Alceste. Not another word.

Philinte. But what . . .

Alceste. I will hear no more.

Philinte. But . . .

Alceste. Again?

Philinte.   People insult . . .

Alceste.   Ah! zounds! this is too much. Do not dog my steps.

Philinte.   You are making fun of me; I shall not leave you.

ACT II

Scene I.—Alceste, Célimène.

Alceste. Will you have me speak candidly to you, madam? Well, then, I am very much dissatisfied with your behaviour. I am very angry when I think of it; and I perceive that we shall have to break with each other. Yes; I should only deceive you were I to speak otherwise. Sooner or later a rupture is unavoidable; and if I were to promise the contrary a thousand times, I should not be able to bear this any longer.

Célmiène. Oh, I see! it is to quarrel with me, that you wished to conduct me home?

Alceste. I do not quarrel. But your disposition, madam, is too ready to give any first comer an entrance into your heart. Too many admirers beset you; and my temper cannot put up with that.

Célimène. Am I to blame for having too many admirers? Can I prevent people from thinking me amiable? and am I to take a stick to drive them away, when they endeavour by tender means to visit me?

Alceste. No, madam, there is no need for a stick, but only a heart less yielding and less melting at their love-tales. I am aware that your good looks accompany you, go where you will; but your reception retains those whom your eyes attract; and that gentleness, accorded to those who surrender their arms, finishes on their hearts the sway which your charms began. The too agreeable expectation which you offer them increases their assiduities towards you; and your complacency, a little less extended, would drive away the great crowd of so many admirers. But, tell me, at least, madam, by what good fortune Clitandre has the happiness of pleasing you so mightily? Upon what basis of merit and sublime virtue do you ground the honour of your regard for him? Is it by the long nail on his little finger that he has acquired the esteem which you display for him? Are you, like all the rest of the fashionable world, fascinated by the dazzling merit of his fair wig? Do his great rolls make you love him? Do his many ribbons charm you? Is it by the attraction of his great German breeches that he has conquered your heart, whilst at the same time he pretended to be your slave? Or have his manner of smiling, and his falsetto voice, found out the secret of moving your feelings?

Célimène. How unjustly you take umbrage at him! Do not you know why I countenance him; and that he has promised to interest all his friends in my lawsuit?

Alceste. Lose your lawsuit, madam, with patience, and do not countenance a rival whom I detest.

Célimène. But you are getting jealous of the whole world.

Alceste. It is because the whole world is so kindly received by you.

Célimène. That is the very thing to calm your frightened mind, because my goodwill is diffused over all: you would have more reason to be offended if you saw me entirely occupied with one.

Alceste. But as for me, whom you accuse of too much jealousy, what have I more than any of them, madam, pray?

Célimène. The happiness of knowing that you are beloved.

Alceste. And what grounds has my love-sick heart for believing it?

Célimène. I think that, as I have taken the trouble to tell you so, such an avowal ought to satisfy you.

Alceste. But who will assure me that you may not, at the same time, say as much to everybody else perhaps?

Célimène. Certainly, for a lover, this is a pretty amorous speech, and you make me out a very nice lady. Well! to remove such a suspicion, I retract this moment everything I have said; and no one but yourself shall for the future impose upon you. Will that satisfy you?

Alceste. Zounds! why do I love you so! Ah! if ever I get heart-whole out of your hands, I shall bless Heaven for this rare good fortune. I make no secret of it; I do all that is possible to tear this unfortunate attachment from my heart; but hitherto my greatest efforts have been of no avail; and it is for my sins that I love you thus.

Célimène. It is very true that your affection for me is unequalled.

Alceste. As for that, I can challenge the whole world. My love for you cannot be conceived; and never, madam, has any man loved as I do.

Célimène. Your method, however, is entirely new, for you love people only to quarrel with them; it is in peevish expression alone that your feelings vent themselves; no one ever saw such a grumbling swain.

Alceste. But it lies with you alone to dissipate this ill-humour. For mercy's sake let us make an end of all these bickerings; deal openly with each other, and try to put a stop . . .

SCENE II.—CÉLIMÈNE, ALCESTE, BASQUE.

Célimène. What is the matter?

Basque. Acaste is below.

Célimène. Very well! bid him come up.

SCENE III.—CÉLIMÈNE, ALCESTE.

Alceste. What! can one never have a little private conversation with you? You are always ready to receive company; and you cannot, for a single instant, make up your mind to be "not at home."

Célimène. Do you wish me to quarrel with Acaste?

Alceste. You have such regard for people, which I by no means like.

Célimène. He is a man never to forgive me, if he knew that his presence could annoy me.

Alceste. And what is that to you, to inconvenience yourself so . . .

Célimène. But, good Heaven! the amity of such as he is of importance; they are a kind of people who, I do not know how, have acquired the right to be heard at Court. They take their part in every conversation; they can do you no good, but they may do you harm; and, whatever support one may find elsewhere, it will never do to be on bad terms with these very noisy gentry.

Alceste. In short, whatever people may say or do, you always find reasons to bear with every one; and your very careful judgment . . .

SCENE IV.—ALCESTE, CÉLIMÈNE, BASQUE.

Basque. Clitandre is here too, madam.

Alceste. Exactly so. (*Wishes to go.*)

Célimène. Where are you running to?

Alceste. I am going.

Célimène. Stay.

Alceste. For what?

Célimène. Stay.

Alceste. I cannot.

Célimène. I wish it.

Alceste. I will not. These conversations only weary me; and it is too bad of you to wish me to endure them.

Célimène. I wish it, I wish it.

Alceste. No, it is impossible.

Célimène. Very well, then; go, begone; you can do as you like.

SCENE V.—ÉLIANTE, PHILINTE, ACASTE, CLITANDRE,
     ALCESTE, CÉLIMÈNE, BASQUE.

Éliante (*to* CÉLIMÈNE). Here are the two marquises
coming up with us. Has anyone told you?

Célimène. Yes. (*To* BASQUE). Place chairs for
everyone. (BASQUE *places chairs, and goes out*). (*To*
ALCESTE). You are not gone?

Alceste. No; but I am determined, madam, to have
you make up your mind either for them or for me.

Célimène. Hold your tongue.

Alceste. This very day you shall explain yourself.

Célimène. You are losing your senses.

Alceste. Not at all. You shall declare yourself.

Célimène. Indeed!

Alceste. You must take your stand.

Célimène. You are jesting, I believe.

Alceste. Not so. But you must choose. I have been
too patient.

Clitandre. Egad! I have just come from the Louvre,
where Cléonte, at the levee, made himself very ridiculous.
Has he not some friend who could charitably enlighten
him upon his manners?

Célimène. Truth to say, he compromises himself very
much in society; everywhere he carries himself with an
air that is noticed at first sight, and when after a short
absence you meet him again, he is still more absurd
than ever.

Acaste. Egad! Talk of absurd people, just now,
one of the most tedious ones was annoying me. That
reasoner, Damon, kept me, if you please, for a full hour
in the broiling sun, away from my Sedan chair.

Célimène. He is a strange talker, and one who always finds the means of telling you nothing with a great
flow of words. There is no sense at all in his tittle-tattle,
and all that we hear is but noise.

Éliante (*to* PHILINTE). This beginning is not bad; and the conversation takes a sufficiently agreeable turn against our neighbours.

Clitandre. Timante, too, Madam, is another original.

Célimène. He is a complete mystery from top to toe, who throws upon you, in passing, a bewildered glance, and who, without having anything to do, is always busy. Whatever he utters is accompanied with grimaces; he quite oppresses people by his ceremonies. To interrupt a conversation, he has always a secret to whisper to you, and that secret turns out to be nothing. Of the merest molehill he makes a mountain, and whispers everything in your ear, even to a "good-day."

Acaste. And Geralde, Madam?

Célimène. That tiresome story-teller! He never comes down from his nobleman's pedestal; he continually mixes with the best society, and never quotes any one of minor rank than a Duke, Prince, or Princess. Rank is his hobby, and his conversation is of nothing but horses, carriages, and dogs. He *thee's* and *thou's* persons of the highest standing, and the word *Sir* is quite obsolete with him.

Clitandre. It is said that he is on the best of terms with Bélise.

Célimène. Poor silly woman, and the dreariest company! When she comes to visit me, I suffer from martyrdom; one has to rack one's brain perpetually to find out what to say to her; and the impossibility of her expressing her thoughts allows the conversation to drop every minute. In vain you try to overcome her stupid silence by the assistance of the most commonplace topics; even the fine weather, the rain, the heat and the cold are subjects, which, with her, are soon exhausted. Yet for all that, her calls, unbearable enough, are prolonged to an insufferable length; and you may consult the clock,

or yawn twenty times, but she stirs no more than a log
of wood.

Acaste.   What think you of Adraste?

Célimène.   Oh! What excessive pride! He is a man
positively puffed out with conceit.   His self-importance
is never satisfied with the Court, against which he in-
veighs daily; and whenever an office, a place, or a living
is bestowed on another, he is sure to think himself unjustly treated.

Clitandre.   But young Cléon, whom the most respectable people go to see, what say you of him?

Célimène.   That it is to his cook he owes his distinction, and to his table that people pay visits.

Éliante.   He takes pains to provide the most dainty
dishes.

Célimène.   True; but I should be very glad if he
would not dish up himself.   His foolish person is a very
ba*d* dish, which, to my thinking, spoils every entertain-
ment which he gives.

Philinte.   His uncle Damis is very much esteemed;
what say you to him, Madam?

Célimène.   He is one of my friends.

Philinte.   I think him a perfect gentleman, and sensible enough.

Célimène.   True; but he pretends to too much wit,
which annoys me.   He is always upon stilts, and, in all
his conversations, one sees him labouring to say smart
things.   Since he took it into his head to be clever, he is
so difficult to please that nothing suits his taste.   He
must needs find mistakes in everything that one writes,
and thinks that to bestow praise does not become a wit,
that to find fault shows learning, that only fools admire
and laugh, and that, by not approving of anything in
the works of our time, he is superior to all other people.
Even in conversations he finds something to cavil at, the
subjects are too trivial for his condescension; and, with

arms crossed on his breast, he looks down from the
height of his intellect with pity on what everyone says.

Acaste. Drat it! his very picture.

Clitandre (to CÉLIMÈNE). You have an admirable
knack of portraying people to the life.

Alceste. Capital, go on, my fine courtly friends. You
spare no one, and everyone will have his turn. Nevertheless, let but any one of those persons appear, and we
shall see you rush to meet him, offer him your hand, and,
with a flattering kiss, give weight to your protestations
of being his servant.

Clitandre. Why this to us? If what is said offends
you, the reproach must be addressed to this lady.

Alceste. No, gadzooks! it concerns you; for your
assenting smiles draw from her wit all these slanderous
remarks. Her satirical vein is incessantly recruited by
the culpable incense of your flattery; and her mind
would find fewer charms in raillery, if she discovered
that no one applauded her. Thus it is that to flatterers
we ought everywhere to impute the vices which are sown
among mankind.

Philinte. But why do you take so great an interest
in those people, for you would condemn the very things
that are blamed in them?

Célimène. And is not this gentleman bound to contradict? Would you have him subscribe to the general
opinion; and must he not everywhere display the spirit
of contradiction with which Heaven has endowed him?
Other people's sentiments can never please him. He
always supports a contrary idea, and he would think
himself too much of the common herd, were he observed
to be of any one's opinion but his own. The honour of
gainsaying has so many charms for him, that he very
often takes up the cudgels against himself; he combats
his own sentiments as soon as he hears them from other
folks' lips.

Alceste. In short, madam, the laughters are on your side; and you may launch your satire against me.

Philinte. But it is very true, too, that you always take up arms against everything that is said; and, that your avowed spleen cannot bear people to be praised or blamed.

Alceste. 'Sdeath! spleen against mankind is always seasonable, because they are never in the right, and I see that, in all their dealings, they either praise impertinently, or censure rashly.

Célimène. But . . .

Alceste. No, Madam, no, though I were to die for it, you have pastimes which I cannot tolerate; and people are very wrong to nourish in your heart this great attachment to the very faults which they blame in you.

Clitandre. As for myself, I do not know; but I openly acknowledge that hitherto I have thought this lady faultless.

Acaste. I see that she is endowed with charms and attractions; but the faults which she has have not struck me.

Alceste. So much the more have they struck me; and far from appearing blind, she knows that I take care to reproach her with them. The more we love any one, the less we ought to flatter her. True love shows itself by overlooking nothing; and, were I a lady, I would banish all those mean-spirited lovers who submit to all my sentiments, and whose mild complacencies every moment offer up incense to my vagaries.

Célimène. In short, if hearts were ruled by you we ought, to love well, to relinquish all tenderness, and make it the highest aim of perfect attachment to rail heartily at the persons we love.

Éliante. Love, generally speaking, is little apt to put up with these decrees, and lovers are always observed to extol their choice. Their passion never sees aught to blame in it, and in the beloved all things become love-able. They think their faults perfections, and invent sweet terms to call them by. The pale one vies with the jessamine in fairness; another, dark enough to frighten people, becomes an adorable brunette; the lean one has a good shape and is lithe; the stout one has a portly and majestic bearing; the slattern, who has few charms, passes under the name of a careless beauty; the giantess seems a very goddess in their sight; the dwarf is an epi-tome of all the wonders of Heaven; the proud one has a soul worthy of a diadem; the artful brims with wit; the silly one is very good-natured; the chatterbox is good-tempered; and the silent one modest and reticent. Thus a passionate swain loves even the very faults of those of whom he is enamoured.

Alceste. And I maintain that . . .

Célimène. Let us drop the subject, and take a turn or two in the gallery. What! are you going, gentlemen?

Clitandre and Acaste. No, no, Madam.

Alceste. The fear of their departure troubles you very much. Go when you like, gentlemen; but I tell you be-forehand that I shall not leave until you leave.

Acaste. Unless it inconveniences this lady, I have nothing to call me elsewhere the whole day.

Clitandre. I, provided I am present when the King retires, I have no other matter to call me away.

Célimène (*to* ALCESTE). You only joke, I fancy.

Alceste. Not at all. We shall soon see whether it is me of whom you wish to get rid.

SCENE VI.—ALCESTE, CÉLIMÈNE, ÉLIANTE, ACASTE, PHILINTE, CLITANDRE, BASQUE.

Basque (*to* ALCESTE). There is a man down stairs, sir, who wishes to speak to you on business which cannot be postponed.

Alceste. Tell him that I have no such urgent business.

Basque. He wears a jacket with large plaited skirts embroidered with gold.

Célimène (*to* ALCESTE). Go and see who it is, or else let him come in.

SCENE VII.—ALCESTE, CÉLIMÈNE, ÉLIANTE, ACASTE, PHILINTE, CLITANDRE, A GUARD OF THE MARÉCHAUSSÉE.

Alceste (*going to meet the guard*). What may be your pleasure? Come in, sir.

Guard. I would have a few words privately with you, sir.

Alceste. You may speak aloud, sir, so as to let me know.

Guard. The Marshals of France, whose commands I bear, hereby summon you to appear before them immediately, sir.

Alceste. Whom? Me, sir?

Guard. Yourself.

Alceste. And for what?

Philinte (*to* ALCESTE). It is this ridiculous affair between you and Oronte.

Célimène (*to* PHILINTE). What do you mean?

Philinte. Oronte and he have been insulting each other just now about some trifling verses which he did not like; and the Marshals wish to nip the affair in the bud.

Alceste. Well, I shall never basely submit.

Philinte. But you must obey the summons: come, get ready.

Alceste. How will they settle this between us? Will the edict of these gentlemen oblige me to approve of the verses which are the cause of our quarrel? I will not retract what I have said; I think them abominable.

Philinte. But with a little milder tone . . .

Alceste. I will not abate one jot; the verses are execrable.

Philinte. You ought to show a more accommodating spirit. Come along.

Alceste. I shall go, but nothing shall induce me to retract.

Philinte. Go and show yourself.

Alceste. Unless an express order from the King himself commands me to approve of the verses which cause all this trouble, I shall ever maintain, egad, that they are bad, and that a fellow deserves hanging for making them. (*To* CLITANDRE *and* ACASTE *who are laughing.*) Hang it! gentlemen, I did not think I was so amusing.

Célimène. Go quickly whither you are wanted.

Alceste. I am going, Madam; but shall come back here to finish our discussion.

ACT III

Scene I.—Clitandre, Acaste.

Clitandre. My dear marquis, you appear mightily pleased with yourself; everything amuses you, and nothing discomposes you. But really and truly, think you, without flattering yourself, that you have good reasons for appearing so joyful?

Acaste. Egad, I do not find, on looking at myself, any matter to be sorrowful about. I am wealthy, I am young, and am descended from a family which, with some appearance of truth, may be called noble; and I think that, by the rank which my lineage confers upon me, there are very few offices to which I might not aspire. As for courage, which we ought especially to value, it is well known—this without vanity—that I do not lack it; and people have seen me carry on an affair of honour in a manner sufficiently vigorous and brisk. As for wit, I have some, no doubt; and as for good taste, to judge and reason upon everything without study; at "first nights," of which I am very fond, to take my place as a critic upon the stage, to give my opinion as a judge, to applaud, and point out the best passages by repeated bravoes, I am sufficiently adroit; I carry myself well, and am good-looking, have particularly fine teeth, and a good figure. I believe, without flattering myself, that, as for dressing in good taste, very few will dispute the palm with me. I find myself treated with every possible consideration, very much beloved by the fair sex; and I stand very well with the King. With all that, I think, dear marquis, that one might be satisfied with oneself anywhere.

Clitandre. True. But, finding so many easy conquests elsewhere, why come you here to utter fruitless sighs?

Acaste. I? Zounds! I have neither the wish nor the disposition to put up with the indifference of any woman. I leave it to awkward and ordinary people to burn constantly for cruel fair maidens, to languish at their feet, and to bear with their severities, to invoke the aid of sighs and tears, and to endeavour, by long and persistent assiduities, to obtain what is denied to their little merit. But men of my stamp, marquis, are not made to love on trust, and be at all the expenses themselves. Be the merit of the fair ever so great, I think, thank Heaven, that we have our value as well as they; that it is not reasonable to enthrall a heart like mine without its costing them anything; and that, to weigh everything in a just scale, the advances should be, at least, reciprocal.

Clitandre. Then you think that you are right enough here, marquis?

Acaste. I have some reason, marquis, to think so.

Clitandre. Believe me, divest yourself of this great mistake: you flatter yourself, dear friend, and are altogether self-deceived.

Acaste. It is true. I flatter myself, and am, in fact, altogether, self-deceived.

Clitandre. But what causes you to judge your happiness to be complete?

Acaste. I flatter myself.

Clitandre. Upon what do you ground your belief?

Acaste. I am altogether self-deceived.

Clitandre. Have you any sure proofs?

Acaste. I am mistaken, I tell you.

Clitandre. Has Célimène made you any secret avowal of her inclinations?

Acaste. No, I am very badly treated by her.

Clitandre. Answer me, I pray.

Acaste. I meet with nothing but rebuffs.

Clitandre. A truce to your raillery; and tell me what hope she has held out to you.

Acaste. I am the rejected, and you are the lucky one. She has a great aversion to me, and one of these days I shall have to hang myself.

Clitandre. Nonsense. Shall we two, marquis, to adjust our love affairs, make a compact together? Whenever one of us shall be able to show a certain proof of having the greater share in Célimène's heart, the other shall leave the field free to the supposed conqueror, and by that means rid him of an obstinate rival.

Acaste. Egad! you please me with these words, and I agree to that from the bottom of my heart. But, hush.

Scene II.—Célimène, Acaste, Clitandre.

Célimène. What! here still?

Clitandre. Love, madam, detains us.

Célimène. I hear a carriage below. Do you know whose it is?

Clitandre. No.

Scene III.—Célimène, Acaste, Clitandre, Basque.

Basque. Arsinoé, Madam, is coming up to see you.

Célimène. What does the woman want with me?

Basque. Éliante is down stairs talking to her.

Célimène. What is she thinking about, and what brings her here?

Acaste. She has everywhere the reputation of being a consummate prude, and her fervent zeal . . .

Célimène. Psha, downright humbug. In her inmost soul she is as worldly as any; and her every nerve is strained to hook some one, without being successful, however. She can only look with envious eyes on the accepted lovers of others; and in her wretched condition, forsaken by all, she is for ever railing against the blind-

ness of the age. She endeavours to hide the dreadful
isolation of her home under a false cloak of prudishness;
and to save the credit of her feeble charms, she brands as
criminal the power which they lack. Yet a swain would
not come at all amiss to the lady; and she has even a
tender hankering after Alceste. Every attention that
he pays me, she looks upon as a theft committed by me,
and as an insult to her attractions; and her jealous spite,
which she can hardly hide, breaks out against me at
every opportunity, and in an underhand manner. In
short, I never saw anything, to my fancy, so stupid. She
is impertinent to the last degree . . .

SCENE IV.—ARSINOÉ, CÉLIMÈNE, CLITANDRE, ACASTE.

Célimène. Ah! what happy chance brings you here,
Madam? I was really getting uneasy about you.

Arsinoé. I have come to give you some advice as a
matter of duty.

Célimène. How very glad I am to see you!
          (*Exeunt* CLITANDRE *and* ACASTE, *laughing*).

SCENE V.—ARSINOÉ, CÉLIMÈNE.

Arsinoé. They could not have left at a more convenient opportunity.

Célimène. Shall we sit down?

Arsinoé. It is not necessary. Friendship, Madam,
must especially show itself in matters which may be of
consequence to us; and as there are none of greater importance than honour and decorum, I come to prove to
you, by an advice which closely touches your reputation,
the friendship which I feel for you. Yesterday I was
with some people of rare virtue, where the conversation
turned upon you; and there, your conduct, which is causing some stir, was unfortunately, Madam, far from being
commended. That crowd of people, whose visits you
permit, your gallantry and the noise it makes, were criti-

cised rather more freely and more severely than I could have wished. You can easily imagine whose part I took. I did all I could to defend you. I exonerated you, and vouched for the purity of your heart, and the honesty of your intentions. But you know there are things in life, which one cannot well defend, although one may have the greatest wish to do so; and I was at last obliged to confess that the way in which you lived did you some harm; that, in the eyes of the world, it had a doubtful look; that there was no story so ill-natured as not to be everywhere told about it; and that, if you liked, your behaviour might give less cause for censure. Not that I believe that decency is in any way outraged. Heaven forbid that I should harbour such a thought! But the world is so ready to give credit to the faintest shadow of a crime, and it is not enough to live blameless one's self. Madam, I believe you to be too sensible not to take in good part this useful counsel, and not to ascribe it only to the inner promptings of an affection that feels an interest in your welfare.

Célimène. Madam, I have a great many thanks to return you. Such counsel lays me under an obligation; and, far from taking it amiss, I intend this very moment to repay the favour, by giving you an advice which also touches your reputation closely; and as I see you prove yourself my friend by acquainting me with the stories that are current of me, I shall follow so nice an example, by informing you what is said of you. In a house the other day, where I paid a visit, I met some people of exemplary merit, who, while talking of the proper duties of a well spent life, turned the topic of the conversation upon you, Madam. There your prudishness and your too fervent zeal were not at all cited as a good example. This affectation of a grave demeanour, your eternal conversations on wisdom and honor, your mincings and mouthings at the slightest shadows of indecency, which an innocent though ambiguous word may convey, that lofty esteem in which you hold yourself, and those pitying glances which you cast upon all, your frequent lectures and your acrid censures on things which are pure and harmless; all this, if I may speak frankly to you, Madam, was blamed unanimously. What is the good, said they, of this modest mien and this prudent exterior, which is belied by all the rest? She says her prayers with the utmost exactness; but she beats her servants and pays them no wages. She displays great fervour in every place of devotion; but she paints and wishes to appear handsome. She covers the nudities in her pictures; but loves the reality. As for me, I undertook your defence against everyone, and positively assured them that it was nothing but scandal; but the general opinion went against me, as they came to the conclusion that you would do well to concern yourself less about the actions of others, and take a little more pains with your own; that one ought to look a long time at one's self before thinking of condemning other people; that when we wish to correct others, we ought to add the weight of a blameless life; and that even then, it would be better to leave it to those whom Heaven has ordained for the task. Madam, I also believe you to be too sensible not to take in good part this useful counsel, and not to ascribe it only to the inner promptings of an affection that feels an interest in your welfare.

Arsinoé. To whatever we may be exposed when we reprove, I did not expect this retort, Madam, and, by its very sting, I see how my sincere advice has hurt your feelings.

Célimène. On the contrary, Madam; and, if we were reasonable, these mutual counsels would become customary. If honestly made use of, it would to a great extent destroy the excellent opinion people have of themselves. It depends entirely on you whether we shall con-

tinue this trustworthy practice with equal zeal, and
whether we shall take great care to tell each other, between ourselves, what we hear, you of me, I of you.

Arsinoé. Ah! Madam, I can hear nothing said of you.
It is in me that people find so much to reprove.

Célimène. Madam, it is easy, I believe, to blame or
praise everything; and everyone may be right, according
to their age and taste. There is a time for gallantry,
there is one also for prudishness. One may out of policy
take to it, when youthful attractions have faded away.
It sometimes serves to hide vexatious ravages of time.
I do not say that I shall not follow your example, one of
these days. Those things come with old age; but twenty,
as everyone well knows, is not an age to play the prude.

Arsinoé. You certainly pride yourself upon a very
small advantage, and you boast terribly of your age.
Whatever difference there may be between your years
and mine, there is no occasion to make such a tremendous fuss about it; and I am at a loss to know,
Madam, why you should get so angry, and what makes
you goad me in this manner.

Célimène. And I, Madam, am at an equal loss to
know why one hears you inveigh so bitterly against me
everywhere. Must I always suffer for your vexations?
Can I help it, if people refuse to pay you any attentions?
If men will fall in love with me, and will persist in offer-
ing me each day those attentions of which your heart
would wish to see me deprived, I cannot alter it, and it
is not my fault. I leave you the field free, and do not
prevent you from having charms to attract people.

Arsinoé. Alas! and do you think that I would trouble
myself about this crowd of lovers of which you are
so vain, and that it is not very easy to judge at what
price they may be attracted now-a-days? Do you wish
to make it be believed, that, judging by what is going on,
your merit alone attracts this crowd; that their affection

for you is strictly honest, and that it is for nothing but
your virtue that they all pay you their court? People
are not blinded by those empty pretences; the world is
not duped in that way; and I see many ladies who are
capable of inspiring a tender feeling, yet who do not
succeed in attracting a crowd of beaux; and from that
fact we may draw our conclusion that those conquests
are not altogether made without some great advances;
that no one cares to sigh for us, for our handsome looks
only; and that the attentions bestowed on us are generally dearly bought. Do not therefore pull yourself up
with vain-glory about the trifling advantages of a poor
victory; and moderate slightly the pride on your good
looks, instead of looking down upon people on account of
them. If I were at all envious about your conquests, I
dare say, that I might manage like other people; be under
no restraint, and thus show plainly that one may have
lovers, when one wishes for them.

Célimène. Do have some then, Madam, and let us
see you try it; endeavour to please by this extraordinary
secret; and without . . .

Arsinoé. Let us break off this conversation, madam,
it might excite too much both your temper and mine;
and I would have already taken my leave, had I not been
obliged to wait for my carriage.

Célimène. Please stay as long as you like, and do not
hurry yourself on that account, madam. But instead of
wearying you any longer with my presence, I am going
to give you some more pleasant company. This gentleman, who comes very opportunely, will better supply my
place in entertaining you.

SCENE VI.—ALCESTE, CÉLIMÈNE, ARSINOÉ.

Célimène. Alceste, I have to write a few lines, which
I cannot well delay. Please to stay with this lady; she
will all the more easily excuse my rudeness.

SCENE VII.—ALCESTE, ARSINOÉ.

Arsinoé.   You see, I am left here to entertain you, until my coach comes round.   She could have devised no more charming treat for me, than such a conversation. Indeed, people of exceptional merit attract the esteem and love of every one; and yours has undoubtedly some secret charm, which makes me feel interested in all your doings.   I could wish that the Court, with a real regard to your merits would do more justice to your deserts. You have reason to complain; and it vexes me to see that day by day nothing is done for you.

Alceste.   For me, Madam?   And by what right could I pretend to anything?   What service have I rendered to the State?   Pray, what have I done, so brilliant in itself, to complain of the Court doing nothing for me?

Arsinoé.   Not everyone whom the State delights to honour, has rendered signal services; there must be an opportunity as well as the power; and the abilities which you allow us to perceive, ought . . .

Alceste.   For Heaven's sake, let us have no more of my abilities, I pray.   What would you have the Court to do?   It would have enough to do, and have its hands full, to discover the merits of people.

Arsinoé.   Sterling merit discovers itself.   A great deal is made of yours in certain places; and let me tell you that, not later than yesterday, you were highly spoken of in two distinguished circles, by people of very great standing.

Alceste.   As for that, Madam, everyone is praised now-a-days, and very little discrimination is shown in our times.   Everything is equally endowed with great merit, so that it is no longer an honour to be lauded.   Praises abound, they throw them at one's head, and even my valet is put in the gazette.

Arsinoé.   As for me, I could wish that, to bring yourself into greater notice, some place at Court might tempt you. If you will only give me a hint that you seriously think about it, a great many engines might be set in motion to serve you; and I know some people whom I could employ for you, and who would manage the matter smoothly enough.

Alceste. And what should I do when I got there, Madam? My disposition rather prompts me to keep away from it. Heaven, when ushering me into the world, did not give me a mind suited for the atmosphere of a Court. I have not the qualifications necessary for success, nor for making my fortune there. To be open and candid is my chief talent; I possess not the art of deceiving people in conversation; and he who has not the gift of concealing his thoughts, ought not to stay long in those places. When not at Court, one has not, doubtless, that standing, and the advantage of those honourable titles which it bestows now-a-days; but, on the other hand, one has not the vexation of playing the silly fool. One has not to bear a thousand galling rebuffs; one is not, as it were, forced to praise the verses of mister so-and-so, to laud Madam such and such, and to put up with the whims of some ingenious marquis.

Arsinoé. Since you wish it, let us drop the subject of the Court: but I cannot help grieving for your amours; and, to tell you my opinions candidly on that head, I could heartily wish your affections better bestowed. You certainly deserve a much happier fate, and she who has fascinated you is unworthy of you.

Alceste. But in saying so, Madam, remember, I pray, that this lady is your friend.

Arsinoé. True. But really my conscience revolts at the thought of suffering any longer the wrong that is done to you. The position in which I see you afflicts my very soul, and I caution you that your affections are betrayed.

Alceste. This is certainly showing me a deal of good feeling, Madam, and such information is very welcome to a lover.

Arsinoé. Yes, for all Célimène is my friend, I do not hesitate to call her unworthy of possessing the heart of a man of honour; and hers only pretends to respond to yours.

Alceste. That is very possible, Madam, one cannot look into the heart; but your charitable feelings might well have refrained from awakening such a suspicion as mine.

Arsinoé. Nothing is easier than to say no more about it, if you do not wish to be undeceived.

Alceste. Just so. But whatever may be openly said on this subject is not half so annoying as hints thrown out; and I for one would prefer to be plainly told that only which could be clearly proved.

Arsinoé. Very well! and that is sufficient; I can fully enlighten you upon this subject. I will have you believe nothing but what your own eyes see. Only have the kindness to escort me as far as my house; and I will give you undeniable proof of the faithlessness of your fair one's heart; and if, after that, you can find charms in anyone else, we will perhaps find you some consolation.

ACT IV

Scene I.—Éliante, Philinte

Philinte. No, never have I seen so obstinate a mind, nor a reconciliation more difficult to effect. In vain was Alceste tried on all sides; he would still maintain his opinion; and never, I believe, has a more curious dispute engaged the attention of those gentlemen. "No, gentlemen," exclaimed he, "I will not retract, and I shall agree with you on every point, except on this one. At what is Oronte offended? and with what does he reproach me? Does it reflect upon his honour that he cannot write well? What is my opinion to him, which he has altogether wrongly construed? One may be a perfect gentleman, and write bad verses; those things have nothing to do with honour. I take him to be a gallant man in every way; a man of standing, of merit, and courage, anything you like, but he is a wretched author. I shall praise, if you wish, his mode of living, his lavishness, his skill in riding, in fencing, in dancing; but as to praising his verses, I am his humble servant; and if one has not the gift of composing better, one ought to leave off rhyming altogether, unless condemned to it on forfeit of one's life." In short, all the modification they could with difficulty obtain from him, was to say, in what he thought a much gentler tone—"I am sorry, Sir, to be so difficult to please; and out of regard to you, I could wish, with all my heart, to have found your sonnet a little better." And they compelled them to settle this dispute quickly with an embrace.

Éliante. He is very eccentric in his doings; but I
214

must confess that I think a great deal of him; and the candour upon which he prides himself has something noble and heroic in it. It is a rare virtue now-a-days, and I, for one, should not be sorry to meet with it everywhere.

Philinte. As for me, the more I see of him, the more I am amazed at that passion to which his whole heart is given up. I cannot conceive how, with a disposition like his, he has taken it into his head to love at all; and still less can I understand how your cousin happens to be the person to whom his feelings are inclined.

Éliante. That shows that love is not always produced by compatibility of temper; and in this case, all the pretty theories of gentle sympathies are belied.

Philinte. But do you think him beloved in return, to judge from what we see?

Éliante. That is a point not easily decided. How can we judge whether it be true she loves? Her own heart is not so very sure of what it feels. It sometimes loves, without being quite aware of it, and at other times thinks it does, without the least grounds.

Philinte. I think that our friend will have more trouble with this cousin of yours than he imagines; and to tell you the truth, if he were of my mind, he would bestow his affections elsewhere; and by a better choice, we should see him, Madam, profit by the kind feelings which your heart evinces for him.

Éliante. As for me, I do not mince matters, and I think that in such cases we ought to act with sincerity. I do not run counter to his tender feelings; on the contrary, I feel interested in them; and, if it depended only on me, I would unite him to the object of his love. But if, as it may happen in love affairs, his affections should receive a check, and if Célimène should respond to the love of any one else, I could easily be prevailed upon to listen to his addresses, and I should have no repugnance whatever to them on account of their rebuff elsewhere.

Philinte. Nor do I, from my side, oppose myself, Madam, to the tender feelings which you entertain for him; and he himself, if he wished, could inform you what I have taken care to say to him on that score. But if, by the union of those two, you should be prevented from accepting his attentions, all mine would endeavour to gain that great favour which your kind feelings offer to him; only too happy, Madam, to have them transferred to myself, if his heart could not respond to yours.

Éliante. You are in the humour to jest, Philinte.

Philinte. Not so, Madam, I am speaking my inmost feelings. I only wait the opportune moment to offer myself openly, and am wishing most anxiously to hurry its advent.

Scene II.—Alceste, Éliante, Philinte.

Alceste. Ah, Madam! obtain me justice, for an offence which triumphs over all my constancy.

Éliante. What ails you? What disturbs you?

Alceste. This much ails me, that it is death to me to think of it; and the upheaving of all creation would less overwhelm me than this accident. It is all over with me . . . My love . . . I cannot speak.

Éliante. Just endeavour to be composed.

Alceste. Oh, just Heaven; can the odious vices of the basest minds be joined to such beauty?

Éliante. But, once more, what can have . . .

Alceste. Alas! All is ruined! I am! I am betrayed! I am stricken to death Célimène . . . would you credit it! Célimène deceives me and is faithless.

Éliante. Have you just grounds for believing so?

Philinte. Perhaps it is a suspicion, rashly conceived; and your jealous temper often harbours fancies . . .

Alceste. Ah! 'Sdeath, please to mind your own business, Sir. (*To* Éliante). Her treachery is but too certain, for I have in my pocket a letter in her own handwriting. Yes, Madam, a letter, intended for Oronte, has placed before my eyes my disgrace and her shame; Oronte, whose addresses I believed she avoided, and whom, of all my rivals, I feared the least.

Philinte. A letter may deceive by appearances, and is sometimes not so culpable as may be thought.

Alceste. Once more, sir, leave me alone, if you please, and trouble yourself only about your own concerns.

Éliante. You should moderate your passion; and the insult . . .

Alceste. You must be left to do that, Madam; it is to you that my heart has recourse to-day to free itself from this goading pain. Avenge me on an ungrateful and perfidious relative who basely deceives such constant tenderness. Avenge me for an act that ought to fill you with horror.

Éliante. I avenge you? How?

Alceste. By accepting my heart. Take it, Madam, instead of the false one; it is in this way that I can avenge myself upon her; and I shall punish her by the sincere attachment, and the profound love, the respectful cares, the eager devotions, the ceaseless attentions which this heart will henceforth offer up at your shrine.

Éliante. I certainly sympathize with you in your sufferings, and do not despise your proffered heart; but the wrong done may not be so great as you think, and you might wish to forego this desire for revenge. When the injury proceeds from a beloved object, we form many designs which we never execute; we may find as powerful a reason as we like to break off the connection, the guilty charmer is soon again innocent; all the harm we wish her quickly vanishes, and we know what a lover's anger means.

Alceste. No, no, Madam, no. The offence is too cruel; there will be no relenting, and I have done with her. Nothing shall change the resolution I have taken, and I should hate myself for ever loving her again. Here she comes. My anger increases at her approach. I shall taunt her with her black guilt, completely put her to the blush, and, after that, bring you a heart wholly freed from her deceitful attractions.

SCENE III.—CÉLIMÈNE, ALCESTE.

Alceste (*aside*). Grant, Heaven, that I may control my temper.

Célimène (*aside*). Ah! (*To* ALCESTE). What is all this trouble that I see you in, and what means those long-drawn sighs, and those black looks which you cast at me?

Alceste. That all the wickedness of which a heart is capable is not to be compared to your perfidy; that neither fate, hell, nor Heaven in its wrath, ever produced anything so wicked as you are.

Célimène. These are certainly pretty compliments, which I admire very much.

Alceste. Do not jest. This is no time for laughing. Blush rather, you have cause to do so; and I have undeniable proofs of your treachery. This is what the agitations of my mind prognosticated; it was not without cause that my love took alarm; by these frequent suspicions, which were hateful to you, I was trying to discover the misfortune which my eyes have beheld; and in spite of all your care and your skill in dissembling, my star foretold me what I had to fear. But do not imagine that I will bear unavenged this slight of being insulted. I know that we have no command over our inclinations, that love will everywhere spring up spontaneously, that there is no entering a heart by force, and that every soul is free to name its conqueror: I should thus have no reason to complain if you had spoken to me without dissembling, and rejected my advances from the very beginning; my heart would then have been justified in blaming fortune alone. But to see my love encouraged by a deceitful avowal on your part, is an action so treacherous and perfidious, that it cannot meet with too great a punishment; and I can allow my resentment to do anything. Yes, yes; after such an outrage, fear everything; I am no longer myself, I am mad with rage. My senses, struck by the deadly blow with which you kill me, are no longer governed by reason; I give way to the outbursts of a just wrath, and am no longer responsible for what I may do.

Célimène. Whence comes, I pray, such a passion? Speak! Have you lost your senses?

Alceste. Yes, yes, I lost them when, to my misfortune, I beheld you, and thus took the poison which kills me, and when I thought to meet with some sincerity in those treacherous charms that bewitched me.

Célimène. Of what treachery have you to complain?

Alceste. Ah! how double-faced she is! how well she knows how to dissemble! But I am fully prepared with the means of driving her to extremities. Cast your eyes here and recognize your writing. This picked-up note is sufficient to confound you, and such proof cannot easily be refuted.

Célimène. And this is the cause of your perturbation of spirits?

Alceste. You do not blush on beholding this writing!

Célimène. And why should I blush?

Alceste. What! You add boldness to craft! Will you disown this note because it bears no name?

Célimène. Why should I disown it, since I wrote it.

Alceste. And you can look at it without becoming confused at the crime of which its style accuses you!

Célimène. You are, in truth, a very eccentric man.

Alceste. What! you thus out-brave this convincing proof! And the contents so full of tenderness for

Oronte, need have nothing in them to outrage me, or to shame you?

Célimène. Oronte! Who told you that this letter is for him?

Alceste. The people who put it into my hands this day. But I will even suppose that it is for some one else. Has my heart any less cause to complain of yours? Will you, in fact, be less guilty toward me?

Célimène. But if it is a woman to whom this letter is addressed, how can it hurt you, or what is there culpable in it?

Alceste. Hem! The prevarication is ingenious, and the excuse excellent. I must own that I did not expect this turn; and nothing but that was wanting to convince me. Do you dare to have recourse to such palpable tricks? Do you think people entirely destitute of common sense? Come, let us see a little by what subterfuge, with what air, you will support so palpable a falsehood; and how you can apply to a woman every word of this note which evinces so much tenderness! Reconcile, if you can, to hide your deceit, what I am about to read. . . .

Célimène. It does not suit me to do so. I think it ridiculous that you should take so much upon yourself, and tell me to my face what you have the daring to say to me!

Alceste. No, no, without flying into a rage, take a little trouble to explain these terms.

Célimène. No, I shall do nothing of the kind, and it matters very little to me what you think upon the subject.

Alceste. I pray you, show me, and I shall be satisfied, if this letter can be explained as meant for a woman.

Célimène. Not at all. It is for Oronte; and I will have you believe it. I accept all his attentions gladly; I admire what he says, I like him, and I shall agree to whatever you please. Do as you like, and act as you think proper; let nothing hinder you and do not harass me any longer.

Alceste (aside). Heavens! can anything more cruel be conceived, and was ever heart treated like mine? What! I am justly angry with her, I come to complain, and I am quarrelled with instead! My grief and my suspicions are excited to the utmost, I am allowed to believe everything, she boasts of everything; and yet, my heart is still sufficiently mean not to be able to break the bonds that hold it fast, and not to arm itself with a generous contempt for the ungrateful object of which it is too much enamoured. (*To* CÉLIMÈNE). Perfidious woman, you know well how to take advantage of my great weakness, and to employ for your own purpose that excessive, astonishing, and fatal love which your treacherous looks have inspired! Defend yourself at least from this crime that overwhelms me, and stop pretending to be guilty. Show me, if you can, that this letter is innocent; my affection will even consent to assist you. At any rate, endeavour to appear faithful, and I shall strive to believe you such.

Célimène. Bah, you are mad with your jealous frenzies, and do not deserve the love which I have for you. I should much like to know what could compel me to stoop for you to the baseness of dissembling; and why, if my heart were disposed towards another, I should not say so candidly. What! does the kind assurance of my sentiments towards you not defend me sufficiently against all your suspicions? Ought they to possess any weight at all with such a guarantee? Is it not insulting me even to listen to them? And since it is with the utmost difficulty that we can resolve to confess our love, since the strict honour of our sex, hostile to our passion, strongly opposes such a confession, ought a lover who sees such an obstacle overcome for his sake, doubt with impunity our avowal? And is he not greatly to blame in not assuring himself of the truth of that which is never said but after a severe struggle with oneself? Begone, such suspicions deserve my anger, and you are not worthy of being cared for. I am silly, and am vexed at my own simplicity in still preserving the least kindness for you. I ought to place my affections elsewhere, and give you a just cause for complaint.

Alceste. Ah! you traitress! mine is a strange infatuation for you; those tender expressions are, no doubt, meant only to deceive me. But it matters little, I must submit to my fate; my very soul is wrapt up in you; I will see to the bitter end how your heart will act towards me, and whether it will be black enough to deceive me.

Célimène. No, you do not love me as you ought to love.

Alceste. Indeed! Nothing is to be compared to my exceeding love; and, in its eagerness to show itself to the whole world, it goes even so far as to form wishes against you. Yes, I could wish that no one thought you handsome, that you were reduced to a miserable existence; that Heaven, at your birth, had bestowed upon you nothing; that you had no rank, no nobility, no wealth, so that I might openly proffer my heart, and thus make amends to you for the injustice of such a lot; and that, this very day, I might have the joy and the glory of seeing you owe everything to my love.

Célimène. This is wishing me well in a strange way! Heaven grant that you may never have occasion . . . But here comes Monsieur Dubois curiously decked out.

SCENE IV.—CÉLIMÈNE, ALCESTE, DUBOIS.

Alceste. What means this strange attire, and that frightened look? What ails you?

Dubois. Sir . . .

Alceste. Well?

Dubois.   The most mysterious event.

Alceste.   What is it?

Dubois.   Our affairs are turning out badly, Sir.

Alceste.   What?

Dubois.   Shall I speak out?

Alceste.   Yes, do, and quickly.

Dubois.   Is there no one there?

Alceste.   Curse your trifling!   Will you speak?

Dubois.   Sir, we must beat a retreat.

Alceste.   What do you mean?

Dubois.   We must steal away from this quietly.

Alceste.   And why?

Dubois.   I tell you that we must leave this place.

Alceste.   The reason?

Dubois.   You must go, Sir, without staying to take leave.

Alceste.   But what is the meaning of this strain?

Dubois.   The meaning is, Sir, that you must make yourself scarce.

Alceste.   I shall knock you on the head to a certainty, booby, if you do not explain yourself more clearly.

Dubois.   A fellow, Sir, with a black dress, and as black a look, got as far as the kitchen to leave a paper with us, scribbled over in such a fashion that old Nick himself could not have read it.   It is about your law-suit, I make no doubt; but the very devil, I believe, could not make head nor tail of it.

Alceste.   Well! what then?   What has the paper to do with the going away of which you speak, you scoundrel?

Dubois.   I must tell you, Sir, that, about an hour afterwards, a gentleman who often calls, came to ask for you quite eagerly, and not finding you at home, quietly told me, knowing how attached I am to you, to let you know . . . Stop a moment, what the deuce is his name?

Alceste.   Never mind his name, you scoundrel, and tell me what he told you.

Dubois. He is one of your friends, in short, that is sufficient. He told me that for your very life you must get away from this, and that you are threatened with arrest.

Alceste. But how! has he not specified anything?

Dubois. No. He asked me for ink and paper, and has sent you a line from which you can, I think, fathom the mystery!

Alceste. Hand it over then.

Célimène. What can all this mean?

Alceste. I do not know; but I am anxious to be informed. Have you almost done, devil take you?

Dubois (*after having fumbled for some time for the note*). After all, Sir, I have left it on your table.

Alceste. I do not know what keeps me from . . .

Célimène. Do not put yourself in a passion, but go and unravel this perplexing business.

Alceste. It seems that fate, whatever I may do has sworn to prevent my having a conversation with you. But, to get the better of her, allow me to see you again, Madam, before the end of the day.

ACT V

SCENE I.—ALCESTE, PHILINTE.

Alceste. I tell you, my mind is made up about it.

Philinte. But, whatever this blow may be, does it compel you . . .

Alceste. You may talk and argue till doomsday if you like, nothing can avert me from what I have said. The age we live in is too perverse, and I am determined to withdraw altogether from intercourse with the world. What! when honour, probity, decency, and the laws, are all against my adversary; when the equity of my claim is everywhere cried up; when my mind is at rest as to the justice of my cause, I meanwhile see myself betrayed by its issue! What! I have got justice on my side, and I lose my case! A wretch, whose scandalous history is well known, comes off triumphant by the blackest falsehood! All good faith yields to his treachery! He finds the means of being in the right, whilst cutting my throat! The weight of his dissimulation, so full of cunning, overthrows the right and turns the scales of justice! He obtains even a decree of court to crown his villainy. And, not content with the wrong he is doing me, there is abroad in society an abominable book, of which the very reading is to be condemned, a book that deserves the utmost severity, and of which the scoundrel has the impudence to proclaim me the author. Upon this, Oronte is observed to mutter, and tries wickedly to support the imposture! He, who holds an honourable position at Court, to whom I have done nothing except having been sincere and candid, who came to ask me in spite of myself of my opinion of some of his verses; and because

I treat him honestly, and will not betray either him or truth, he assists in overwhelming me with a trumped-up crime. Behold him now my greatest enemy! And I shall never obtain his sincere forgiveness, because I did not think that his sonnet was good! 'Sdeath! to think that mankind is made thus! The thirst for fame induces them to do such things! This is the good faith, the virtuous zeal, the justice and the honour to be found amongst them! Let us begone; it is too much to endure the vexations they are devising; let us get out of this wood, this cut-throat hole; and since men behave towards each other like real wolves, wretches, you shall never see me again as long as I live.

Philinte. I think you are acting somewhat hastily; and the harm done is not so great as you would make it out. Whatever your adversary dares to impute to you has not had the effect of causing you to be arrested. We see his false reports defeating themselves, and this action is likely to hurt him much more than you.

Alceste. Him? he does not mind the scandal of such tricks as these. He has a license to be an arrant knave; and this event, far from damaging his position, will obtain him a still better standing to-morrow.

Philinte. In short, it is certain that little notice has been taken of the report which his malice spread against you; from that side you have already nothing to fear; and as for your law-suit, of which you certainly have reason to complain, it is easy for you to bring the trial on afresh, and against this decision . . .

Alceste. No, I shall leave it as it is. Whatever cruel wrong this verdict may inflict, I shall take particular care not to have it set aside. We see too plainly how right is maltreated in it, and I wish to go down to posterity as a signal proof, as a notorious testimony of the wickedness of the men of our age. It may indeed cost me twenty thousand francs, but at the cost of twenty thousand francs I shall have the right of railing against the iniquity of human nature, and of nourishing an un-dying hatred of it.

Philinte. But after all . . .

Alceste. But after all, your pains are thrown away. What can you, sir, say upon this head? Would you have the assurance to wish, to my face, to excuse the villainy of all that is happening?

Philinte. No, I agree with you in all that you say. Everything goes by intrigue, and by pure influence. It is only trickery which carries the day in our time, and men ought to act differently. But is their want of equity a reason for wishing to withdraw from their society? All human failings give us, in life, the means of exer-cising our philosophy. It is the best employment for virtue; and if probity reigned everywhere, if all hearts were candid, just, and tractable, most of our virtues would be useless to us, inasmuch as their functions are to bear, without annoyance, the injustice of others in our good cause; and just in the same way as a heart full of virtue . . .

Alceste. I know that you are a most fluent speaker, sir; that you always abound in fine arguments; but you are wasting your time, and all your fine speeches. Rea-son tells me to retire for my own good. I cannot com-mand my tongue sufficiently; I cannot answer for what I might say, and should very probably get myself into a hundred scrapes. Allow me, without any more words, to wait for Célimène. She must consent to the plan that brings me here. I shall see whether her heart has any love for me; and this very hour will prove it to me.

Philinte. Let us go upstairs to Éliante, and wait her coming.

Alceste. No, my mind is too harassed. You go and see her, and leave me in this little dark corner with my black care.

Philinte. That is strange company to leave you in; I will induce Éliante to come down.

SCENE II.—CÉLIMÈNE, ORONTE, ALCESTE.

Oronte. Yes, Madam, it remains for you to consider whether, by ties so dear, you will make me wholly yours. I must be absolutely certain of your affection: a lover dislikes to be held in suspense upon such a subject. If the ardour of my affection has been able to move your feelings, you ought not to hesitate to let me see it; and the proof, after all, which I ask of you, is not to allow Alceste to wait upon you any longer; to sacrifice him to my love, and, in short, to banish him from your house this very day.

Célimène. But why are you so incensed against him; you, whom I have so often heard speak of his merits?

Oronte. There is no need, Madam, of these explanations; the question is, what are your feelings? Please to choose between the one or the other; my resolution depends entirely upon yours.

Alceste (coming out of his corner). Yes, this gentleman is right, Madam, you must make a choice; and his request agrees perfectly with mine. I am equally eager, and the same anxiety brings me here. My love requires a sure proof. Things cannot go on any longer in this way, and the moment has arrived for explaining your feelings.

Oronte. I have no wish, Sir, in any way to disturb, by an untimely affection, your good fortune.

Alceste. And I have no wish, Sir, jealous or not jealous, to share aught in her heart with you.

Oronte. If she prefers your affection to mine . . .

Alceste. If she has the slightest inclination towards you . . .

Oronte. I swear henceforth not to pretend to it again.

Alceste. I peremptorily swear never to see her again.

Oronte. Madam, it remains with you now to speak openly.

Alceste. Madam, you can explain yourself fearlessly.

Oronte. You have simply to tell us where your feelings are engaged.

Alceste. You may simply finish the matter, by choosing between us two.

Oronte. What! you seem to be at a loss to make such a choice.

Alceste. What! your heart still wavers, and appears uncertain!

Célimène. Good Heavens, how out of place is this persistence, and how very unreasonable you both show yourselves! It is not that I do not know whom to prefer, nor is it my heart that wavers. It is not at all in doubt between you two; and nothing could be more quickly accomplished than the choice of my affections. But to tell the truth, I feel too confused to pronounce such an avowal before you; I think that disobliging words ought not to be spoken in people's presence; that a heart can give sufficient proof of its attachment without going so far as to break with everyone; and gentler intimations suffice to inform a lover of the ill success of his suit.

Oronte. No, no, I do not fear a frank avowal; for my part I consent to it.

Alceste. And I demand it; it is just its very publicity that I claim, and I do not wish you to spare my feelings in the least. Your great study has always been to keep friends with everyone; but no more trifling, no more uncertainty. You must explain yourself clearly, or I shall take your refusal as a verdict; I shall know, for my part, how to interpret your silence, and shall consider it as a confirmation of the worst.

Oronte. I owe you many thanks, sir, for this wrath, and I say in every respect as you do.

Célimène. How you weary me with such a whim! Is there any justice in what you ask? And have I not told you what motive prevents me? I will be judged by Éliante, who is just coming.

SCENE III.—ÉLIANTE, PHILINTE, CÉLIMÈNE, ORONTE, ALCESTE.

Célimène. Good cousin, I am being persecuted here by people who have concerted to do so. They both demand, with the same warmth, that I should declare whom my heart has chosen, and that, by a decision which I must give before their very faces, I should forbid one of them to tease me any more with his attentions. Say, has ever such a thing been done?

Éliante. Pray, do not consult me upon such a matter. You may perhaps address yourself to a wrong person, for I am decidedly for people who speak their mind.

Oronte. Madam, it is useless for you to decline.

Alceste. All your evasions here will be badly supported.

Oronte. You must speak, you must, and no longer waver.

Alceste. You need do no more than remain silent.

Oronte. I desire but one word to end our discussions.

Alceste. To me your silence will convey as much as speech.

SCENE IV.—ARSINOÉ, CÉLIMÈNE, ÉLIANTE, ALCESTE, PHILINTE, ACASTE, CLITANDRE, ORONTE.

Acaste (*to* CÉLIMÈNE). We have both come, by your leave, Madam, to clear up a certain little matter with you.

Clitandre (*to* ORONTE *and* ALCESTE). Your presence happens fortunately, gentlemen; for this affair concerns you also.

Arsinoé (to CÉLIMÈNE). No doubt you are surprised at seeing me here, Madam; but these gentlemen are the cause of my intrusion. They both came to see me, and complained of a proceeding which I could not have credited. I have too high an opinion of your kindness of heart ever to believe you capable of such a crime; my eyes even have refused to give credence to their strongest proofs, and in my friendship, forgetting trivial disagreements, I have been induced to accompany them here, to hear you refute this slander.

Acaste. Yes, Madam, let us see, with composure, how you will manage to bear this out. This letter has been written by you, to Clitandre.

Clitandre. And this tender epistle you have addressed to Acaste.

Acaste (to ORONTE *and* ALCESTE). This writing is not altogether unknown to you, gentlemen, and I have no doubt that her kindness has before now made you familiar with her hand. But this is well worth the trouble of reading.

"You are a strange man to condemn my liveliness of spirits, and to reproach me that I am never so merry as when I am not with you. Nothing could be more unjust; and if you do not come very soon to ask my pardon for this offence, I shall never forgive you as long as I live. Our great hulking booby of a Viscount." He ought to have been here. *"Our great hulking booby of a Viscount, with whom you begin your complaints, is a man who would not at all suit me; and ever since I watched him for full three-quarters of an hour spitting in a well to make circles in the water, I never could have a good opinion of him. As for the little Marquis . . ."* that is myself, ladies and gentlemen, be it said without the slightest vanity, . . . *"as for the little Marquis, who held my hand yesterday for a long while, I think that there is nothing*

so diminutive as his whole person, and his sole merit con-
sists in his cloak and sword. As to the man with the
green shoulder knot." (*To* ALCESTE). It is your turn
now, Sir. *"As to the man with the green shoulder knot,*
he amuses me sometimes with his bluntness and his
splenetic behaviour; but there are hundreds of times
when I think him the greatest bore in the world. Re-
specting the man with the big waistcoat . . ." (*To*
ORONTE). This is your share. *"Respecting the man*
with the big waistcoat, who has thought fit to set up as a
wit, and wishes to be an author in spite of everyone, I
cannot even take the trouble to listen to what he says;
and his prose bores me just as much as his poetry. Take
it for granted that I do not always enjoy myself so much
as you think; and that I wish for you, more than I care
to say, amongst all the entertainments to which I am
dragged; and that the presence of those we love is an ex-
cellent relish to our pleasures."

Clitandre. Now for myself.

"Your Clitandre, whom you mention to me, and who
has always such a quantity of soft expressions at his com-
mand, is the last man for whom I could feel any affection.
He must be crazed in persuading himself that I love him;
and you are so too in believing that I do not love you.
You had better change your fancies for his, and come and
see me as often as you can, to help me in bearing the an-
noyance of being pestered by him." This shows the
model of a lovely character, Madam; and I need not tell
you what to call it. It is enough. We shall, both of us,
show this admirable sketch of your heart everywhere and
to everybody.

Acaste. I might also say something, and the subject
is tempting; but I deem you beneath my anger; and I
will show you that little marquises can find worthier
hearts than yours to console themselves

SCENE V.—CÉLIMÈNE, ÉLIANTE, ARSINOÉ, ALCESTE,
ORONTE, PHILINTE.

Oronte. What! Am I to be pulled to pieces in this
fashion, after all that you have written to me? And does
your heart, with all its semblance of love, plight its faith
to all mankind by turns! Bah, I have been too great a
dupe, but I shall be so no longer. You have done me a
service, in showing yourself in your true colours to me. I
am the richer by a heart which you thus restore to me,
and find my revenge in your loss. (*To* ALCESTE.) Sir, I
shall no longer be an obstacle to your flame, and you
may settle matters with this lady as soon as you please.

SCENE VI.—CÉLIMÈNE, ÉLIANTE, ARSINOÉ, ALCESTE,
PHILINTE.

Arsinoé (to CÉLIMÈNE). This is certainly one of the
basest actions which I have ever seen; I can no longer
be silent, and feel quite upset. Has any one ever seen
the like of it? I do not concern myself much in the
affairs of other people, but this gentleman (*pointing to*
ALCESTE), who has staked the whole of his happiness on
you, an honourable and deserving man like this, and
who worshipped you to madness, ought he to have
been . . .

Alceste. Leave me, I pray you, madam, to manage
my own affairs; and do not trouble yourself unneces-
sarily. In vain do I see you espouse my quarrel. I
am unable to repay you for this great zeal; and if ever
I intended to avenge myself by choosing some one else,
it would not be you whom I would select.

Arsinoé. And do you imagine, sir, that I ever har-
boured such a thought, and that I am so very anxious
to secure you? You must be very vain, indeed, to flatter yourself with such an idea. Célimène's leavings are
a commodity, of which no one needs be so very much

enamoured. Pray, undeceive yourself, and do not carry
matters with so high a hand. People like me are not
for such as you. You will do much better to remain
dangling after her skirts, and I long to see so beautiful
a match.

SCENE VII.—CÉLIMÈNE, ÉLIANTE, ALCESTE, PHILINTE.

Alceste (*to* CÉLIMÈNE). Well! I have held my
tongue, notwithstanding all I have seen, and I have let
everyone have his say before me. Have I controlled
myself long enough? and will you now allow me . . .

Célimène. Yes, you may say what you like; you are
justified when you complain, and you may reproach me
with anything you please. I confess that I am in the
wrong; and overwhelmed by confusion I do not seek by
any idle excuse to palliate my fault. The anger of the
others I have despised; but I admit my guilt towards
you. No doubt, your resentment is just; I know how
culpable I must appear to you, that everything speaks
of my treachery to you, and that, in short, you have cause
to hate me. Do so, I consent to it.

Alceste. But can I do so, you traitress? Can I thus
get the better of all my tenderness for you? And although I wish to hate you with all my soul, shall I find
a heart quite ready to obey me. (*To* ÉLIANTE *and*
PHILINTE.) You see what an unworthy passion can do,
and I call you both as witnesses of my infatuation.
Nor, truth to say, is this all, and you will see me carry
it out to the bitter end, to show you that it is wrong
to call us wise, and that in all hearts there remains still
something of the man. (*To* CÉLIMÈNE.) Yes, perfidious creature, I am willing to forget your crimes. I can
find, in my own heart, an excuse for all your doings,
and hide them under the name of a weakness into which
the vices of the age betrayed your youth, provided your

heart will second the design which I have formed of avoiding all human creatures, and that you are determined to follow me without delay into the solitude in which I have made a vow to pass my days. It is by that only, that, in everyone's opinion, you can repair the harm done by your letters, and that, after the scandal which every noble heart must abhor, it may still be possible for me to love you.

Célimène. What! I renounce the world before I grow old, and bury myself in your wilderness!

Alceste. If your affection responds to mine what need the rest of the world signify to you? Am I not sufficient for you?

Célimène. Solitude is frightful to a widow of twenty. I do not feel my mind sufficiently grand and strong to resolve to adopt such a plan. If the gift of my hand can satisfy your wishes, I might be induced to tie such bonds; and marriage . . .

Alceste. No. My heart loathes you now, and this refusal alone effects more than all the rest. As you are not disposed, in those sweet ties, to find all in all in me, as I would find all in all in you, begone, I refuse your offer, and this much-felt outrage frees me for ever from your unworthy toils.

SCENE VIII.—ÉLIANTE, ALCESTE, PHILINTE.

Alceste (*to* ÉLIANTE). Madam, your beauty is adorned by a hundred virtues; and I never saw anything in you but what was sincere. For a long while I thought very highly of you; but allow me to esteem you thus for ever, and suffer my heart in its various troubles not to offer itself for the honour of your acceptance. I feel too unworthy, and begin to perceive that Heaven did not intend me for the marriage bond; that the homage of only the remainder of a heart unworthy of you, would be below your merit, and that in short . . .

Eliante.   You may pursue this thought.   I am not at all embarrassed with my hand; and here is your friend, who, without giving me much trouble, might possibly accept it if I asked him.

Philinte.   Ah!   Madam, I ask for nothing better than that honour, and I could sacrifice my life and soul for it.

Alceste.   May you, to taste true contentment, preserve for ever these feelings towards each other!   Deceived on all sides, overwhelmed with injustice, I will fly from an abyss where vice is triumphant, and seek out some small secluded nook on earth, where one may enjoy the freedom of being an honest man.

Philinte.   Come, Madam, let us leave nothing untried to deter him from the design on which his heart is set.

THE PHYSICIAN
IN SPITE OF HIMSELF

THE PHYSICIAN
IN SPITE OF HIMSELF

(Le Médecin malgré lui)

DRAMATIS PERSONÆ.

Géronte, *father to Lucinde.*
Léandre, *Lucinde's lover.*
Sganarelle, *husband to Martine.*
M. Robert, *Sganarelle's neighbour.*
Lucas, *husband to Jacqueline.*
Valère, *Géronte's servant.*
Thibaut, } *peasants,*
Perrin, *his son,* }
Lucinde, *Géronte's daughter.*
Martine, *Sganarelle's wife.*
Jacqueline, *nurse at Géronte's, and Lucas' wife.*

The Scene represents a Forest.

ACT I

Scene I.—Sganarelle, Martine (*appearing on the stage, quarrelling*).

Sganarelle. No; I tell you that I will do nothing of the kind, and that it is for me to speak, and to be master.

Martine. And I tell you that I will have you live as I like, and that I am not married to you to put up with your vargaries.

Sganarelle. Oh! what a nuisance it is to have a wife!

and Aristotle is perfectly right in saying that a woman is worse than a demon.

Martine. Look at Master Clever, with his silly Aristotle!

Sganarelle. Yes, Master Clever. Find me another faggot-binder who can argue upon things as I can, who has served a famous physician for six years, and who, when only a boy, knew his grammar by heart!

Martine. Plague on the arrant fool.

Sganarelle. Plague on the slut!

Martine. Cursed be the hour and the day when I took it into my head to say yes.

Sganarelle. Cursed be the cuckold of a notary that made me sign my own ruination.

Martine. Certainly it well becomes you to complain on that score. Ought you not rather to thank Heaven every minute of the day that you have me for a wife? and did you deserve to marry a woman like me?

Sganarelle. It is true you did me too much honour, and I had great occasion to be satisfied with my wedding-night. Zounds! do not make me open my mouth too wide: I might say certain things . . .

Martine. What? What could you say?

Sganarelle. Enough; let us drop the subject. It is enough that we know what we know, and that you were very glad to meet with me.

Martine. What do you call very glad to meet with you? A fellow who will drive me to the hospital—a debauched, deceitful wretch, who gobbles up every farthing I have got!

Sganarelle. That is a lie: for I drink part of it.

Martine. Who sells piecemeal every stick of furniture in the house!

Sganarelle. That is living upon one's means.

Martine. Who has taken the very bed from under me!

Sganarelle. You will get up all the earlier.

Martine. In short, who does not leave me a stick in the whole house.

Sganarelle. There will be less trouble in moving.

Martine. And who from morning to night does nothing but gamble and drink!

Sganarelle. That is done in order not to get in the dumps.

Martine. And what am I to do all the while with my family?

Sganarelle. Whatever you like.

Martine. I have got four poor children on my hands.

Sganarelle. Put them down.

Martine.—Who keep asking me every moment for bread.

Sganarelle. Whip them. When I have had enough to eat and to drink, every one in the house ought to be satisfied.

Martine. And do you mean to tell me, you sot, that things can always go on so?

Sganarelle. Wife, let us proceed gently, if you please.

Martine. That I am to bear forever with your insolence and your debauchery?

Sganarelle. Do not let us get into a passion, wife.

Martine. And that I do not know the way to bring you back to your duty?

Sganarelle. Wife, you know that I am not very patient, and that my arm is somewhat heavy.

Martine. I laugh at your threats.

Sganarelle. My sweet wife, my pet, your skin is itching as usual.

Martine. I will let you see that I am not afraid of you.

Sganarelle. My dearest rib, you have set your heart upon a thrashing.

Martine. Do you think that I am frightened at your talk?

Sganarelle. Sweet object of my affections, I shall box your ears for you.

Martine. Sot that you are!

Sganarelle. I shall thrash you.

Martine. Walking wine-cask!

Sganarelle. I shall pummel you.

Martine. Infamous wretch!

Sganarelle. I shall curry your skin for you.

Martine. Wretch! villain! deceiver! cur! scoundrel! gallows-bird! churl! rogue! scamp! thief! . . .

Sganarelle. You will have it, will you? (*Takes a stick and beats her.*)

Martine (*shrieking*). Help! help! help! help!

Sganarelle. That is the real way of quieting you.

SCENE II.—M. ROBERT, SGANARELLE, MARTINE.

M. Robert. Hulloa, hulloa, hulloa! Fie! What is this? What a disgraceful thing! Plague take the scamp to beat his wife so.

Martine (*her arms akimbo, speaks to* M. ROBERT, *and makes him draw back; at last she gives him a slap on the face*). And I like him to beat me, I do.

M. Robert. If that is the case, I consent with all my heart.

Martine. What are you interfering with?

M. Robert. I am wrong.

Martine. Is it any of your business?

M. Robert. You are right.

Martine. Just look at this jackanapes, who wishes to hinder husbands from beating their wives!

M. Robert. I apologize.

Martine. What have you got to say to it?

M. Robert. Nothing.

Martine. Is it for you to poke your nose into it?

M. Robert. No.

Martine. Mind your own business.

M. Robert. I shall not say another word.

Martine. It pleases me to be beaten.

M. Robert. Agreed.

Martine. It does not hurt you.

M. Robert. That is true.

Martine. And you are an ass to interfere with what does not concern you.

M. Robert. Neighbour, I ask your pardon with all my heart. Go on, thrash and beat your wife as much as you like; I shall help you, if you wish it. (*He goes towards* SGANARELLE, *who also speaks to him, makes him draw back, beats him with the stick he has been using, and puts him to flight*).

Sganarelle. I do not wish it.

M. Robert. Ah! that is a different thing.

Sganarelle. I will beat her if I like; and I will not beat her if I do not like.

M. Robert. Very good.

Sganarelle. She is my wife, and not yours.

M. Robert. Undoubtedly.

Sganarelle. It is not for you to order me about.

M. Robert. Just so.

Sganarelle. I do not want your help.

M. Robert. Exactly so.

Sganarelle. And it is like your impertinence to meddle with other people's business. Remember that Cicero says that between the tree and the finger you should not put the bark. (*He drives him away, then comes back to his wife, and says to her, squeezing her hand:*)

SCENE III.—SGANARELLE, MARTINE.

Sganarelle. Come, let us make it up. Shake hands.

Martine. Yes, after having beaten me thus!

Sganarelle. Never mind that. Shake hands.

Martine. I will not.

Sganarelle. Eh?

Martine. No.

Sganarelle. Come, wife!

Martine. I shall not.

Sganarelle. Come, I tell you.

Martine. I will do nothing of the kind.

Sganarelle. Come, come, come.

Martine. No; I will be angry.

Sganarelle. Bah! it is a trifle. Do.

Martine. Leave me alone.

Sganarelle. Shake hands, I tell you.

Martine. You have treated me too ill.

Sganarelle. Well! I beg your pardon; put your hand there.

Martine. I forgive you (*aside, softly*); but I shall make you pay for it.

Sganarelle. You are silly to take notice of it; these are trifles that are necessary now and then to keep up good feeling; and five or six strokes of a cudgel between people who love each other, only brighten the affections. There now! I am going to the wood, and I promise you that you shall have more than a hundred faggots to-day.

Scene IV.—Martine, *alone.*

Go, my lad, whatever look I may put on, I shall not forget to pay you out; and I am dying to hit upon something to punish you for the blows you gave me. I know well enough that a wife has always the means of being revenged upon her husband; but that is too delicate a punishment for my gallows-bird; I want a revenge that shall strike home a little more, or it will not be satisfaction for the insult which I have received.

Scene V.—Valère, Lucas, Martine.

Lucas (*to* Valère, *without seeing* Martine). I'facks we have undertaken a curious errand; and I do not know, for my part, what we shall get by it.

Valère (*to* Lucas, *without seeing* Martine). What is the use of grumbling, good foster-father? We are bound to do as our master tells us; and, besides, we have both of us some interest in the health of his daughter, our mistress; for her marriage, which is put off through her illness, will no doubt bring us in something. Horace, who is generous, is the most likely to succeed among her suitors; and although she has shown some inclination for a certain Léandre, you know well enough that her father would never consent to receive him for his son-in-law.

Martine (*musing on one side, thinking herself alone*). Can I not find out some way of revenging myself?

Lucas (*to* Valère). But what an idea has he taken into his head, since the doctors are quite at a loss.

Valère (*to* Lucas). You may sometimes find by dint of seeking, what cannot be found at once; and often in the most unlikely spots you may . . .

Martine (*still thinking herself alone*). Yes; I must pay him out, no matter at what cost. Those cudgel blows lie heavy on my stomach; I cannot digest them; and . . . (*She is saying all this musingly, and as she moves, she comes in contact with the two men*). Ah, gentlemen, I beg your pardon, I did not notice you, and was puzzling my brain about something that perplexes me.

Valère. Every one has his troubles in this world, and we also are looking for something that we should be very glad to find.

Martine. Is it something in which I can assist you?

Valère. Perhaps. We are endeavouring to meet with some clever man, some special physician, who could give some relief to our master's daughter, seized with an illness which has at once deprived her of the use of her tongue. Several physicians have already exhausted all their knowledge on her behalf; but sometimes one may find people with wonderful secrets, and certain peculiar remedies, who very often succeed where others have failed; and that is the sort of man we are looking for.

Martine (*softly and aside*). Ah! This is an inspiration from Heaven to revenge myself on my rascal. (*Aloud*). You could never have addressed yourselves to any one more able to find what you want; and we have a man here, the most wonderful fellow in the world for desperate maladies.

Valère. Ah! for mercy's sake, where can we meet with him?

Martine. You will find him just now in that little spot yonder, where he is amusing himself in cutting wood.

Lucas. A doctor who cuts wood!

Valère. Who is amusing himself in gathering some simples, you mean to say?

Martine. No; he is a strange fellow who takes a delight in this; a fantastic, eccentric, whimsical man, whom you would never take to be what he really is. He goes about dressed in a most extraordinary fashion, pretends sometimes to be very ignorant, keeps his knowledge to himself, and dislikes nothing so much every day as using the marvellous talents which God has given him for the healing art.

Valère. It is a wonderful thing that all these great men have always some whim, some slight grain of madness mixed with their learning.

Martine. The madness of this man is greater than can be imagined, for sometimes he has to be beaten before he will own his ability; and I warn you beforehand that you will not succeed, that he will never own that he is a physician, unless you take each a stick, and compel him, by dint of blows, to admit at last what he will conceal at first. It is thus that we act when we have need of him.

Valère. What a strange delusion!

Martine. That is true; but, after that, you shall see that he works wonders.

Valère. What is his name?

Martine. His name is Sganarelle. But it is very easy to recognise him. He is a man with a large black beard, and wears a ruff, and a yellow and green coat.

Lucas. A yellow and green coat! He is then a par-rot-doctor?

Valère. But is it really true that he is as clever as you say?

Martine. As clever. He is a man who works mir-acles. About six months ago, a woman was given up by all the other physicians; she was considered dead at least six hours, and they were going to bury her, when they dragged by force the man we are speaking of to her bedside. Having seen her, he poured a small drop of something into her mouth; and at that very instant she rose from her bed, and began immediately to walk in her room as if nothing had happened.

Lucas. Ah!

Valère. It must have been a drop of liquid gold.

Martine. Possibly so. Not more than three weeks ago, a young child, twelve years old, fell from the top of the belfry, and smashed his head, arms, and legs on the stones. No sooner took they our man to it, than he rubbed the whole body with a certain ointment, which he knows how to prepare; and the child immediately rose on its legs, and ran away to play at chuck-farthing.

Lucas. Hah!

Valère. This man must have the universal cure-all.

Martine. Who doubts it?

Lucas. Odds-bobs! that is the very man we want Let us go quickly and fetch him.

Valère. We thank you for the service you have rendered us.

Martine. But do not fail to remember the warning I have given you.

Lucas. Hey! Zooks! leave it to us. If he wants nothing but a thrashing, we will gain our point.

Valère (*to* LUCAS). We are very glad to have met with this woman; and I conceive the best hopes in the world from it.

SCENE VI.—SGANARELLE, VALÈRE, LUCAS.

Sganarelle (*singing behind the Scene*). La, la, la . . .

Valère. I hear some one singing and cutting wood.

Sganarelle (*coming on, with a bottle in his hand, without perceiving* VALÈRE *or* LUCAS). La, la, la. . . . Really I have done enough to deserve a drink. Let us take a little breath. (*He drinks*). This wood is as salt as the very devil. (*Sings*).

> *How sweet to hear,*
> *My pretty flask,*
> *How sweet to hear,*
> *Your little gull, gull!*
> *No fate with mine could vie,*
> *If never you ran dry,*
> *Oh! darling little flask,*
> *But constantly were full!*

Come! Zounds! we must take care not to get the blues.

Valère (*softly to* LUCAS). This is the very man.

Lucas (*softly to* VALÈRE). I think you are right, and that we have just hit upon him.

Valère. Let us look a little closer.

Sganarelle (*hugging the bottle*). Ah! you little rogue! I love you, my pretty dear! (*He sings; but perceiving* LUCAS *and* VALÈRE, *who are examining him, he lowers his voice.*)

> *No fate . . . with mine . . . could . . . vie,*
> *Is . . .*

(*Seeing that they examine him more closely*). Whom the deuce do these people want?

Valère (*to* LUCAS). It is surely he.

Lucas (*to* VALÈRE). There he is, exactly as he has been described to us.

Sganarelle (*aside*). (*At this point he puts down his bottle; and when* VALÈRE *stoops down to bow to him, he thinks that it is in order to snatch it away, and puts it on the other side. As* LUCAS *is doing the same thing as* VALÈRE, SGANARELLE *takes it up again, and hugs it to his breast, with various grimaces which make a great deal of by-play.*) They are consulting each other, while looking at me. What can be their intentions!

Valère. Sir, is not your name Sganarelle?

Sganarelle. Hey! What!

Valère. I ask you if your name is not Sganarelle.

Sganarelle (*turning first to* VALÈRE, *then to* LUCAS). Yes, and no. It depends on what you want with him.

Valère. We want nothing with him, but to offer him our utmost civilities.

Sganarelle. In that case my name is Sganarelle.

Valère. We are delighted to see you, Sir. We have been recommended to you for what we are in search of; and we have come to implore your help, of which we are in want.

Sganarelle. If it be anything, gentlemen, that belongs to my little trade, I am quite ready to oblige you.

Valère. You are too kind to us, Sir. But put your hat on, Sir, if you please; the sun might hurt you.

Lucas. Pray, Sir, put it on.

Sganarelle (*aside*). What a deal of ceremony these people use. (*He puts his hat on*).

Valère. You must not think it strange, Sir, that we have addressed ourselves to you. Clever people are always much sought after, and we have been informed of your capacity.

Sganarelle. It is true, gentlemen, that I am the best hand in the world at making faggots.

Valère. Oh! Sir . . .

Sganarelle. I spare no pains, and make them in a fashion that leaves nothing to be desired.

Valère. That is not the question we have come about, Sir.

Sganarelle. But I charge a hundred and ten sous the hundred.

Valère. Let us not speak about that, if you please.

Sganarelle. I pledge you my word that I could not sell them for less.

Valère. We know what is what, Sir.

Sganarelle. If you know what is what, you know that I charge that price.

Valère. This is a joke, Sir, but . . .

Sganarelle. It is no joke at all, I cannot bate a farthing.

Valère. Let us talk differently, please.

Sganarelle. You may find some elsewhere for less; there be faggots and faggots; but for those which I make . . .

Valère. Let us change the conversation, pray, Sir.

Sganarelle. I take my oath that you shall not have them for less, not a fraction.

Valère. Fie! Fie!

Sganarelle. No, upon my word, you shall have to pay that price. I am speaking frankly, and I am not the man to overcharge.

Valère. Ought a gentleman like you, Sir, to amuse himself with those clumsy pretences, to lower himself to talk thus? Ought so learned a man, such a famous physician as you are, wish to disguise himself in the eyes of the world and keep buried his great talents?

Sganarelle (*aside*). He is mad.

Valère. Pray, Sir, do not dissemble with us.

Sganarelle. What do you mean?

Lucas. All this beating about the bush is useless. We know what we know.

Sganarelle. What do you know? What do you want with me? For whom do you take me?

Valère. For what you are, a great physician.

Sganarelle. Physician yourself; I am not one, and I have never been one.

Valère (aside). Now the fit is on him. *(Aloud).* Sir, do not deny things any longer, and do not, if you please, make us have recourse to unpleasant extremities.

Sganarelle. Have recourse to what?

Valère. To certain things that we should be sorry for.

Sganarelle. Zounds! Have recourse to whatever you like. I am not a physician, and do not understand what you mean.

Valère (aside). Well, I perceive that we shall have to apply the remedy. *(Aloud.)* Once more, Sir, I pray you to confess what you are.

Lucas. Odds-bobs, do not talk any more nonsense; and confess plainly that you are a physician.

Sganarelle (aside). I am getting in a rage.

Valère. What is the good of denying what all the world knows?

Lucas. Why all these funny falsehoods? What is the good of it?

Sganarelle. One word is as good as a thousand, gentlemen. I tell you that I am not a physician.

Valère. You are not a physician?

Sganarelle. No.

Lucas. You are not a physician?

Sganarelle. No, I tell you.

Valère. Since you will have it so, we must make up our minds to do it. *(They each take a stick, and thrash him.)*

Sganarelle. Hold! hold! hold, gentlemen! I will be anything you like

Valère. Why, Sir, do you oblige us to use this violence?

Lucas. Why do you make us take the trouble of giving you a beating?

Valère. I assure you that I regret it with all my heart.

Lucas. Upon my word I am sorry for it too.

Sganarelle. What the devil does it all mean, gentlemen? For pity's sake, is it a joke, or are you both gone out of your minds, to wish to make me out a physician?

Valère. What! you do not give in yet, and you still deny being a physician?

Sganarelle. The devil take me if I am one!

Lucas. Are you not a physician?

Sganarelle. No, plague choke me! (*They begin to thrash him again*). Hold! hold! Well gentlemen, yes, since you will have it so, I am a physician, I am a physician—an apothecary into the bargain, if you like. I prefer saying yes to everything to being knocked about so.

Valère. Ah! that is right, Sir; I am delighted to see you so reasonable.

Lucas. It does my heart good to hear you speak in this way.

Valère. I beg your pardon with all my heart.

Lucas. I hope you will forgive me for the liberty I have taken.

Sganarelle (aside). Bless my soul! Am I perhaps myself mistaken, and have I become a physician without being aware of it?

Valère. You shall not regret, Sir, having shown us what you are; and you shall certainly be satisfied.

Sganarelle. But, tell me, gentlemen, may you not be

yourselves mistaken? Is it quite certain that I am a physician?

Lucas. Yes, upon my word!

Sganarelle. Really and truly.

Valère. Undoubtedly.

Sganarelle. The devil take me if I knew it!

Valère. Nonsense! You are the cleverest physician in the world.

Sganarelle. Ha, ha!

Lucas. A physician who has cured I do not know how many complaints.

Sganarelle. The dickens I have!

Valère. A woman was thought dead for six hours; she was ready to be buried when you, with a drop of something, brought her to again, and made her walk at once about the room.

Sgnarelle. The deuce I did!

Lucas. A child of twelve fell from the top of the belfry, by which he had his head, his legs, and his arms smashed; and you, with I do not know what ointment, made him immediately get up on his feet, and off he ran to play chuck-farthing.

Sganarelle. The devil I did!

Valère. In short, Sir, you will be satisfied with us, and you shall earn whatever you like, if you allow us to take you where we intend.

Sganarelle. I shall earn whatever I like?

Valère. Yes.

Sganarelle. In that case I am a physician: there is no doubt of it. I had forgotten it; but I recollect it now. What is the matter? Where am I to go?

Valère. We will conduct you. The matter is to see a girl who has lost her speech.

Sganarelle. Indeed! I have not found it.

Valère (softly to Lucas). How he loves his joke! (*To* Sganarelle). Come along, Sir!

Sganarelle. Without a physician's gown!

Valère. We will get one.

Sganarelle (*presenting his bottle to* VALÈRE). You carry this: I put my juleps in there (*turning round to* LUCAS *and spitting on the ground*). And you, stamp on this, by order of the physician.

Lucas. Odds sniggers! this is a physician I like. I think he will do, for he is a comical fellow.

ACT II

(The scene represents a room in GÉRONTE'S *house.)*

SCENE I.—GÉRONTE, VALÈRE, LUCAS, JACQUELINE.

Valère. Yes, sir, I think you will be satisfied; we have brought the greatest physician in the world with us.

Lucas. Oh! Zooks! this one beats everything; all the others are not worthy to hold the candle to him.

Valère. He is a man who has performed some mar∙vellous cures.

Lucas. Who has put dead people on their legs again.

Valère. He is somewhat whimsical, as I have told you; and at times there are moments when his senses wander, and he does not seem what he really is.

Lucas. Yes, he loves a joke, and one would say sometimes that he has got a screw loose somewhere.

Valère. But in reality he is quite scientific; and very often he says things quite beyond any one's com∙prehension.

Lucas. When he sets about it, he talks as finely as if he were reading a book.

Valère. He has already a great reputation hereabout, and everybody comes to consult him.

Géronte. I am very anxious to see him; send him to me quickly.

Valère. I am going to fetch him.

SCENE II.—GÉRONTE, JACQUELINE, LUCAS.

Jacqueline. Upon my word, Sir, this one will do jus∙ the same as all the rest. I think it will be six of th∙

255

one and half-a-dozen of the others; and the best medicine to give to your daughter would, in my opinion, be a handsome strapping husband, for whom she could have some love.

Géronte. Lord bless my soul, nurse dear, you are meddling with many things!

Lucas. Hold your tongue, mother Jacqueline; it is not for you to poke your nose there.

Jacqueline. I tell you, and a dozen more of you, that all these physicians do her no good; that your daughter wants something else than rhubarb and senna, and that a husband is a plaster which cures all girls' complaints.

Géronte. Would any one have her in her present state, with that affliction on her? and when I intended her to marry, has she not opposed my wishes?

Jacqueline. No wonder. You wished to give her a man whom she does not like. Why did you not give her to Monsieur Léandre, who takes her fancy? She would have been very obedient, and I vouch for it that he will take her as she is, if you but give her to him.

Géronte. Léandre is not the man we want; he has not got a fortune like the other.

Jacqueline. He has got an uncle who is so rich, and he is the heir.

Géronte. All these expectations seem to me but moon-shine. Brag is a good dog, but Holdfast is a better; and we run a great risk in waiting for dead men's shoes. Death is not always at the beck and call of gentlemen heirs; and while the grass grows, the cow starves.

Jacqueline. That is all well and good, but I have always heard that in marriage, as in everything else, happiness excels riches. Fathers and mothers have this cursed habit of asking always, "How much has he got?" and "How much has she got?" And gaffer Peter has married his Simonette to that lout Thomas, because he has got a few more vineyards than young Robin, for whom the girl had a fancy; and now the poor creature is as yellow as a guinea, and has not looked like herself ever since. That is a good example for you, Sir. After all, folks have but their pleasure in this world; and I would sooner give my daughter a husband whom she likes than have all the riches in the country.

Géronte. Bless me, nurse, how you chatter! Hold your tongue, let me beg of you; you take too much upon yourself, and you will spoil your milk.

Lucas (*slapping* GÉRONTE'S *shoulder at every word*). Indeed, be silent; you are too saucy. The master does not want your speeches, and he knows what he is about. All you have got to do is to suckle your baby, without arguing so much. Our master is the girl's father, and he is good and clever enough to know what she wants.

Géronte. Gently, gently.

Lucas (*still slapping* GÉRONTE'S *shoulder*). I wish to show her her place, and teach her the respect due to you, Sir.

Géronte. Very well. But it does not need all this gesticulating.

SCENE III.—VALÈRE, SGANARELLE, GÉRONTE, LUCAS. JACQUELINE.

Valère. Look out, Sir, here is our physician coming.

Géronte (*to* SGANARELLE). I am delighted to see you, Sir, at my house, and we have very great need of you.

Sganarelle (*in a physician's gown with a very pointed cap*). Hippocrates says . . . that we should both put our hats on.

Géronte. Hippocrates says that?

Sganarelle. Yes.

Géronte. In which chapter, if you please?

Sganarelle. In his chapter . . . on hats.

Géronte. Since Hippocrates says so, we must obey.

Sganarelle. Doctor, having heard of the marvellous things . . .

Géronte. To whom are you speaking, pray?

Sganarelle. To you.

Géronte. I am not a physician.

Sganarelle. You are not a physician?

Géronte. Indeed I am not.

Sganarelle. Really?

Géronte. Really. (SGANARELLE *takes a stick and thrashes* GÉRONTE.) Oh! Oh! Oh!

Sganarelle. Now you are a physician, I have never taken any other degree.

Géronte (*to* VALÈRE). What a devil of a fellow you have brought me here!

Valère. Did I not tell you that he was a funny sort of a physician?

Géronte. Yes; but I shall send him about his business with his fun.

Lucas. Do not take any notice of it, Sir. It is only his joking.

Géronte. The joking does not suit me.

Sganarelle. Sir; I beg your pardon for the liberty I have taken.

Géronte. I am your humble servant, Sir.

Sganarelle. I am sorry . . .

Géronte. It is nothing.

Sganarelle. For the cudgelling I . . .

Géronte. There is no harm done.

Sganarelle. Which I have had the honour to give you.

Géronte. Do not say any more about it, Sir. I have a daughter who is suffering from a strange complaint.

Sganarelle. I am delighted, Sir, that your daughter has need of my skill; and I wish, with all my heart, that you stood in the same need of it, you and all your family, in order to show you my wish to serve you.

Geronte. I am obliged to you for these kind feelings.

Sganarelle. I assure you that I am speaking from my
very heart.

Géronte. You really do me too much honour.

Sganarelle. What is your daughter's name?

Géronte. Lucinde.

Sganarelle. Lucinde! Ah! a pretty name to physic!
Lucinde!

Géronte. I will just see what she is doing.

Sganarelle. Who is that tall woman?

Géronte. She is my baby's nurse.

SCENE IV.—SGANARELLE, JACQUELINE, LUCAS.

Sganarelle (*aside*). The deuce! that is a fine piece of
household furniture. (*Aloud*). Ah, nurse! Charming
nurse! my physic is the very humble slave of your nurse-
ship, and I should like to be the fortunate little nursling
to suck the milk of your good graces. (*He puts his
hand on her bosom.*) All my nostrums, all my skill, all
my cleverness, is at your service; and . . .

Lucas. By your leave, M. Doctor; leave my wife
alone, I pray you.

Sganarelle. What! is she your wife?

Lucas. Yes.

Sganarelle. Oh! indeed! I did not know that, but
I am very glad of it for the love of both. (*He pretends
to embrace* LUCAS, *but embraces the nurse.*)

Lucas (*pulling* SGANARELLE *away, and placing himself
between him and his wife*). Gently, if you please.

Sganarelle. I assure you that I am delighted that you
should be united together. I congratulate her upon having such a husband as you; and I congratulate you upon
having a wife so handsome, so discreet, and so well-
shaped as she is. (*He pretends once more to embrace*
LUCAS, *who holds out his arms, he slips under them and
embraces the nurse*).

Lucas (*pulling him away again*). Do not pay so many compliments, I beg of you.

Sganarelle. Shall I not rejoice with you about such a lovely harmony?

Lucas. With me as much as you like; but a truce to compliments with my wife.

Sganarelle. I have both your happiness equally at heart; and if I embrace you to show my delight in you, I embrace her to show my delight in her. (*Same by-play*).

Lucas (*pulling him away for the third time*). Odds boddikins, Doctor, what capers you cut!

SCENE V.—GÉRONTE, SGANARELLE, LUCAS, JACQUELINE.

Géronte. My daughter will be here directly, Sir.

Sganarelle. I am awaiting her, Sir, with all my physic.

Géronte. Where is it?

Sganarelle (*touching his forehead*). In there.

Géronte. That is good.

Sganarelle. But as I feel much interested in your family, I should like to test the milk of your nurse, and examine her breasts. (*He draws close to* JACQUELINE).

Lucas (*pulling him away, and swinging him round*). Nothing of the sort, nothing of the sort. I do not wish it.

Sganarelle. It is the physician's duty to see the breasts of the nurse.

Lucas. Duty or no duty, I will not have it.

Sganarelle. Have you the audacity to contradict a physician? Out with you.

Lucas. I do not care a straw about a physician.

Sganarelle (*looking askance at him*). I will give you a fever.

Jacqueline (*taking* LUCAS *by the arm, and swinging him round also*). Get out of the way. Am I not big enough to take my own part, if he does anything to me which he ought not to do?

Lucas. I will not have him touch you, I will not.

Sganarelle. For shame you rascal, to be jealous of your wife.

Géronte. Here comes my daughter.

SCENE VI.—LUCINDE, GÉRONTE, SGANARELLE, VALÈRE, LUCAS, JACQUELINE.

Sganarelle. Is this the patient?

Géronte. Yes, I have but one daughter; and I would never get over it if she were to die.

Sganarelle. Do not let her do anything of the kind. She must not die without a prescription of the physician.

Géronte. A chair here!

Sganarelle (seated between GÉRONTE *and* LUCINDE*).* This is not at all an unpleasant patient, and I am of the opinion that she would not be at all amiss for a man in very good health.

Géronte. You have made her laugh, Sir.

Sganarelle. So much the better. It is the best sign in the world when a physician makes the patient laugh. (*To* LUCINDE.) Well, what is the matter? What ails you? What is it you feel?

Lucinde (replies by motions, by putting her hand to her mouth, her head, and under her chin). Ha, hi, ho, ha!

Sganarelle. What do you say?

Lucinde (continues the same motions). Ha, hi, ho, ha, ha, hi, ho!

Sganarelle. What is that?

Lucinde. Ha, hi, ho!

Sganarelle (imitating her). Ha, hi, ho, ha, ha! I do not understand you. What sort of language do you call that?

Géronte. That is just where her complaint lies, Sir. She has become dumb, without our having been able till now to discover the cause. This accident has obliged us to postpone her marriage.

Sganarelle. And why so?

Géronte. He whom she is going to marry wishes to wait for her recovery to conclude the marriage.

Sganarelle. And who is this fool that does not want his wife to be dumb? Would to Heaven that mine had that complaint! I should take particular care not to have her cured.

Géronte. To the point, Sir. We beseech you to use all your skill to cure her of this affliction.

Sganarelle. Do not make yourself uneasy. But tell me, does this pain oppress her much?

Géronte. Yes, Sir.

Sganarelle. So much the better. Is the suffering very acute?

Géronte. Very acute.

Sganarelle. That is right. Does she go to . . . you know where?

Géronte. Yes.

Sganarelle. Freely?

Géronte. That I know nothing about.

Sganarelle. Is the matter healthy?

Géronte. I do not understand these things.

Sganarelle (*turning to the patient*). Give me your hand. (*To* Géronte.) The pulse tells me that your daughter is dumb.

Géronte. Sir, that is what is the matter with her; ah! yes, you have found it out at the first touch.

Sganarelle. Of course!

Jacqueline. See how he has guessed her complaint.

Sganarelle. We great physicians, we know matters at once. An ignoramus would have been nonplussed, and would have told you: it is this, that, or the other; but I hit the nail on the head from the very first, and I tell you that your daughter is dumb.

Géronte. Yes; but I should like you to tell me whence it arises.

Sganarelle. Nothing is easier; it arises from loss of speech.

Géronte. Very good. But the reason of her having lost her speech, pray?

Sganarelle. Our best authorities will tell you that it is because there is an impediment in the action of her tongue.

Géronte. But, once more, your opinion upon this impediment in the action of her tongue.

Sganarelle. Aristotle on this subject says . . . a great many clever things.

Géronte. I dare say.

Sganarelle. Ah! He was a great man!

Géronte. No doubt.

Sganarelle. Yes, a very great man. (*Holding out his arm, and putting a finger of the other hand in the bend*). A man who was, by this, much greater than I. But to come back to our argument: I hold that this impediment in the action of her tongue is caused by certain humours, which among us learned men, we call peccant humours; peccant—that is to say . . . peccant humours; inasmuch as the vapours formed by the exhalations of the influences which rise in the very region of diseases, coming, . . . as we may say to. . . . Do you understand Latin?

Géronte. Not in the least.

Sganarelle (*suddenly rising*). You do not understand Latin?

Géronte. No.

Sganarelle (*assuming various comic attitudes*). *Cabricias arci thuram, catalamus, singulariter, nominativo, hæc musa*, the muse, *bonus, bona, bonum. Deus sanctus, estne oratio latinas? Etiam*, Yes. *Quare?* Why.

Quia substantivo et adjectivum, concordat in generi, numerum, et casus.

Géronte. Ah! Why did I not study?

Jacqueline. What a clever man!

Lucas. Yes, it is so beautiful that I do not understand a word of it.

Sganarelle. Thus these vapours which I speak of, passing from the left side, where the liver is, to the right side, where we find the heart, it so happens that the lungs, which in Latin we call *armyan*, having communication with the brain, which in Greek we style *nasmus*, by means of the *vena cava*, which in Hebrew, is termed *cubile*, meet in their course the said vapours, which fill the ventricles of the omoplata; and because the said vapours . . . now understand well this argument, pray . . . and because these said vapours are endowed with a certain malignity . . . listen well to this, I beseech you.

Géronte. Yes.

Sganarelle. Are endowed with a certain malignity which is caused . . . pay attention here, if you please.

Géronte. I do.

Sganarelle. Which is caused by the acridity of these humours engendered in the concavity of the diaphragm, it happens that these vapours. . . . *Ossabandus, nequeis, nequer, potarinum, puipsa milus.* That is exactly the reason that your daughter is dumb.

Jacqueline. Ah! How well this gentleman explains all this.

Lucas. Why does not my tongue wag as well as his?

Géronte. It is undoubtedly impossible to argue better. There is but one thing that I cannot exactly make out: that is the whereabouts of the liver and the heart. It appears to me that you place them differently from what they are; that the heart is on the left side, and the liver on the right.

Sganarelle. Yes; this was so formerly; but we have

changed all that, and we now-a-days practise the medical art on an entirely new system.

Géronte. I did not know that, and I pray you pardon my ignorance.

Sganarelle. There is no harm done; and you are not obliged to be so clever as we are.

Géronte. Certainly not. But what think you, Sir, ought to be done for this complaint?

Sganarelle. What do I think ought to be done?

Géronte. Yes.

Sganarelle. My advice is to put her to bed again, and make her, as a remedy, take plenty of bread soaked in wine.

Géronte. Why so, sir?

Sganarelle. Because there is in bread and wine mixed together a sympathetic virtue which produces speech. Do you not see that they give nothing else to parrots, and that, by eating it, they learn to speak?

Géronte. That is true. Oh! the great man! Quick, plenty of bread and wine.

Sganarelle. I shall come back to-night to see how the patient is getting on.

SCENE VII.—GÉRONTE, SGANARELLE, JACQUELINE.

Sganarelle (to JACQUELINE). Stop a little you. (*To* GÉRONTE.) Sir, I must give some medicine to your nurse.

Jacqueline. To me, Sir? I am as well as can be.

Sganarelle. So much the worse, nurse, so much the worse. This excess of health is dangerous, and it would not be amiss to bleed you a little gently, and to administer some little soothing injection.

Géronte. But, my dear Sir, that is a method which I cannot understand. Why bleed folks when they are not ill?

Sganarelle. It does not matter, the method is salutary;

and as we drink for the thirst to come, so must we bleed for the disease to come.

Jacqueline (*going*). I do not care a fig for all this, and I will not have my body made an apothecary's shop.

Sganarelle. You object to my remedies; but we shall know how to bring you to reason.

SCENE VIII.—GÉRONTE, SGANARELLE.

Sganarelle. I wish you good day.

Géronte. Stay a moment, if you please.

Sganarelle. What are you going to do?

Géronte. Give you your fee, sir.

Sganarelle (*putting his hands behind him, from under his gown, while* GÉRONTE *opens his purse*). I shall not accept it, Sir.

Géronte. Sir.

Sganarelle. Not at all.

Géronte. One moment.

Sganarelle. On no consideration.

Géronte. Pray!

Sganarelle. You are jesting.

Géronte. That is settled.

Sganarelle. I shall do nothing of the kind.

Géronte. What!

Sganarelle. I do not practise for money's sake.

Géronte. I am convinced of that.

Sganarelle (*after having taken the money*). Are they good weight?

Géronte. Yes, Sir.

Sganarelle. I am not a mercenary physician.

Géronte. I am well aware of it.

Sganarelle. I am not actuated by interest.

Géronte. I do not for a moment think so.

Sganarelle (*alone, looking at the money he has received*). Upon my word, this does not promise badly; and provided . . .

SCENE IX.—LÉANDRE, SGANARELLE.

Léandre. I have been waiting some time for you, Sir, and I have come to beg your assistance.

Sganarelle (*feeling his pulse*). That is a very bad pulse.

Léandre. I am not ill, Sir; and it is not for that I am come to you.

Sganarelle. If you are not ill, why the devil do you not tell me so?

Léandre. No. To tell you the matter in a few words, my name is Léandre. I am in love with Lucinde to whom you have just paid a visit; and as all access to her is denied to me, through the ill-temper of her father, I venture to beseech you to serve me in my love affair, and to assist me in a stratagem that I have invented, so as to say a few words to her, on which my whole life and happiness absolutely depend.

Sganarelle (*in apparent anger*). Whom do you take me for? How dare you address yourself to me to assist you in your love affair, and to wish me to lower the dignity of a physician by an affair of that kind!

Léandre. Do not make a noise, Sir!

Sganarelle (*driving him back*). I will make a noise. You are an impertinent fellow.

Léandre. Ah! gently, Sir.

Sganarelle. An ill-mannered jackanapes.

Léandre. Pray!

Sganarelle. I will teach you that I am not the kind of man you take me for, and that it is the greatest insolence . . .

Léandre (*taking out a purse*). Sir . . .

Sganarelle. To wish to employ me . . . (*taking the purse*). I am not speaking about you, for you are a gentleman; and I should be delighted to be of any use to you; but there are certain impertinent people in this world who take folks for what they are not; and I tell you candidly that this puts me in a passion.

Léandre. I ask your pardon, Sir, for the liberty I have . . .

Sganarelle. You are jesting. What is the affair in question?

Léandre. You must know then, Sir, that this disease which you wish to cure is a feigned complaint. The physicians have argued about it, as they ought to do, and they have not failed to give it as their opinion,— this one, that it arose from the brain; that one, from the intestines; another, from the spleen; another, again, from the liver; but the fact is that love is its real cause, and that Lucinde has only invented this illness in order to free herself from a marriage with which she has been harassed. But for fear that we may be seen together, let us retire; and I will tell you as we go along, what I wish you to do.

Sganarelle. Come along, then, Sir. You have inspired me with an inconceivable interest in your love; and if all my medical science does not fail me, the patient shall either die or be yours.

ACT III

(The scene represents a spot near GÉRONTE'S *house.)*

SCENE I.—LÉANDRE, SGANARELLE.

Léandre. I think that I am not at all badly got up for an apothecary; and as her father has scarcely ever seen me, this change of dress and wig is likely enough, I think, to disguise me.

Sganarelle. There is no doubt of it.

Léandre. Only I should like to know five or six big medical words to leaven my conversation with, and to give me the air of a learned man.

Sganarelle. Go along, go along; it is not at all necessary. The dress is sufficient; and I know no more about it than you do.

Léandre. How is that!

Sganarelle. The devil take me if I understand anything about medicine! You are a gentleman, and I do not mind confiding in you, as you have confided in me.

Léandre. What! Then you are not really . . .

Sganarelle. No, I tell you. They have made me a physician in the teeth of my protests. I have never attempted to be so learned as that; and all my studies did not go farther than the lowest class at school. I do not know how the idea has come to them; but when I saw that in spite of everything they would have it that I was a physician, I made up my mind to be so at somebody's expense. You would not believe, however, how this error has spread, and how everyone is possessed, and believes me to a learned man. They come seeking me on all sides; and if things go on in this way, I am resolved to stick to the profession all my life. I find that it is the best trade of all; for, whether we manage well or ill, we are paid just the same. Bad workmanship never recoils on us; and we cut the material we have to work with pretty much as we like. A shoemaker, in making a pair of shoes, cannot spoil a scrap of leather without having to bear the loss; but in our business we may spoil a man without its costing us a farthing. The blunders are never put down to us, and it is always the fault of the fellow who dies. The best of this profession is, that there is the greatest honesty and discretion among the dead; for you never find them complain of the physician who has killed them.

Léandre. It is true that the dead are very honourable in that respect.

Sganarelle (*seeing some people advancing towards him*). There come some people, who seem anxious to consult me. (*To* Léandre). Go and wait for me near the house of your lady-love.

Scene II.—Thibaut, Perrin, Sganarelle.

Thibaut. Sir, we come to look for you, my son Perrin and myself.

Sganarelle. What is the matter?

Thibaut. His poor mother, whose name is Perrette, has been on a bed of sickness for the last six months.

Sganarelle (*holding out his hand as if to receive money*). What would you have me do to her?

Thibaut. I would like you to give me some little doctor's stuff to cure her.

Sganarelle. We must first see what is the matter with her.

Thibaut. She is ill with the hypocrisy, Sir.

Sganarelle. With the hypocrisy?

Thibaut. Yes; I mean she is swollen everywhere. They say that there is a lot of seriosities in her inside, and that her liver, her belly, or her spleen, as you would call it, instead of making blood makes nothing but water. She has, every other day, the quotiguian fever, with lassitude and pains in the muscles of her legs. We can hear in her throat phlegms that are ready to choke her, and she is often taken with syncoles and conversions, so that we think she is going off the hooks. We have got in our village an apothecary—with respect be it said— who has given her, I do not know how much stuff; and it has cost me more than a dozen good crowns in clysters, saving your presence, in apostumes which he has made her swallow, in infections of hyacinth, and in cordial potions. But all this, as people say, was nothing but an ointment of fiddle-faddle. He wanted to give her a certain drug called ametile wine; but I was downright afeard that this would send her to the other world altogether; because they tell me that those big physicians kill, I do not know how many, with that new-fangled notion.

Sganarelle (*still holding out his hand, and moving it about to show that he wants money*). Let us come to the point, friend, let us come to the point.

Thibaut. The point is, Sir, that we have come to beg of you to tell us what we must do.

Sganarelle. I do not understand you at all.

Perrin. My mother is ill, Sir, and here are two crowns which we have brought you to give us some stuff.

Sganarelle. Ah! you I do understand. There is a lad who speaks clearly, and explains himself as he should. You say that your mother is ill with the dropsy; that she is swollen all over her body; that she has a fever, with pains in the legs; that she sometimes is taken with syncopes and convulsions, that is to say with fainting fits.

Perrin. Indeed, Sir! that is just it.

Sganarelle. I understand you at once. Your father does not know what he says. And now you ask me for a remedy?

Perrin. Yes, sir.

Sganarelle. A remedy to cure her?

Perrin. That is just what I mean.

Sganarelle. Take this then. It is a piece of cheese which you must make her take.

Perrin. A piece of cheese, Sir?

Sganarelle. Yes; it is a kind of prepared cheese, in which there is gold, coral, and pearls, and a great many other precious things.

Perrin. I am very much obliged to you, Sir, and I shall go and make her take it directly.

Sganarelle. Go, and if she dies, do not fail to bury her in the best style you can.

SCENE III.—(*The Scene changes, and represents, as in the Second Act, a room in* GÉRONTE'S *house*)— JACQUELINE, SGANARELLE, LUCAS, *at the far end of the stage.*

Sganarelle. Here is the pretty nurse. Ah! you darling nurse, I am delighted at this meeting; and the sight of you is like rhubarb, cassia, and senna to me, which purges all melancholy from my mind.

Jacqueline. Upon my word, M. Physician, it is no good talking to me in that style, and I do not understand your Latin at all.

Sganarelle. Get ill, nurse, I beg of you; get ill for my sake. I shall have all the pleasure in the world of curing you.

Jacqueline. I am your humble servant; I would much rather not be cured.

Sganarelle. How I grieve for you, beautiful nurse, in having such a jealous and troublesome husband.

Jacqueline. What am I to do, Sir? It is as a penance for my sins; and where the goat is tied down she must browse.

Sganarelle. What! Such a clod-hopper as that! a fellow who is always watching you, and will let no one speak to you!

Jacqueline. Alas! you have seen nothing yet; and that is only a small sample of his bad temper.

Sganarelle. Is it possible? and can a man have so mean a spirit as to ill-use a woman like you? Ah! I know some, sweet nurse, and who are not very far off, who would only be too glad to kiss your little feet! Why should such a handsome woman have fallen into such hands! and a mere animal, a brute, a stupid, a fool. . . . Excuse me, nurse, for speaking in that way of your husband.

Jacqueline. Oh! Sir, I know full well that he deserves all these names.

Sganarelle. Undoubtedly, nurse, he deserves them; and he also deserves that you should plant something on his head to punish him for his suspicions.

Jacqueline. It is true enough that if I had not his interest so much at heart, he would drive me to do some strange things.

Sganarelle. Indeed it would just serve him right if you were to revenge yourself upon him with some one. The fellow richly deserves it all, I tell you, and if I were fortunate enough, fair nurse, to be chosen by you . . .

(*While* Sganarelle *is holding out his arms to embrace* Jacqueline, Lucas *passes his head under them, and comes between the two.* Sganarelle *and* Jacqueline *stare at* Lucas, *and depart on opposite sides, but the doctor does so in a very comic manner.*)

SCENE IV.—Géronte, Lucas.

Géronte. I say, Lucas, have not you seen our physician here?

Lucas. Indeed I have seen him, by all the devils, and my wife, too.

Géronte. Where can he be?

Lucas. I do not know; but I wish he were with the devil.

Géronte. Just go and see what my daughter is doing.

SCENE V.—SGANARELLE, LÉANDRE, GÉRONTE.

Géronte. I was just inquiring after you, Sir.

Sganarelle. I have just been amusing myself in your court with expelling the superfluity of drink. How is the patient?

Géronte. Somewhat worse since your remedy.

Sganarelle. So much the better; it shows that it takes effect.

Géronte. Yes; but while it is taking effect, I am afraid it will choke her.

Sganarelle. Do not make yourself uneasy; I have some remedies that will make it all right! and I will wait until she is at death's door.

Géronte (*pointing to* LÉANDRE). Who is this man that is with you?

Sgnarelle (*intimates by motions of his hands that it is an apothecary*). It is. . . .

Géronte. What?

Sganarelle. He who . . .

Géronte. Oh!

Sganarelle. Who . . .

Géronte. I understand.

Sganarelle. Your daughter will want him.

SCENE VI.—LUCINDE, GÉRONTE, LÉANDRE, JACQUELINE, SGANARELLE.

Jacqueline. Here is your daughter, Sir, who wishes to stretch her limbs a little.

Sganarelle. That will do her good. Go to her, M.

Apothecary, and feel her pulse, so that I may consult with you presently about her complaint. (*At this point he draws* GÉRONTE *to one end of the stage, and putting one arm upon his shoulder, he places his hand under his chin, with which he makes him turn towards him, each time that* GÉRONTE *wants to look at what is passing between his daughter and the apothecary, while he holds the following discourse with him.*) Sir, it is a great and subtle question among physicians to know whether women or men are more easily cured. I pray you to listen to this, if you please. Some say "no," others say "yes": I say both "yes" and "no"; inasmuch as the incongruity of the opaque humours, which are found in the natural temperament of women, causes the brutal part to struggle for the mastery over the sensitive, we find that the conflict of their opinion depends on the oblique motion of the circle of the moon; and as the sun, which darts its beams on the concavity of the earth, meets . . .

Lucinde (*to* LÉANDRE). No; I am not at all likely to change my feelings.

Géronte. Hark! my daughter speaks! O great virtue of the remedy! O excellent physician! How deeply am I obliged to you, Sir, for this marvellous cure! And what can I do for you after such a service?

Sganarelle (*strutting about the stage, fanning himself with his hat*). This case has given me some trouble.

Lucinde. Yes, father, I have recovered my speech; but I have recovered it to tell you that I will never have any other husband than Léandre, and that it is in vain for you to wish to give me to Horace.

Géronte. But . . .

Lucinde. Nothing will shake the resolution I have taken.

Géronte. What . . .

Lucinde. All your fine arguments will be in vain.

Géronte. If . . .

Lucinde. All your talking will be of no use.

Géronte. I . . .

Lucinde. I have made up my mind about the matter.

Géronte. But . . .

Lucinde. No paternal authority can compel me to marry against my will.

Géronte. I have . . .

Lucinde. You may try as much as you like.

Géronte. It . . .

Lucinde. My heart cannot submit to this tyranny.

Géronte. The . . .

Lucinde. And I will sooner go into a convent than marry a man I do not love.

Géronte. But . . .

Lucinde (*in a loud voice*). No. By no means. It is of no use. You waste your time. I shall do nothing of the kind. I am fully determined.

Géronte. Ah! what a torrent of words! One cannot hold out against it. (*To* SGANARELLE). I beseech you, Sir, to make her dumb again.

Sganarelle. That is impossible. All that I can do in your behalf is to make you deaf, if you like.

Géronte. I thank you. (*To* LUCINDE). Do you think . . .

Lucinde. No; all your reasoning will not have the slightest effect upon me.

Géronte. You shall marry Horace this very evening.

Lucinde. I would sooner marry death itself.

Sganarelle (*to* GÉRONTE). Stop, for Heaven's sake! stop. Let me doctor this matter; it is a disease that has got hold of her, and I know the remedy to apply to it.

Géronte. Is it possible, indeed, Sir, that you can cure this disease of the mind also?

Sganarelle. Yes; let me manage it. I have remedies for everything; and our apothecary will serve us capitally for this cure. (*To* LÉANDRE.) A word with you. You perceive that the passion she has for this Léandre is altogether against the wishes of the father; that there is no time to lose; that the humours are very acrimonious; and that it becomes necessary to find speedily a remedy for this complaint, which may get worse by delay. As for myself, I see but one, which is a dose of purgative flight, mixed, as it should be, with two drachms of matrimonium, made up into pills. She may, perhaps, make some difficulty about taking this remedy; but as you are a clever man in your profession, you must induce her to consent to it, and make her swallow the thing as best you can. Go and take a little turn in the garden with her to prepare the humours, while I converse here with her father; but, above all, lose not a moment. Apply the remedy quick! apply the specific!

Scene VII.—Géronte, Sganarelle.

Géronte. What drugs are those you have just mentioned, Sir? It seems to me that I never heard of them before.

Sganarelle. They are drugs which are used only in urgent cases.

Géronte. Did you ever see such insolence as hers?

Sganarelle. Daughters are a little headstrong at times.

Géronte. You would not believe how she is infatuated with this Léandre.

Sganarelle. The heat of the blood produces those things in young people.

Géronte. As for me, the moment I discovered the violence of this passion, I took care to keep my daughter under lock and key.

Sganarelle. You have acted wisely.

Géronte. And I have prevented the slightest communication between them.

Sganarelle. Just so.

Géronte. They would have committed some folly, if they had been permitted to see each other.

Sganarelle. Undoubtedly.

Géronte. And I think she would have been the girl to run away with him.

Sganarelle. You have argued very prudently.

Géronte. I was informed, that he tried every means to get speech of her.

Sganarelle. The rascal!

Géronte. But he will waste his time.

Sganarelle. Aye! Aye!

Géronte. And I will effectually prevent him from seeing her.

Sganarelle. He has no fool to deal with, and you know some tricks of which he is ignorant. One must get up very early to catch you asleep.

SCENE VIII.—LUCAS, GÉRONTE, SGANARELLE.

Lucas. Odds-bobs! Sir, here is a pretty to do. Your daughter has fled with her Léandre. It was he that played the apothecary, and this is the physician who has performed this nice operation.

Géronte. What! to murder me in this manner! Quick, fetch a magistrate, and take care that he does not get away. Ah villain! I will have you punished by the law.

Lucas. I am afraid, Master Doctor, that you will be hanged. Do not stir a step, I tell you.

SCENE IX.—MARTINE, SGANARELLE, LUCAS.

Martine (to LUCAS). Good gracious! what a difficulty I have had to find this place! Just tell me what has become of the physician I recommended to you?

Lucas. Here he is; just going to be hanged.

Martine. What! my husband hanged! Alas, and for what?

Lucas. He has helped some one to run away with master's daughter.

Martine. Alas, my dear husband, is it true that you are going to be hanged?

Sganarelle. Judge for yourself. Ah!

Martine. And must you be made an end of in the presence of such a crowd.

Sganarelle. What am I to do?

Martine. If you had only finished cutting our wood I should be somewhat consoled.

Sganarelle. Leave me, you break my heart.

Martine. No, I will remain to encourage you to die; and I will not leave you until I have seen you hanged.

Sganarelle. Ah!

SCENE X.—GÉRONTE, SGANARELLE, MARTINE.

Géronte (*to* SGANARELLE). The magistrate will be here directly, and we shall put you in a place of safety where they will be answerable for you.

Sganarelle (*on his knees, hat in hand*). Alas! will not a few strokes with a cudgel do instead?

Géronte. No; no; the law shall decide. But what do I see?

SCENE XI.—GÉRONTE, LÉANDRE, LUCINDE, SGANARELLE, LUCAS, MARTINE.

Léandre. Sir, I appear before you as Léandre, and am come to restore Lucinde to your authority. We intended to run away, and get married; but this design has given away to a more honourable proceeding. I will not presume to steal away your daughter, and it is from your hands alone that I will obtain her. I must at the same time acquaint you, that I have just now received some letters informing me of the death of my uncle, and that he has left me heir to all his property.

Géronte. Really, Sir, your virtue is worthy of my

utmost consideration, and I give you my daughter with the greatest pleasure in the world.

Sganarelle (*aside*). The physician has had a narrow escape!

Martine. Since you are not going to be hanged, you may thank me for being a physician; for I have procured you this honour.

Sganarelle. Yes, it is you who procured me, I do not know how many thwacks with a cudgel.

Léandre (*to* SGANARELLE). The result has proved too happy to harbour any resentment.

Sganarelle. Be it so. (*To* MARTINE.) I forgive you the blows on account of the dignity to which you have elevated me; but prepare yourself henceforth to behave with great respect towards a man of my consequence; and consider that the anger of a physician is more to be dreaded than people imagine.

THE MISER

THE MISER
(*L'AVARE*)

DRAMATIS PERSONÆ

HARPAGON, *father to* CLÉANTE *and* ELISE, *in love with*
    MARIANE.
CLÉANTE, HARPAGON'S *son*, MARIANE'S *lover*.
VALÈRE, *son of* ANSELME, ELISE'S *lover*.
ANSELME, *father to* VALÈRE *and* MARIANE.
MASTER SIMON, *agent*.
MASTER JACQUES, *cook and coachman to* HARPAGON.
LA FLÈCHE, CLÉANTE'S *valet*.
BRINDAVOINE } HARPAGON'S *lacqueys*.
LA MERLUCHE
A MAGISTRATE *and his* CLERK.
ELISE, HARPAGON'S *daughter*, VALÈRE'S *sweetheart*.
MARIANE, CLÉANTE'S *sweetheart*, *beloved by* HARPAGON
FROSINE, *a designing woman*.
MISTRESS CLAUDE, HARPAGON'S *servant*.

    The scene is in PARIS, *in* HARPAGON'S HOUSE.

ACT I

SCENE I.—VALÈRE, ELISE.

Valère. Eh, what! charming Elise, you are growing
melancholy, after the kind assurances which you were
good enough to give me of your love! Alas! I see you
sighing in the midst of my joy! Tell me, is it with
regret at having made me happy? And do you repent

of that engagement to which my affection has induced you?

Elise. No, Valère, I cannot repent of anything that I do for you. I feel myself attracted to it by too sweet a power, and I have not even the will to wish that things were otherwise. But, to tell you the truth, our success causes me uneasiness; and I am very much afraid of loving you a little more than I ought.

Valère. Eh! what is there to fear, Elise, in the affection you have for me?

Elise. Alas! a hundred things at once: the anger of a father, the reproaches of my family, the censure of the world; but more than all, Valère, the change of your heart, and that criminal coolness with which those of your sex most frequently repay the too ardent proofs of an innocent love.

Valère. Ah! do not wrong me thus, to judge of me by others! Suspect me of anything, Elise, rather than of failing in my duty to you. I love you too well for that: and my affection for you will last as long as my life.

Elise. Ah, Valère, every one talks in the same strain! All men are alike in their words; their actions only show them to be different.

Valère. Since actions only can show what we are, wait then, at least, to judge of my heart by them; and do not search for crimes because you unjustly fear, and wrongly anticipate. Pray do not kill me with the poignant blows of an outrageous suspicion; and give me time to convince you, by many thousand proofs, of the sincerity of my affection.

Elise. Alas, how easily we are persuaded by those we love! Yes, Valère, I hold your heart incapable of deceiving me. I believe that you truly love me, and that you will be constant. I will no longer doubt of it, and

I will confine my grief to the apprehensions of the blame
which people may utter against me.

Valère. But why this uneasiness?

Elise. I should have nothing to fear, if every one
could see you with the eyes with which I look upon you;
and in your own person I see sufficient to justify me in
what I do for you. For its defence, my heart pleads all
your merits, supported by the help of a gratitude with
which Heaven has bound me to you. At every moment I
call to mind that supreme danger which first made us
acquainted with each other; that wonderful generosity
which made you risk your life in order to snatch mine
from the fury of the waves; those most tender attentions
which you lavished upon me, after having dragged me
out of the water, and the assiduous homage of that ardent
affection, which neither time nor obstacles have been
able to discourage, and which, causing you to neglect
relatives and country, detains you in this spot, and keeps
your position unrecognized all on my account, and has
reduced you to assume the functions of servant to my
father, in order to see me. All this produces, no doubt,
a marvellous effect on me, and quite sufficient to justify,
in my own eyes, the engagement to which I have consented; but it is not perhaps enough to justify it in that
of others, and I am not certain that the world will enter
into my sentiments.

Valère. Of all that you have mentioned, it is only by
my love that I pretended to deserve anything from you;
and as for the scruples which you have; your father himself takes but too good care to justify you before the
world; and the excess of his avarice, and the austere way
in which he treats his children, might authorize stranger
things still. Pardon me, charming Elise, for speaking
thus before you. You know that, on that subject, no
good can be said. But in short, if I can, as I hope I
shall, find my relatives again, we shall have very little

difficulty in rendering them favourable to us. I am impatient to receive some tidings of them; and should they be delayed much longer, I will myself go in search of them.

Elise. Ah! Valère, do not stir from this, I beseech you; and think only how to ingratiate yourself with my father.

Valère. You see how I go about it, and the artful wheedling which I have been obliged to make use of to enter his service; beneath what mask of sympathy and affinity of sentiments I disguise myself, in order to please him; and what part I daily play with him, that I may gain his affection. I am making admirable progress in it; and experience teaches me that to find favour with men, there is no better method than to invest ourselves in their eyes with their hobbies; than to act according to their maxims, to flatter their faults and to applaud their doings. One needs not fear to overdo this complaisance; the way in which one fools them may be as palpable as possible; even the sharpest are the greatest dupes when flattery is in the question; and there is nothing too impertinent or too ridiculous for them to swallow, if it be only seasoned with praises. Sincerity suffers somewhat by the trade which I follow; but, when we have need of people, we must suit ourselves to their tastes; and since they are to be gained over only in that way, it is not the fault of those who flatter, but of those who wish to be flattered.

Elise. But why do you not try to gain the support of my brother, in case the servant should take it into her head to reveal our secret?

Valère. There is no managing them both at once; and the disposition of the father and that of the son are so opposed to each other, that it becomes difficult to arrange a confidence with both. But you, on your part, act upon your brother, and make use of the affection between you two, to bring him over to our interests. He is just coming. I go. Take this opportunity of speaking to him, and reveal our business to him, only when you judge the fit time come.

Elise. I do not know whether I shall have the courage to entrust this confidence to him.

Scene II.—Cléante, Elise.

Cléante. I am very glad to find you alone, sister; I was dying to speak to you, to unburden myself to you of a secret.

Elise. You find me quite ready to listen, brother. What have you to tell me?

Cléante. Many things, sister, all contained in one word. I am in love.

Elise. You are in love?

Cléante. Yes, I am in love. But before going farther, I know that I am dependent on my father, and that the name of son subjects me to his will; that we ought not to pledge our affection without the consent of those to whom we owe our life; that Heaven has made them the masters of our affection, and that we are enjoined not to dispose of it but by their direction; that, not being biassed by any foolish passion, they are less likely to deceive themselves than we are, and to see much better what is proper for us; that we ought rather to be guided by the light of their prudence than by the blindness of our passion; and that the ardour of our youth often drags us to dangerous precipices. I tell you all this, sister, that you may save yourself the trouble of telling it to me; for, frankly, my love will not listen to anything, and I pray you not to make any remonstrances.

Elise. Have you pledged yourself, brother, with her whom you love?

Cléante. No; but I am determined to do so, and I

implore you, once more, not to advance any reasons to dissuade me from it.

Elise. Am I then so strange a person, brother?

Cléante. No, sister; but you are not in love; you are ignorant of the sweet empire which a tender passion exercises over our hearts; and I dread your wisdom.

Elise. Alas! dear brother, let us not speak of my wisdom: there is no one who does not fail in it, at least once in his life; and were I to open my heart to you, perhaps I would appear less wise in your eyes than yourself.

Cléante. Ah! would to Heaven that your heart, like mine . . .

Elise. Let us first finish your affair, and tell me who it is whom you love.

Cléante. A young person, who has lately come to live in this neighbourhood, and who seems to be made to inspire love in all who behold her. Nature, sister, has created nothing more amiable; and I felt myself carried away the moment I saw her. Her name is Mariane, and she lives under the protection of a good motherly woman who is nearly always ill, and for whom this dear girl entertains feelings of friendship not to be imagined. She waits upon her, condoles with her, and cheers her with a tenderness that would touch you to the very soul. She does things with the most charming air in the world; a thousand graces shine through her every action, a gentleness full of attraction, a most prepossessing kindness, an adorable simplicity, a. . . . Ah! sister, I wish you could have seen her!

Elise. I see much, brother, in the things you tell me; and to understand what she really is, it is sufficient that you love her.

Cléante. I have learned, secretly, that they are not too well off; and that even their careful way of living has some difficulty in making both ends meet with the small means at their command. Imagine, dear sister, the pleasure it must be to improve the condition of her whom we love; to convey, delicately, some small assistance to the modest wants of a virtuous family; and then conceive how annoying it is to me to find myself, through the avarice of a father, powerless to taste that joy, and to be unable to show this fair one any proof of my love.

Elise. Yes, I can conceive well enough, brother, what must be your grief.

Cléante. Ah! sister, it is greater than you can believe. For, in short, can anything be more cruel than this rigorous meanness that is exercised over us, this strange niggardliness in which we are made to languish? What good will it do us to have means, when we shall no longer be of an age to enjoy them, and if, to maintain myself, I am now obliged to run in debt on all sides; if I, as well as you, am obliged to crave daily the aid of tradesmen in order to wear decent clothes? In short, I wished to speak to you to help me to sound my father upon my present feelings; and should I find him opposed to them, I am resolved to go elsewhere, with this dear girl, to enjoy whatever fortune providence may have in store for us. I have endeavoured to raise money everywhere for this purpose, and if your affairs, sister, are similar to mine, and if our father runs counter to our wishes, we shall both leave him, and emancipate ourselves from that tyranny in which his insupportable avarice has so long held us.

Elise. It is true enough that every day he gives us more cause to regret the death of our mother, and that . . .

Cléante. I hear his voice; let us go a little farther to finish our confidences; and afterwards we will join our forces to attack the ruggedness of his temper.

Scene III.—Harpagon, La Flèche.

Harpagon. Clear out of this immediately, and let me
have no reply! Get out of my house, you consummate
cheat, you veritable gallow's bird!

La Flèche (aside). I have never seen anything more
vicious than this cursed old man; and I really think—I
speak under correction—that he has got the devil in him.

Harpagon. You are muttering between your teeth!

La Flèche. Why are you sending me away?

Harpagon. It well becomes you, you hang-dog, to ask
me my reasons. Out with you, quickly, that I may not
knock you down.

La Flèche. What have I done to you?

Harpagon. You have done so much to me that I wish
you to get out.

La Flèche. Your son, my master, has ordered me to
wait.

Harpagon. Go and wait for him in the street, then;
but do not remain in my house, planted bolt upright as
a sentry, taking notice of everything that goes on, and
making the best use of it. I will not have a spy over my
concerns eternally before my eyes, a wretch, whose cursed
eyes watch every one of my actions, covet all I have,
and ferret about everywhere to see if there is nothing to
pilfer.

La Flèche. How the deuce could one manage to rob
you? Are you a likely man to have aught stolen from
you, when you lock up everything, and keep guard day
and night?

Harpagon. I shall lock up whatever I think fit, and
keep guard as long as I please. A nice pass it has come
to with these spies, who take notice of everything one
does. (*Softly, aside*). I quake for fear he should suspect something about my money. (*Aloud*). Ah! are you
not just the fellow who would think nothing of bruiting

the tale about that I have money hidden in my house?

La Flèche. You have money hidden?

Harpagon. No, you scoundrel, I do not say that. (*To himself*). I am bursting with rage. (*Aloud*). I ask whether you would not from sheer malice, bruit the story about that I have some.

La Flèche. Eh! what does it matter to us whether you have any or not, as long as it comes to the same thing to us?

Harpagon (*lifting up his hand, to slap* LA FLÈCHE's *face*). You are arguing the matter! I will give you something for this reasoning on your ears. Once more, get out of this.

La Flèche. Very well! I am going.

Harpagon. Wait: you are not taking anything away with you?

La Flèche. What should I take from you?

Harpagon. I do not know until I look. Show me your hands?

La Flèche. Here they are.

Harpagon. The others.

La Flèche The others?

Harpagon. Yes.

La Flèche. Here they are.

Harpagon (*pointing to the breeches of* LA FLÈCHE) Have you put nothing in there?

La Flèche. Look for yourself!

Harpagon (*feeling the outside of* LA FLÈCHE's *pockets*). Those wide breeches are just fit to become receivers for things purloined, and I wish one of them had been hanged at the gallows.

La Flèche (*aside*). Ah, how a man like this well deserves the thing he fears! and how much pleasure I would have in robbing him!

Harpagon. Eh?

La Flèche. What?

Harpagon.   What are you muttering about robbing!

La Flèche.   I am saying that you feel carefully everywhere to see if I have robbed you.

Harpagon.   That is what I mean to do.   (HARPAGON *fumbles in* LA FLÈCHE'S *pockets*).

La Flèche (*aside*).   May the plague take avarice and all avaricious people!

Harpagon.   What! what are you saying?

La Flèche.   What am I saying?

Harpagon.   Yes; what are you saying about avarice and avaricious people?

La Flèche.   I say may the plague take avarice and all avaricious people.

Harpagon.   To whom are you alluding?

La Flèche.   To avaricious people.

Harpagon.   And who are they, these avaricious people?

La Flèche.   Villains and curmudgeons.

Harpagon.   But whom do you mean by that?

La Flèche.   What are you troubling yourself about?

Harpagon.   I am troubling myself about what concerns me.

La Flèche.   Do you think that I am speaking of you?

Harpagon.   I think what I think; but I wish you to tell me to whom you are addressing yourself when you say that.

La Flèche.   I am addressing myself . . . I am addressing myself to my cap.

Harpagon.   And I might address myself to the head that is in it.

La Flèche.   Will you prevent me from cursing avaricious people?

Harpagon.   No: but I will prevent you from jabbering, and from being insolent.   Hold your tongue!

La Flèche.   I name no one.

Harpagon.   I shall thrash you if you say another word.

La Flèche. Whom the cap fits, let him wear it.

Harpagon. Will you hold your tongue?

La Flèche. Yes, against my will.

Harpagon. Ah! Ah!

La Flèche (showing HARPAGON *a pocket in his doublet).* Just look, there is another pocket; are you satisfied?

Harpagon. Come, you had better give it up without my searching you.

La Flèche. What?

Harpagon. What you have taken from me.

La Flèche. I have taken nothing at all from you.

Harpagon. Assuredly?

La Flèche. Assuredly.

Harpagon. Good-bye, then, and go to the devil.

La Flèche (aside). That is a pretty dismissal.

Harpagon. I leave you to your own conscience, at least.

SCENE IV.—HARPAGON, *alone.*

There is a hang-dog of a valet who is very much in my way; I do not at all care to see this limping cur about the place. It is certainly no small trouble to keep such a large sum of money in one's house; and he is a happy man who has all his well laid out at interest, and keeps only so much by him as is necessary for his expenses. One is not a little puzzled to contrive, in the whole house, a safe hiding-place; for, as far as I am concerned, I distrust safes, and would never rely on them. I look upon them just as a distinct bait to burglars; for it is always the first thing which they attack.

SCENE V.—HARPAGON; ELISE *and* CLÉANTE *conversing together at the farther end of the stage.*

Harpagon (still thinking himself alone). For all that, I am not quite sure if I have done right in burying in

my garden these ten thousand crowns, which were paid
to me yesterday. Ten thousand golden crowns in one's
house is a sum sufficient. . . . (*Aside, perceiving* ELISE
and CLÉANTE). Oh, Heavens! I have betrayed myself!
The excitement has carried me too far, and I verily believe I have spoken aloud, while arguing to myself. (*To*
CLÉANTE *and* ELISE). What is the matter?

Cléante. Nothing, father?

Harpagon. Have you been there long?

Elise. We were just coming in.

Harpagon. You have heard . . .

Cléante. What, father?

Harpagon. There . . .

Elise. What?

Harpagon. What I said just now.

Cléante. No.

Harpagon. Yes, you have.

Elise. I beg your pardon.

Harpagon. I see well enough that you overheard some
words. I was talking to myself about the difficulty one
experiences now-a-days in finding money, and I was saying how pleasant it must be to have ten thousand crowns
in the house.

Cléante. We hesitated to speak to you, for fear of interrupting you.

Harpagon. I am very glad to tell you this, so that
you may not take things the wrong way, and imagine
that I said that I myself had ten thousand crowns.

Cléante. We have no wish to enter into your concerns.

Harpagon. Would to Heaven that I had them, ten
thousand crowns!

Cléante. I do not think . . .

Harpagon. It would be a capital affair for me.

Elise. These are things . . .

Harpagon. I am greatly in need of them.

Cléante. I think . . .

Harpagon. That would suit me very well.

Elise. You are . . .

Harpagon. And I should not have to complain as I do now, about the hard times.

Cléante. Good Heavens! father, you have no need to complain, and we know that you have wealth enough.

Harpagon. How! I wealth enough! Those who say so surely tell a lie. Nothing could be more false; and they are but a pack of rascals who spread all these reports about.

Elise. Do not put yourself in a rage.

Harpagon. A strange thing, that my own children should betray me, and become my enemies.

Cléante. Is it becoming your enemy to say that you have wealth?

Harpagon. Yes. Such talk, and the expenses you indulge in will be the cause that one of these fine days people will come and cut my throat, in my own house, in the belief that I am stuffed with gold pieces.

Cléante. What great expenses do I indulge in?

Harpagon. Expenses? Can anything be more scandalous than this sumptuous attire, which you exhibit about the town? I scolded your sister yesterday; but this is much worse. This cries aloud to Heaven for vengeance; for, take you from top to toe, there is enough to ensure a handsome competency. I have told you twenty times, son, that all your manners displease me; you are furiously aping the aristocracy; and to go dressed as you do, you must rob me.

Cléante. Eh! how rob you?

Harpagon. How do I know? Where can you get the means of keeping up such an appearance?

Cléante. I, father? it is because I play; and, as I am very lucky, I put my winnings on my back.

Harpagon. That is very bad. If you are lucky at

play, you should profit by it, and lay out the money you win at decent interest, that you may provide for a rainy day. I should much like to know, leaving all other things aside, what the good can be of all these ribbons with which you are decked out from head to foot, and if half-a-dozen tacks are not sufficient to fasten your breeches. Is it at all necessary to spend money upon wigs? when one can wear hair of home grow th, which costs nothing! I would bet that your wig and ribbons cost far more than twenty pistoles, and twenty pistoles, at a little more than eight per cent. bring in eighteen livres, six pence, and eight groats a year.

Cléante. You are perfectly right.

Harpagon. Let us leave the subject, and talk of other things. (*Perceiving that* CLÉANTE *and* ELISE *interchange glances*). Eh! (*Softly, aside*). I believe that they are making signs to each other to rob me of my purse. (*Aloud*). What mean those gestures?

Elise. My brother and I are arguing who shall speak first. We have each something to say to you.

Harpagon. And I have something to say to you both.

Cléante. It is about marriage that we wish to speak to you, father.

Harpagon. And it is also about marriage that I wish to converse with you.

Elise. Ah, father!

Harpagon. Why this cry? Is it the word, or the thing itself that frightens you, daughter?

Cléante. The way you may look at marriage may frighten us both; and we fear that your sentiments may not happen to chime in with our choice.

Harpagon. A little patience; do not alarm yourselves. I know what is good for you both, and neither the one nor the other shall have cause to complain of what I intend to do. To begin at one end of the story (*to*

CLÉANTE), tell me, have you noticed a young person called Mariane, who lodges not far from here?

Cléante. Yes, father.

Harpagon. And you?

Elise. I have heard her spoken of.

Harpagon. How do you like that girl, son?

Cléante. A very charming person.

Harpagon. What do you think of her countenance?

Cléante. Very genteel, and full of intelligence.

Harpagon. Her air and manner?

Cléante. Without doubt, admirable.

Harpagon. Do you not think that a girl like that deserves to be taken notice of?

Cléante. Yes, father.

Harpagon. That it would be a desirable match?

Cléante. Very desirable.

Harpagon. That she looks as if she would make a good wife?

Cléante. Undoubtedly.

Harpagon. And that a husband would have reason to be satisfied with her?

Cléante. Assuredly.

Harpagon. There is a slight difficulty. I fear that she has not as much money as one might reasonably pretend to.

Cléante. Ah! father, money is not worth considering when there is a question of marrying a respectable girl.

Harpagon. Not so, not so. But this much may be said, that if one finds not quite so much money as one might wish, there is a way of regaining it in other things.

Cléante. Of course.

Harpagon. Well, I am very glad to see that you share my sentiments; for her genteel behaviour and her gentleness have quite gained my heart, and I have made up my mind to marry her, provided she has some dowry.

Cléante. Eh!

Harpagon. What now?

Cléante. You have made up your mind, you say . . .

Harpagon. To marry Mariane.

Cléante. Who? You, you?

Harpagon. Yes, I, I, I. What means this?

Cléante. I feel a sudden giddiness, and I had better go.

Harpagon. It will be nothing. Go quickly into the kitchen, and drink a large glassful of cold water.

Scene VI.—Harpagon, Elise.

Harpagon. A lot of flimsy sparks, with no more strength than chickens. Daughter, this is what I have resolved upon for myself. As for your brother, I intend him for a certain widow, of whom they spoke to me this morning; and you, I will give to M. Anselme.

Elise. To M. Anselme?

Harpagon. Yes, a staid, prudent, and careful man, who is not above fifty, and whose wealth is spoken of everywhere.

Elise (making a curtsey). I have no wish to get married, father, if you please.

Harpagon (imitating her). And I, my dear girl, my pet, I wish you to get married, if you please.

Elise (curtseying once more). I beg your pardon, father.

Harpagon (imitating Elise*).* I beg your pardon, daughter.

Elise. I am M. Anselme's most humble servant (*curtseying again*); but, with your leave, I shall not marry him.

Harpagon. I am your most humble slave, but (*imitating* Elise*),* with your leave, you shall marry him not later than this evening.

Elise. Not later than this evening?

Harpagon. Not later than this evening.

Elise (*curtseying again*). That shall not be, father.

Harpagon (*imitating her again*). This shall be, daughter.

Elise. No.

Harpagon. Yes.

Elise. No, I tell you.

Harpagon. Yes, I tell you.

Elise. That is a thing you shall not drive me to.

Harpagon. That is a thing I shall drive you to.

Elise. I will kill myself sooner than marry such a husband.

Harpagon. You shall not kill yourself, and you shall marry him. But has such boldness ever been seen! Has ever a daughter been heard to speak to her father in this manner?

Elise. But has any one ever seen a father give away his daughter in marriage in this manner?

Harpagon. It is a match to which no one can object; and I bet that every one will approve of my choice.

Elise. And I bet that no reasonable being will approve of it.

Harpagon (*perceiving* VALÈRE *in the distance*). Here comes Valère. Shall we make him judge betwixt us in this matter?

Elise. I consent to it.

Harpagon. Will you submit to his judgment?

Elise. Yes; I will submit to what he shall decide.

Harpagon. That is agreed.

SCENE VII.—VALÈRE, HARPAGON, ELISE.

Harpagon. Come here, Valère. We have elected you to tell us who is in the right, my daughter or I.

Valère. You, Sir, beyond gainsay.

Harpagon. Are you aware of what we are talking?

Valère. No. But you could not be in the wrong. You are made up of right.

Harpagon. I intend, this evening, to give her for a husband a man who is as rich as he is discreet; and the jade tells me to my face that she will not take him. What say you to this?

Valère. What do I say to it?

Harpagon. Yes.

Valère. Eh! eh!

Harpagon. What?

Valère. I say, that in the main, I am of your opinion; and you cannot but be right. But on the other side, she is not altogether wrong, and . . .

Harpagon. How is that? M. Anselme is a desirable match; he is a gentleman who is noble, kind, steady, discreet, and very well to do, and who has neither chick nor child left him from his first marriage. Could she meet with a better match?

Valère. That is true. But she might say to you that it is hurrying things a little too much, and that you should give her some time at least to see whether her inclinations would agree with . . .

Harpagon. This is an opportunity which should be taken by the forelock. I find in this marriage an advantage which I could not find elsewhere; and he agrees to take her without a dowry.

Valère. Without a dowry?

Harpagon. Yes.

Valère. In that case, I say no more. Do you see, this is altogether a convincing reason; one must yield to that.

Harpagon. It is a considerable saving to me.

Valère. Assuredly; it cannot be gainsaid. It is true that your daughter might represent to you that marriage is a more important matter than you think; that it involves a question of being happy or miserable all one's life; and that an engagement which must last till death

ought never to be entered upon except with great precautions.

Harpagon. Without a dowry!

Valère. You are right. That decides it all, of course
There are people who might tell you that on such an
occasion the wishes of a daughter are something, no doubt,
that ought to be taken into consideration; and that this
great disparity of age, of temper, and of feelings makes
a marriage subject to very sad accidents.

Harpagon. Without a dowry!

Valère. Ah! there is no reply to that; I know that
well enough. Who the deuce could say anything against
that? Not that there are not many fathers who would
prefer to humour the wishes of their daughters to the
money they could give them; who would not sacrifice
them to their own interests, and who would, above all
things, try to infuse into marriage that sweet conformity,
which, at all times, maintains honour, peace, and joy;
and which . . .

Harpagon. Without a dowry!

Valère. It is true; that closes one's mouth at once.
Without a dowry! There are no means of resisting an
argument like that.

Harpagon (aside, looking towards the garden). Bless
my soul! I think I hear a dog barking. Most likely it
is some one with a design upon my money. (*To* VALÈRE)
Do not stir; I am coming back directly.

SCENE VIII.—ELISE, VALÈRE.

Elise. Are you jesting, Valère, to speak to him in
that manner?

Valère. It is in order not to sour his temper, and to
gain my end the better. To run counter to his opinions
is the way to spoil everything; and there are certain
minds which cannot be dealt with in a straightforward
manner; temperaments averse to all resistance; restive

characters, whom the truth causes to rear, who always
set their faces against the straight road of reason, and
whom you cannot lead except by turning them with their
back towards the goal. Pretend to consent to what he
wishes, you will gain your end all the better; and . . .

Elise. But this marriage, Valère!

Valère. We will find some pretext to break it off.

Elise. But what to invent, if it is to be consum-
mated this evening?

Valère. You must ask for a delay, and pretend to
be ill.

Elise. But the feint will be discovered, if they call in
the doctors.

Valère. Are you jesting? What do they know about
it? Come, come, with them you may have whatever illness you please; they will find you some reasons to tell
you whence it proceeds.

Scene IX.—Harpagon, Elise, Valère.

Harpagon (*aside, at the further end of the stage*). It
is nothing, thank Heaven.

Valère (*not seeing* Harpagon). In short, our last
resource is flight, which will shelter us from everything;
and if your love, fair Elise, be capable of acting with
firmness . . . (*Perceiving* Harpagon). Yes, a daughter
ought to obey her father. She ought not to look at the
shape of a husband; and when the great argument of
without a dowry is added to it, she must be ready to
accept what is given to her.

Harpagon. Good: that is well spoken.

Valère. I crave your pardon, Sir, if I am a little
warm, and take the liberty of speaking as I do.

Harpagon. How now! I am delighted with it, and I
wish you to take an absolute control over her. (*To*
Elise). Yes, you may run away as much as you like, I
invest him with the authority which Heaven has given

me over you, and I will have you do all that he tells you.

Valère (*to* ELISE). After that, resist my remonstrances.

SCENE X.—HARPAGON, VALÈRE.

Valère. With your leave, Sir, I will follow her, to continue the advice which I was giving her.

Harpagon. Yes, you will oblige me. By all means . . .

Valère. It is as well to keep her tight in hand.

Harpagon. True. We must . . .

Valère. Do not be uneasy. I think that I shall succeed.

Harpagon. Do, do. I am going to take a little stroll in town, and I shall be back presently.

Valère (*addressing himself to* ELISE, *leaving by the door, through which she went out*). Yes, money is more precious than anything else in this world, and you ought to thank Heaven for having given you such an honest man for a father. He knows how to go through life. When any one offers to take a girl without a dowry, one should look no farther. It sums up everything; and *without dowry* makes up for beauty, youth, birth, honour, wisdom, and probity.

Harpagon. Ah! the honest fellow! He speaks like an oracle. It is a rare piece of luck to have such a servant!

ACT II

Scene I.—Cléante, La Flèche.

Cléante. Ah! wretch that you are! where have you been? Did I not give you the order . . .

La Flèche. Yes, Sir; and I came here to wait for you without stirring: but your father, the most surly of men, ordered me out in spite of myself, at the risk of a thrashing.

Cléante. How is our affair getting on? Matters press more than ever, and since I have seen you, I have found out that my father is my rival.

La Flèche. Your father in love?

Cléante. Yes; and I have had the utmost difficulty in concealing from him the trouble which these tidings have caused me.

La Flèche. He meddle with love! What the devil put that in his head? Is he making fun of every one? and has love been made for people like him?

Cléante. This passion must have got into his head to punish me for my sins.

La Flèche. But for what reason do you keep your love a secret from him?

Cléante. In order to give him less suspicion, and to keep, if needs be, the means open for dissuading him from this marriage. What answer have they made to you?

La Flèche. Upon my word, Sir, borrowers are very unlucky people; and one must put up with strange things, when one is compelled, like you, to pass through the hands of money-lenders.

Cléante. Will the affair fall through?

La Flèche. I beg your pardon. Our Master Simon, the agent who has been recommended to us, an active and zealous man, says that he has done wonders for you, and he assures me that your face alone has won his heart.

Cléante. Shall I have the fifteen thousand francs which I want?

La Flèche. Yes, but with some trifling conditions which you must accept, if you purpose that the affair should be carried through.

Cléante. Has he allowed you to speak to the person who is to lend the money?

La Flèche. Ah! really, things are not managed in that way. He takes even more care to remain unknown than you do; and these things are much greater mysteries than you think. Simon would not tell me his name at all, and he will be confronted with you to-day in a house borrowed for the occasion, to be informed by you, personally, of your own substance and that of your family; and I have no doubt that the very name of your father may make things go smoothly.

Cléante. And above all our mother being dead, whose property cannot be alienated.

La Flèche. Here are some clauses, which he has himself dictated to our go-between, to be shown to you before doing anything:—"Provided that the lender see all his securities, and that the borrower be of age, and of a family whose estate is ample, solid, secure, and undoubted, and free from all incumbrance, a binding and correct bond shall be executed before a notary, the most honest man to be found, and who, for this purpose, shall be chosen by the borrower, to whom it is of the greatest importance that the instrument shall be regularly drawn up."

Cléante. There is nothing to object to that.

La Flèche. "The lender, in order not to charge his

conscience with the least scruple, will only lend his money at a little more than five and a half per cent."

Cléante. At a little more than five and a half per cent? Zounds! that is honest enough. There is no reason to complain.

La Flèche. That is true. "But as the lender has not the sum in question by him, and as, to oblige the borrower, he is himself obliged to borrow it of some one at the rate of twenty per cent., it shall be agreed that the said first borrower shall pay this interest. without prejudice of the rest, seeing that it is only to oblige him that the said lender takes up that loan."

Cléante. What the devil! what Jew, what Arab is this? This is more than twenty-five per cent.

La Flèche. It is true, that is what I have said. It is for you to see to that.

Cléante. What can I see? I want the money, and I am bound to consent to everything.

La Flèche. That is the answer which I made.

Cléante. There is something else still?

La Flèche. Nothing but a small matter. "Of the fifteen thousand francs required, the lender can count down in cash only twelve thousand; and, for the remaining thousand crowns, the borrower will have to take them out in chattels, clothing, and jewelry, of which the following is the memorandum, and which the lender has set down honestly at the lowest possible price."

Cléante. What does this mean?

La Flèche. Listen to the memorandum. "First, a four-post bed, elegantly adorned with Hungary-lace bands, with hangings of olive coloured cloth, with six chairs, and a counterpane of the same; the whole in very good condition, and lined with a shot taffetas, red and blue. Item: a tester for this bed, of good Aumale, pale rose-coloured serge, with large and small silk fringes."

Cléante. What does he want me to do with it?

La Flèche. Wait. "Item: Tapestry hangings, representing the loves of Gombaud and Macée. Item: a large walnut wood table, with twelve columns or turned legs, which draws out at both sides, provided with six stools underneath it."

Cléante. What have I to do, egad! . . .

La Flèche. Only have patience. "Item: three large muskets inlaid with mother-of-pearl, with the necessary rests. Item: a brick furnace, with two retorts, and three receivers very useful for those who have a turn for distilling."

Cléante. I am going mad.

La Flèche. Gently. "Item: a Bologna lute with all its strings, or nearly all. Item: a trou-madame table, a draught-board, with the game of mother goose, restored from the Greeks, very agreeable to pass the time when one has nothing else to do. Item: a lizzard's skin of three feet and a half, stuffed with hay: a very pretty curiosity to hang at the ceiling of a room. The whole of the above-mentioned, really worth more than four thousand five hundred francs, and brought down to the value of a thousand crowns, through the discretion of the lender."

Cléante. May the plague choke him with his discretion, the wretch, the cut-throat that he is! Has one ever heard of similar usury? Is he not satisfied with the tremendous interest which he demands, but must needs force me to take for the three thousand francs the old lumber which he picks up? I shall not get two hundred crowns for the whole of it; and nevertheless I must make up my mind to consent to what he wishes; for he has it in his power to make me accept anything: and the scoundrel holds me with a knife to my throat.

La Flèche. Without offence, Sir, I see you exactly on the high road which Panurge took to ruin himself: taking money in advance, buying dear, selling cheap, and eating his corn whilst it was but grass.

Cléante. What am I to do? See to what young people are reduced by the cursed stinginess of their fathers, and then people are surprised when sons wish their fathers dead!

La Flèche. One must confess that yours, with his stinginess, would incense the steadiest man in the world. I have, Heaven be praised, no very great inclination to be hanged; and, among my colleagues whom I see dabbling in many trifling things, I know well enough how to get cleverly out of a scrape, and to keep as clear as possible of those little amenities which savour more or less of the rope; but, to tell you the truth, he would, by his way of acting, give me the temptation to rob him; and I verily believe that, by doing so, I would commit a meritorious action.

Cléante. Give me this memorandum, that I may have another look at it.

SCENE II.—HARPAGON, MASTER SIMON, CLÉANTE *and* LA FLÈCHE *at the farther end of the stage.*

Simon. Yes, Sir, it is a young man who is in want of money; his affairs compel him to find some, and he will consent to all that you dictate to him.

Harpagon. But think you, Master Simon, that there is no risk to run? and do you know the name, the property, and the family of him for whom you speak?

Simon. No. In reality I cannot well inform you about that, and it is only by chance that I have been recommended to him; but he will himself explain all these things to you, and his servant has assured me that you will be satisfied when you shall know him. All that I am able to tell you is that his family is very rich, that he has already lost his mother, and he will engage himself, if you wish it, that his father shall die before eight months are over.

Harpagon. That is something. Charity, Master Simon, enjoins us to be agreeable to people when we can.

Simon. That needs no comment.

La Flèche (*softly, to* CLÉANTE, *recognizing* MASTER SIMON). What does this mean? Master Simon who is speaking to your father?

Clèante (*softly, to* LA FLÈCHE). Can any one have told him who I am and are you perhaps betraying me?

Simon (*to* CLÉANTE *and* LA FLÈCHE). Ah, ah! you are in a great hurry! Who told you that it was here. (*To* HARPAGON). It is not I, at least, Sir, who have given them your name and address; but, in my opinion, there is no great harm in this; they are discreet persons, and you can here come to an understanding with one another.

Harpagon. How?

Simon (*pointing to* CLÉANTE). This gentleman is the party who wishes to borrow the fifteen thousand francs of which I spoke.

Harpagon. What, hangdog, it is you who abandon yourself to these culpable extravagances.

Cléante. What! it is you, father, who lend yourself to these shameful deeds!

(MASTER SIMON *runs away, and* LA FLÈCHE *hides himself*).

SCENE III.—HARPAGON, CLÉANTE.

Harpagon. It is you who wish to ruin yourself by such censurable loans?

Cléante. It is you who seek to enrich yourself by such criminal usury?

Harpagon. Can you dare, after this, to appear before me?

Cléante. Can you dare, after this, to show your face to the world.

Harpagon. Are you not ashamed, tell me, to practice this sort of excess, to rush into these dreadful expenses, and to dissipate so shamefully the property which your parents have amassed for you by the sweat of their brow?

Cléante. Do you not blush to dishonour your station by the trade you are engaged in; to sacrifice glory and reputation to the insatiable desire of piling crown upon crown, and to surpass, in matters of interest, the most infamous tricks that were ever invented by the most notorious usurers?

Harpagon. Begone out of my sight, scoundrel! begone out of my sight!

Cléante. Who, think you, is the more criminal—he who buys the money of which he is in need, or he who steals money for which he has no use?

Harpagon. Begone, I say, and do not break the drums of my ears. (*Alone*). After all, I am not so vexed about this adventure; it will be a lesson to me to keep more than ever an eye upon his proceedings.

Scene IV.—Frosine, Harpagon.

Frosine. Sir.

Harpagon. Wait a moment: I shall be back directly to speak to you. (*Aside*). I had better go and take a look at my money.

Scene V.—La Flèche, Frosine.

La Flèche (*without seeing* Frosine). The adventure is altogether funny! He must have somewhere a large store of furniture; for we could recognize nothing here from what is in the memorandum.

Frosine. Eh! is it you, my poor La Flèche! How comes this meeting?

La Flèche. Ah! ah! it is you, Frosine! What brings you here?

Frosine. The same that brings me everywhere else; to fetch and carry, to render myself serviceable to people, and to profit as much as possible by the small talents of which I am possessed. You know that in this world we must live by our wits, and that to persons like me, Heaven has given no other income than intrigue and industry.

La Flèche. Have you any dealings with the master of this house?

Frosine. Yes. I am arranging some small matter for him, for which I expect a reward.

La Flèche. From him? Ah! you will have to be wide-awake enough if you get anything out of him; and I warn you that money is very scarce in this house.

Frosine. There are certain services that touch to the quick marvellously.

La Flèche. I am your humble servant. You do not know M. Harpagon yet. M. Harpagon is of all human beings the least human, of all mortals the hardest and most close-fisted. There is no service that touches his gratitude deeply enough to make him unloose his purse-strings. Praise, esteem, kindness in words, and friendship, as much as you like; but money, nothing of the kind. There is nothing drier and more arid than his good graces and his caresses; and *to give* is a word for which he has such an aversion, that he never says: *I give you,* but *I lend you good day.*

Frosine. Gad! I have the art of drawing something out of people; I have the secret of entering into their affections, of tickling their hearts, and of finding out their most sensitive spots.

La Flèche. Of no avail here. I defy you to soften the man we are speaking of, so that he will give money. Upon this subject he is a Turk, but of a turkishness to cause the despair of everyone; and one might starve, and he would not budge. In one word, he loves money better than reputation, than honour, and than virtue; and the very sight of one who asks for it sends him into fits; it is touching him in his mortal part, it is piercing his heart, it is tearing out his very entrails; and if . . . But he is coming back; I am going.

SCENE VI.—HARPAGON, FROSINE.

Harpagon (*aside*). Everything is going on right. (*Aloud*). Well! what is it, Frosine?

Frosine. Gad, how well you are looking; you are the very picture of health!

Harpagon. Who? I!

Frosine. I never saw you with such a fresh and jolly complexion.

Harpagon. Really?

Frosine. How? You never in your life looked so young as you do now; I see people of five-and-twenty who look older than you.

Harpagon. I am over sixty, nevertheless, Frosine.

Frosine. Well! what does that signify, sixty years? that is nothing to speak of! It is the very flower of one's age, that is; and you are just entering the prime of manhood.

Harpagon. That is true; but twenty years less would do me no harm, I think.

Frosine. Are you jesting? You have no need of that, and you are made of the stuff to live a hundred.

Harpagon. Do you think so?

Frosine. Indeed I do. You show all the signs of it. Hold up your head a moment. Yes, it is there, well enough between your eyes, a sign of long life!

Harpagon. You are a judge of that sort of thing?

Frosine. Undoubtedly I am. Show me your hand. Good heavens, what a line of life!

Harpagon.   How?

Frosine.   Do you not see how far this line goes?

Harpagon.   Well! what does it mean?

Frosine.   Upon my word, I said a hundred; but you shall pass six score.

Harpagon.   Is it possible?

Frosine.   They will have to kill you, I tell you; and you shall bury your children, and your children's children.

Harpagon.   So much the better!   How is our affair getting on?

Frosine.   Need you ask?   Does one ever see me meddle with anything that I do not bring to an issue?   But for match-making, especially, I have a marvellous talent. There are not two people in the world whom I cannot manage, in a very short time, to couple together; and I believe that, if I took it into my head, I should marry the grand Turk to the republic of Venice.   To be sure, there were no very great difficulties in this matter.   As I am intimate with the ladies, I have often spoken to each of them, of you; and I have told the mother of the design which you had upon Mariane, from seeing her pass in the street, and taking the fresh air at her window.

Harpagon.   Who answered . . .

Frosine.   She has received your proposal with joy; and when I gave her to understand that you very much wished her daughter to be present this evening at the marriage-contract, which was to be signed for yours, she consented without difficulty, and has entrusted her to me for the purpose.

Harpagon.   It is because I am obliged to offer a supper to M. Anselme; and I shall be glad that she share the treat.

Frosine.   You are right.   She is to pay a visit after dinner to your daughter, whence she intends to take a turn in the fair, to come and sup here afterwards.

Harpagon. Well! they shall go together in my coach, which I will lend them.

Frosine. That will do very nicely.

Harpagon. But, Frosine, have you spoken to the mother respecting the portion she can give her daughter? Have you told her that she must bestir herself a little; that she should make some effort; that she must even bleed herself a little on an occasion like that? For, after all, one does not marry a girl without her bringing something.

Frosine. How something! She is a girl who brings you twelve thousand francs a year.

Harpagon. Twelve thousand francs!

Frosine. Yes To begin with; she has been brought up and accustomed to strict economy in feeding. She is a girl used to live on salad, milk, cheese, and apples; and who, in consequence, will neither want a well-appointed table, nor exquisite broths, nor peeled barley, at every turn, nor other delicacies which would be necessary to any other woman; and let these things cost ever so little, they always mount to about three thousand francs a-year at the least. Besides this, she has no taste for anything but the utmost simplicity, and does not care for sumptuous dresses, or valuable jewels or magnificent furniture, to which other young ladies are so much given; and that comes to more than four thousand francs per annum. In addition, she has a terrible aversion to gambling, not a common thing in women of the present day; for I know one in our neighbourhood who has lost more than twenty thousand francs this year at *trente-et-quar-ante*. But let us only estimate it at a fourth of that. Five thousand francs a year at play, and four thousand in jewelry and dresses, that makes nine thousand; and a thousand crowns, say, for the food: are there not your twelve thousand francs a year?

Harpagon.   Yes: that is not so bad; but this reckoning contains, after all, nothing real.

Frosine.   Pardon me. Is it not something real to bring you for a marriage portion great sobriety, the inheritance of a great love for simplicity of dress, and the acquisition of a great hatred for gambling?

Harpagon.   Surely it is a joke to wish to make up her dowry to me out of expenses to which she will not go. I am not going to give a receipt for what I do not receive; and I shall have to get something down on the nail.

Frosine.   Good gracious! you shall get enough; and they have spoken to me of a certain country where they have some property, whereof you will become the master.

Harpagon.   That remains to be seen. But, Frosine, there is something else still which makes me uneasy The girl is young, as you can see; and young people ordinarily love only their equals, and seek only their society. I am afraid that a man of my age may not be to her taste, and that this might produce certain little troubles in my house, which would not at all suit me.

Frosine.   Ah! how little you know her! This is another peculiarity which I had to mention to you. She has a frightful aversion to young people, and cares for none except for old men.

Harpagon.   She?

Frosine.   Yes, she. I should like you to have heard her speak upon that subject. She cannot at all bear the sight of a young man; but nothing gives her greater delight, she says, than to behold a handsome old man with a majestic beard. The oldest are the most charming to her; so I warn you beforehand not to make yourself look younger than you really are. She wishes one at least to be a sexagenarian; and it is not more than four months ago, that, on the point of being married, she flatly broke off the match, when it came out that her lover was but fifty-six years of age, and that he did not put spectacles on to sign the contract.

Harpagon. Only for that?

Frosine. Yes. She says fifty-six will not do for her; and that above all things she cares for noses that wear spectacles.

Harpagon. You certainly tell me something new there.

Frosine. She carries it farther than I could tell you. One may see some pictures and a few prints in her room; but what do you think they are? Portraits of Adonis, of Cephalus, of Paris, and of Apollo? Not at all. Beautiful likenesses of Saturn, of King Priam, of old Nestor, and of good father Anchises on his son's back.

Harpagon. This is admirable. That is what I should never have thought, and I am very glad to hear that she is of that disposition. In fact, had I been a woman, I should never have cared for young men.

Frosine. I should think so. A nice lot they are these young men, to care for them! pretty beauties, indeed, these fine sparks to be enamoured of! I should like to know what one can see in them!

Harpagon. As for me, I cannot understand it at all. I do not know how there are women who like them so much.

Frosine. They must be downright fools. Does it sound like common sense to think youth amiable? Are they men at all, these young fops, and can one love such animals?

Harpagon. That is what I say every day; with their voices like chicken-hearted fellows, three small hairs in the beard twirled like a cat's whiskers; their tow-wigs, their breeches quite hanging down, and their open breasts!

Frosine. Indeed! they are well built compared with a person like you! That is what I call a man; there is something there to please the sight; and that is the way to be made and dressed to inspire love.

Harpagon.   Then you like my appearance?

Frosine.   Do I like your appearance!   You are charming; your figure is worth painting.   Turn round a little, if you please.   Nothing could be better.   Let me see you walk.   That is a well-built body, free and easy as it ought to be, and without a sign of illness.

Harpagon.   None to speak of, thank Heaven.   Nothing but my cough, which worries me now and then.

Frosine.   That is nothing.   It does not become you badly, seeing that you cough very gracefully.

Harpagon.   Just tell me: has Mariane not seen me yet?   She has not taken any notice of me in going past?

Frosine.   No; but we have spoken a great deal of you. I have tried to paint your person to her, and I have not failed to vaunt your merits, and the advantage which it would be to her to have a husband like you.

Harpagon.   You have done well and I thank you for it.

Frosine.   I have, Sir, a slight request to make to you. I have a law-suit which I am on the point of losing for want of a little money (HARPAGON *assumes a serious look*); and you might easily enable me to gain this suit by doing me a little kindness.   You would not believe how delighted she will be to see you.   (HARPAGON *resumes his liveliness*).   How you will charm her, and how this old-fashioned ruff will take her fancy!   But above all things, she will like your breeches fastened to your doublet with tags; that will make her mad for you; and a lover who wears tags will be most acceptable to her.

Harpagon.   Certainly, I am delighted to hear you say so.

Frosine.   Really, sir, this law-suit is of the utmost consequence to me.   (HARPAGON *resumes his serious air.*) If I lose it, I am ruined; and some little assistance would set my affairs in order . . . I should like you to have seen her delight at hearing me speak of you. (HARPAGON *resumes his liveliness*). Joy shone in her eyes at the enumeration of your good qualities; and, in short, I have made her very anxious to have this match entirely concluded.

Harpagon. You have pleased me very much, Frosine; and I confess that I am extremely obliged to you.

Frosine. I pray you, Sir, to give me the little assistance which I ask of you. (HARPAGON *resumes his serious air.*) It will put me on my legs again, and I shall be for ever grateful to you.

Harpagon. Good-bye. I am going to finish my letters.

Frosine. I assure you, Sir, that you could never come to my relief in a greater need.

Harpagon. I will give orders that my coach be ready to take you to the fair.

Frosine. I would not trouble you, if I were not compelled to it from necessity.

Harpagon. And I will take care that the supper shall be served early, so as not to make you ill.

Frosine. Do not refuse me the service which I ask of you. You would not believe, Sir, the pleasure which . . .

Harpagon. I must begone. Some one is calling me. Till by-and-by.

Frosine (*alone*). May ague seize you, and send you to the devil, you stingy cur! The rascal has resisted firmly all my attacks. But I must, for all that, not abandon the attempt; and I have got the other side, from whom, at any rate, I am certain to draw a good reward.

ACT III

Scene I.—HARPAGON, CLÉANTE, ELISE, VALÈRE; MIS-TRESS CLAUDE *holding a broom,* MASTER JACQUES, LA MERLUCHE, BRINDAVOINE.

Harpagon. Come here, all of you, that I may give you my orders for just now, and tell every one what he has to do. Come here, Mistress Claude; let us begin with you. (*Looking at her broom.*) That is right, arms in hand. I trust to you for cleaning up everywhere: and above all, take care not to rub the furniture too hard, for fear of wearing it out. Besides this, I appoint you to look after the bottles during the supper; and, if one is missing, or if something gets broken, I shall hold you responsible, and deduct it from your wages.

Jacques (aside). There is policy in that punishment.

Harpagon (to MISTRESS CLAUDE). You can go.

Scene II.—HARPAGON, CLÉANTE, ELISE, VALÈRE, MAS-TER JACQUES, BRINDAVOINE, LA MERLUCHE.

Harpagon. You, Brindavoine, and you, La Merluche, I confide to you the care of rinsing the glasses, and of serving out the drink, but only when the people are thirsty, and not in the manner of these impertinent lacqueys who come and provoke them, and put drinking into their heads when they have no thought of such a thing. Wait till you are asked for it more than once, and bear in mind always to bring a good deal of water.

Jacques (aside). Yes. Wine undiluted mounts to the head.

La Merluche. Shall we throw off our smocks, Sir?

Harpagon. Yes, when you see the people coming; and take care not to spoil your clothes.

Brindavoine. You know, Sir, that the front of my doublet is covered with a large stain of oil from the lamp.

La Merluche. And I, Sir, I have a large hole in the seat of my breeches, and saving your presence, people can see . . .

Harpagon. Peace; keep it adroitly to the side of the wall, and always show your front to the world. (*To* BRINDAVOINE, *showing him how he is to keep his hat before his doublet, in order to hide the stain*). And you, always hold your hat thus while you are waiting upon the guests.

SCENE III.—HARPAGON, CLÉANTE, ELISE, VALÈRE, MASTER JACQUES.

Harpagon. As for you, daughter, you will keep an eye upon what goes away from the table, and take care that nothing be wasted. It becomes girls to do so. Meanwhile, get yourself ready to receive my intended properly. She is coming to visit you, and will take you to the fair with her. Do you hear what I say to you?

Elise. Yes, father.

SCENE IV.—HARPAGON, CLÉANTE, VALÈRE, MASTER JACQUES.

Harpagon. And you, my foppish son, to whom I have been good enough to forgive what has happened just now, do not take it into your head to show her a sour face.

Cléante. I! father? a sour face. And for what reason?

Harpagon. Egad! we know the ways of children whose fathers marry again, and with what sort of eyes they are in the habit of looking at their so-called stepmothers. But if you wish me to lose the recollection of this last escapade of yours, I recommend you, above all, to show this lady a friendly countenance, and to give her, in fact, the best possible reception.

Cléante. To tell you the truth, father, I cannot promise you to be glad that she is to become my stepmother. I should tell a lie if I said so to you; but as for receiving her well and showing her a friendly countenance, I promise to obey you punctually on this head.

Harpagon. Take care you do, at least.

Cléante. You shall see that you shall have no cause to complain.

Harpagon. You had better.

SCENE V.—HARPAGON, VALÈRE, MASTER JACQUES.

Harpagon. You will have to help me in this, Valère. Now, Master Jacques, draw near, I have left you for the last.

Jacques. Is it to your coachman, Sir, or to your cook, that you wish to speak? For I am both the one and the other.

Harpagon. It is to both.

Jacques. But to which of the two first?

Harpagon. To the cook.

Jacques. Then wait a minute, if you please.

(MASTER JACQUES *takes off his livery coat, and appears in a cook's dress*).

Harpagon. What the deuce does that ceremony mean?

Master Jacques. You have but to speak now.

Harpagon. I have promised, Master Jacques, to give a supper to-night.

Jacques (*aside*). Most miraculous!

Harpagon. Just tell me: will you dish us up something good?

Jacques. Yes, if you give me plenty of money.

Harpagon. The deuce, always money. It seems to

me as if they could speak of nothing else; money, money, money! It is the only word they have got on their lips; money! they always speak of money. That is their chief argument, money.

Valère. I have never heard a more impertinent answer than that. A great wonder to dish up something good with plenty of money! It is the easiest thing in the world; any fool can do as much; but a clever man should speak of dishing up something good with little money.

Jacques. Something good with little money!

Valère. Yes.

Jacques (*to* VALÈRE). Upon my word, Master Steward, you would oblige us by showing us that secret, and by taking my place as cook; you that are meddling with everything in this house, and playing the factotum.

Harpagon. Hold your tongue. What shall we want?

Jacques. Apply to your steward here, who will dish you up something good for little money.

Harpagon. Enough! I wish you to answer me.

Jacques. How many people are to sit down?

Harpagon. We shall be eight or ten; but you must not count upon more than eight. If there is enough for eight, there is enough for ten.

Valère. That needs no comment.

Jacques. Very well! we must have four first-rate soups and five small dishes. Soups . . . Entrées . . .

Harpagon. What the devil! there is enough to feed a whole town.

Jacques. Roast . . .

Harpagon (*putting his hand over* JACQUES' *mouth*) Hold! wretch, you will eat up all my substance.

Jacques. Side-dishes.

Harpagon (*putting his hand over* JACQUES' *mouth again*). What! more still?

Valère (*to* JACQUES). Do you intend to make every

one burst? and think you that master has invited people with the intention of killing them with food? Go and read a little the precepts of health, and ask the doctors whether there is aught more prejudicial to man than eating to excess.

Harpagon. He is right.

Valère. Learn, Master Jacques, you and the like of you, that a table overloaded with viands is a cut-throat business; that, to show one's self the friend of those whom one invites, frugality should reign in the meals which one offers; and that according to the saying of an ancient, *we must eat to live, and not live to eat.*

Harpagon. Ah! how well that is said! Come here, that I may embrace you for that saying. This is the finest sentence that I ever heard in my life; *one must live to eat and not eat to li* . . . No, that is not it. How do you put it?

Valère. *That we must eat to live and not live to eat.*

Harpagon (*to* MASTER JACQUES). That is it. Do you hear it? (*To* VALÈRE). Who is the great man who has said that?

Valère. I do not recollect his name just now.

Harpagon. Just remember to write down these words for me: I wish to have them engraved in letters of gold on the mantel-piece of my dining-room.

Valère. I shall not forget it. And as for your supper, you have but to leave it to me; I shall manage everything right enough.

Harpagon. Do so.

Jacques. So much the better! I shall have less trouble.

Harpagon (*to* VALÈRE). We must have some of these things of which people eat very little, and which fill quickly; some good fat beans, with a potted pie, well stuffed with chestnuts. Let there be plenty of that.

Valère. Depend upon me.

Harpagon. And now, Master Jacques, you must clean my coach.

Jacques. Wait; that is a matter for the coachman. (*Puts his livery coat on.*) You were saying . . .

Harpagon. That you must clean my coach, and hold the horses in readiness to drive to the fair . . .

Jacques. Your horses, Sir? Upon my word, they are not at all in a fit state to go. I will not tell you that they are on the straw; the poor beasts have not got even that much, and it would not be telling the truth; but you make them keep such austere fasts that they are no longer anything but ghosts or shadows, with horses' shapes.

Harpagon. They are very ill, and yet they are doing nothing!

Jacques. And because they do nothing, Sir, must they not eat? It would be far better to work the poor brutes much, and to feed them the same. It breaks my heart to see them in such a wretched condition; for, after all, I have got tender feeling for my horses; it seems to me it is myself, when I see them suffer. Not a day passes but I take the meat out of my own mouth to feed them; and, Sir, it is being too cruel to have no pity for one's neighbour.

Harpagon. The work will not be very hard to go as far as the fair.

Jacques. No, Sir, I have not the heart to drive them, and I would not have it on my conscience to give them the whip in the state they are in. How can you wish them to draw a coach when they can hardly drag themselves along?

Valère. Sir, I will make our neighbour, Picard, take charge of them and drive them; he will be at the same time needed to get the supper ready.

Jacques. Be it so; I prefer their dying under other people's hands than under mine.

Valère. Master Jacques is getting considerate!

Jacques. Sir Steward is getting indispensable!

Harpagon. Peace.

Jacques. I cannot bear flatterers, Sir; and I see what he makes of it; that his perpetual looking after the bread, the wine, the wood, the salt, the candles, is done only with the view of currying favour with you, and getting into your good books. This drives me mad, and I am sorry to hear every day what the world says of you; for, after all, I have some feeling for you; and, after my horses, you are the person whom I love most.

Harpagon. Might I know, Master Jacques, what people say of me.

Jacques. Yes, Sir, if I could be sure that it would not make you angry.

Harpagon. No, not in the least.

Jacques. I beg your pardon; I know full well that I shall put you in a rage.

Harpagon. Not at all. On the contrary, it will be obliging me, and I shall be glad to learn how people speak of me.

Jacques. Since you will have it, Sir, I shall tell you frankly that people everywhere make a jest of you, that they pelt us with a thousand jokes from every quarter on your account, and that they are never more delighted than when holding you up to ridicule, and continually relating stories of your meanness. One says that you have special almanacks printed, in which you double the ember weeks and vigils, in order to profit by the fast days, which you compel your people to keep; another that you have always a quarrel ready for your servants at New Year's day, or when they leave you, so that you may find a reason for not giving them anything. That one tells that you once sued one of your neighbour's cats for having eaten the remainder of a leg of mutton; this one again that you were surprised one night in purloining the hay of your own horses, and that your coachman, that is, the one who was here before me, dealt you I do not know how many blows in the dark, of which you never broached a word. In short, shall I tell you? one can go nowhere without hearing you hauled over the coals on all sides. You are the byword and laughing-stock of every one; and you are never spoken of, except under the names of miser, curmudgeon, hunks and usurer.

Harpagon (*thrashing* MASTER JACQUES). You are a numscull, a rascal, a scoundrel, and an impudent fellow.

Jacques. Well! did I not say so beforehand? You would not believe me. I told you well enough that I should make you angry by telling you the truth.

Harpagon. That will teach you how to speak.

SCENE VI.—VALÈRE, MASTER JACQUES.

Valère (*laughing*). From what I can see, Master Jacques, your candour is ill rewarded.

Jacques. Zounds! Master Upstart, who assume the man of consequence, it is not your business. Laugh at your cudgel-blows when you shall receive them, but do not come here to laugh at mine.

Valère. Ah! Sir Master Jacques, do not get angry, I beg of you.

Jacques (*aside*). He is knuckling under. I shall bully him, and, if he is fool enough to be afraid of me, I shall give him a gentle drubbing. (*Aloud*). Are you aware, Master Laughter, that I am not in a laughing humour, and that if you annoy me, I will make you laugh on the wrong side of your mouth?

(MASTER JACQUES *drives* VALÈRE *to the far end of the stage, threatening him*).

Valère. Eh! gently.

Jacques. How, gently? it does not suit me.

Valère. Pray.

Jacques. You are an impertinent fellow.

Valère. Sir Master Jacques . . .

Jacques. There is no Sir Master Jacques at all. If I had a stick, I would give you a good drubbing.

Valère. How, a stick! (VALÈRE *makes* MASTER JACQUES *retreat in his turn*).

Jacques. Eh! I was not speaking of that.

Valère. Are you aware, Master Boaster, that I am the very man to give you a drubbing myself?

Jacques. I do not doubt it.

Valère. That you are, in all, nothing but a scrub of a cook?

Jacques. I am well aware of it.

Valère. And that you do not know me yet?

Jacques. I ask your pardon.

Valère. You will thrash me, say you?

Jacques. I said so only in jest.

Valère. And I say, that I do not relish your jests. (*Thrashing him with a stick.*) This will teach you, that you are but a sorry clown.

Jacques (*alone*). The plague take my candour! it is a bad business: I give it up for the future, and I will no more speak the truth. I might put up witn it from my master; he has some right to thrash me; but as for this Master Steward, I will have my revenge if I can.

SCENE VII.—MARIANE, FROSINE, MASTER JACQUES.

Frosine. Do you know, Master Jacques, if your master is at home?

Jacques. Yes, indeed, he is; I know it but too well.

Frosine. Tell him, pray, that we are here.

SCENE VIII.—MARIANE, FROSINE.

Mariane. Ah! I feel very strange. Frosine! and, if I must tell you what I feel, I dread this interview!

Frosine. But why, and whence this uneasiness?

Mariane. Alas! can you ask me? and can you not imagine the alarms of any one at the sight of the rack to which she is going to be tied?

Frosine. I see well enough, that to die pleasantly Harpagon is not exactly the rack which you would care to embrace; and I can see by your face, that this young spark, of whom you spoke to me, comes afresh into your head.

Mariane. Yes! it is an accusation, Frosine, from which I shall not defend myself; and the respectful visits which he has paid us, have, I confess, made some impression on my heart.

Frosine. But have you ascertained who he is?

Mariane. No, I do not know who he is. But this I know, that he is made to be beloved: that, if things could be left to my choice, I would sooner have him than any other, and that he is the chief cause in making me feel that the husband whom they wish to give me is a terrible torment.

Frosine. Egad, all these youngsters are agreeable, and play their part well enough, but most of them are as poor as church mice: it will be much better for you to take an old husband who will make you a good settlement. I grant you that the senses will not find their account so well on the side I speak of, and that there are some little distastes to overcome with such a spouse; but that cannot last, and his death, believe me, will soon put you in a position to take one who is more amiable, and who will mend all things.

Mariane. Good gracious! Frosine, it is a strange thing that, to be happy, we should wish for or await the death of some one; the more so as death does not always accommodate itself to our projects.

Frosine. Are you jesting? You marry him only on condition of soon leaving you a widow; and that must be one of the articles of the contract. It would be impertinent in him not to die within three months! **Here he is** himself!

Mariane. Ah! Frosine, what a figure!

SCENE IX.—HARPAGON, MARIANE, FROSINE.

Harpagon (*to* MARIANE). Do not be offended, my beauty, that I come to you with my spectacles on. I know that your charms strike the eye sufficiently, are visible enough by themselves, and that there is no need of spectacles to perceive them; but after all, it is through them that we look at the stars, and I maintain and vouch for it that you are a star; but a star, the brightest in the land of stars. Frosine, she does not answer a word, and does not testify, from what I can perceive, the slightest joy in seeing me.

Frosine. It is because she is as yet taken all aback; and besides, girls are always ashamed to show at first sight what passes in their hearts.

Harpagon. You are right. (*To* MARIANE). Here comes my daughter, sweet child, to welcome you.

SCENE X.—HARPAGON, ELISE, MARIANE, FROSINE.

Mariane. I am much behind, Madam, in acquitting myself of such a visit.

Elise. You have done, Madam, what it was my duty to do, and it was my place to have been beforehand with you.

Harpagon. You see what a great girl she is; but ill weeds grow apace.

Mariane (*in a whisper, to* FROSINE). Oh! what an unpleasant man!

Harpagon (*in a whisper, to* FROSINE). What says the fair one?

Frosine. That she thinks you admirable.

Harpagon. You do me too much honour, adorable pet.

Mariane (*aside*). What a brute!

Harpagon. I am much obliged to you for these sentiments.

Mariane (*aside*). I can hold out no longer.

SCENE XI.—HARPAGON, MARIANE, ELISE, CLÉANTE,
FROSINE, BRINDAVOINE.

Harpagon. There comes my son also, to pay his re-
spects to you.

Mariane (*in a whisper, to* FROSINE). Ah! Frosine,
what a meeting! It is the very person of whom I spoke
to you.

Frosine (*to* MARIANE). The adventure is wonderful.

Harpagon. I see that you are surprised at my having
such grown-up children; but I shall soon be rid of one
and the other.

Cléante (*to* MARIANE). Madam, to tell you the truth,
this is an adventure, which no doubt, I did not expect;
and my father has not a little astonished me, when, a
short time ago, he communicated to me the plan which
he had formed.

Mariane. I may say the same thing. It is an unfore-
seen meeting which surprises me as much as it does you;
and I was not at all prepared for such an adventure.

Cléante. It is true that my father, Madam, could not
make a better choice, and that the honour of seeing you
gives me unfeigned joy, but for all that, I cannot give
you the assurance that I rejoice at the design which you
may have of becoming my step-mother. I avow to you
that it would be too much for me to pay you that compliment; and by your leave, it is a title which I do not
wish you. This speech may become coarse to some; but
I am sure that you will be the one to take it in the
proper sense; that it is a marriage, Madam, for which,
as you may well imagine, I can have only repugnance;
that you are not unaware, knowing what I am, how it

clashes with my interests; and that, in short, you will not take it amiss when I tell you, with the permission of my father, that, if matters depended upon me, this marriage would not take place.

Harpagon. This is a most impertinent compliment! What a pretty confession to make to her!

Mariane. And I, in reply, must tell you, that things are pretty equal; and that, if you have any repugnance in seeing me your step-mother, I shall have, doubtless, no less in seeing you my step-son. Do not think, I pray you, that it is I who seek to give you that uneasiness. I should be very sorry to cause you any displeasure; and unless I see myself compelled to it by an absolute power, I give you my word that I shall not consent to a marriage that vexes you.

Harpagon. She is right. To a silly compliment, a similar retort is necessary. I beg your pardon, my dear, for the impertinence of my son; he is a young fool, who does not as yet know the consequence of what he says.

Mariane. I promise you that what he has said has not at all offended me; on the contrary, he has pleased me by explaining thus his real feelings. I like such an avowal from his lips; and if he had spoken in any other way, I should have esteemed him the less for it.

Harpagon. It is too good of you to be willing thus to condone his faults. Time will make him wiser, and you shall see that he will alter his sentiments.

Cléante. No, father, I am incapable of changing upon that point, and I beg urgently of this lady to believe me.

Harpagon. But see what madness! he goes still more strongly.

Cléante. Do you wish me to go against my own heart?

Harpagon. Again! Perhaps you will be kind enough to change the conversation.

Cléante. Well! since you wish to speak in a different manner, allow me, Madam, to put myself in my

father's place, and to confess to you that I have seen
nothing in the world so charming as you; that I conceive
nothing equal to the happiness of pleasing you, and that
the title of your husband is a glory, a felicity which I
would prefer to the destinies of the greatest princes on
earth. Yes, Madam, the happiness of possessing you is,
in my eyes, the best of all good fortunes; the whole of
my ambition points to that. There is nothing which I
would shrink from to make so precious a conquest; and
the most powerful obstacles . . .

Harpagon. Gently, son, if you please.

Cléante. It is a compliment which I pay for you to
this lady.

Harpagon. Good Heavens! I have a tongue to explain myself, and I have no need of an interpreter like
you. Come, hand chairs.

Frosine. No; it is better that we should go to the
fair now, so that we may return the sooner, and have
ample time afterwards to converse with you.

Harpagon (*to* BRINDAVOINE). Have the horses put to
the carriage.

SCENE XII.—HARPAGON, MARIANE, ELISE, CLÉANTE,
VALÈRE, FROSINE.

Harpagon (*to* MARIANE). I pray you to excuse me,
fair child, if I forgot to offer you some refreshments before going.

Cléante. I have provided for it, father, and have ordered some plates of China oranges, sweet citrons, and
preserves, which I have sent for in your name.

Harpagon (*softly to* VALÈRE). Valère!

Valère (*to* HARPAGON). He has lost his senses.

Cléante. Do you think, father, that it is not sufficient? This lady will have the goodness to excuse that,
if it please her.

Mariane. It was not at all necessary.

Cléante. Have you ever seen, Madam, a diamond more sparkling than the one which you see on my father's finger?

Mariane. It sparkles much indeed.

Cléante (taking the diamond off his father's finger, and handing it to MARIANE). You must see it close.

Mariane. It is no doubt very beautiful, and throws out a deal of light.

Cléante (placing himself before MARIANE, *who is about to return the diamond*). No, Madam, it is in hands too beautiful. It is a present which my father makes you.

Harpagon. I?

Cléante. Is it not true, father, that you wish this lady to keep it for your sake.

Harpagon (softly to his son). How?

Cléante (to MARIANE). A pretty request indeed! He has given me a sign to make you accept it.

Mariane. I do not wish to . . .

Cléante (to MARIANE). Are you jesting? He does not care to take it back.

Harpagon (aside). I am bursting with rage!

Mariane. It would be . . .

Cléante (preventing MARIANE *from returning the diamond*). No, I tell you; you would offend him.

Mariane. Pray . . .

Cléante. Not at all.

Harpagon (aside). May the plague . .

Cléante. He is getting angry at your refusal.

Harpagon (softly to his son). Ah! you wretch!

Cléante (to MARIANE). You see that he is getting desperate.

Harpagon (in a suppressed tone to his son, threatening him). Murderer that you are!

Cléante. It is not my fault, father. I am doing all that I can to make her keep it; but she is obstinate.

Harpagon (*in a great passion, whispering to his son*).
Hang-dog!

Cléante. You are the cause, Madam, of my father's
upbraiding me.

Harpagon (*same as before, to his son*). The scoundrel!

Cléante (*to* MARIANE). You will make him ill. Pray,
Madam, do not resist any longer.

Frosine (*to* MARIANE). Good Heavens, what ceremonies! Keep the ring, since the gentleman wishes it.

Mariane (*to* HARPAGON). Not to put you into a passion, I shall keep it now, and I shall take another opportunity of returning it to you.

SCENE XIII.—HARPAGON, MARIANE, ELISE, CLÉANTE,
VALÈRE, FROSINE, BRINDAVOINE.

Brindavoine. Sir, there is a man who wishes to speak
to you.

Harpagon. Tell him that I am engaged, that he is to
return at another time.

Brindavoine. He says that he brings you some money.

Harpagon (*to* MARIANE). I beg your pardon; I shall
be back directly.

SCENE XIV.—HARPAGON, MARIANE, ELISE, CLÉANTE,
VALÈRE, FROSINE, LA MERLUCHE.

Merluche (*running against* HARPAGON, *whom he
knocks down*). Sir . . .

Harpagon. Oh! I am killed!

Cléante. What is it, father? have you hurt yourself?

Harpagon. The wretch has surely been bribed by
my debtors to make me break my neck.

Valère (*to* HARPAGON). That will be nothing.

Merluche (*to* HARPAGON). I beg your pardon, Sir;
I thought I was doing well in running quickly.

Harpagon. What have you come here for, you hang-dog?

Merluche. To tell you that your two horses have lost their shoes.

Harpagon. Let them be taken to the farrier immediately.

Cléante. While waiting for their being shod, I will do the honours of your house for you, father, and conduct this lady into the garden, whither I shall have the refreshments brought.

SCENE XV.—HARPAGON, VALÈRE.

Harpagon. Valère, keep your eye a little on this, and take care, I pray you, to save as much of it as you can, to send back to the tradespeople.

Valère. I know.

Harpagon (alone). Oh, impertinent son! do you mean to ruin me?

ACT IV

SCENE I.—CLÉANTE, MARIANE, ELISE, FROSINE.

Cléante. Let us go in here; we shall be much better. There is no suspicious person near us now, and we can converse freely.

Elise. Yes, Madam, my brother has confided to me the affection which he feels for you. I am aware of the grief and unpleasantness which such obstacles are capable of causing; and it is, I assure you, with the utmost tenderness that I interest myself in your adventure.

Mariane. It is a sweet consolation to see some one like you in one's interest; and I implore you, Madam, always to reserve for me this generous friendship, so capable of alleviating the cruelties of fortune.

Frosine. You are, upon my word, both unlucky people, in not having warned me before this of your affair. I would, no doubt, have warded off this uneasiness from you, and not have carried matters so far as they now are.

Cléante. Whose fault is it? It is my evil destiny that has willed it so. But fair Mariane, what have you resolved to do?

Mariane. Alas! am I able to make any resolutions? And, in the dependent position in which you see me, can I form aught else than wishes?

Cléante. No other support in your heart for me than mere wishes? No strenuous pity? No helping kindness? No energetic affection?

Mariane. What can I say to you? Put yourself in my place, and see what I can do. Advise, command yourself: I leave the matter to you; and I think you too reasonable to wish to exact from me aught but what may be consistent with honour and decency.

Cléante. Alas! to what straits do you reduce me by driving me back to what the annoying dictates of a rigorous honour and a scrupulous decency only will permit?

Mariane. But what would you have me to do? Even if I could forego the many scruples to which my sex compels me, I have some consideration for my mother. She has always brought me up with the utmost tenderness, and I could not make up my mind to cause her any displeasure. Treat, transact with her; use all your means to gain her mind. You may say and do whatever you like, I give you full power; and if nothing is wanting but to declare myself in your favour, I am willing, myself, to make to her the avowal of all that I feel for you.

Cléante. Frosine, dear Frosine, will you try to serve us?

Frosine. Upon my word, need you ask? I should like it with all my heart. You know that, naturally, I am kind-hearted enough. Heaven has not given me a heart of iron, and I have only too much inclination for rendering little services when I see people who love each other in all decency and honour. What can we do in this matter?

Cléante. Pray consider a little.

Mariane. Give us some advice.

Elise. Invent some means of undoing what you have done.

Frosine. That is difficult enough. (*To* Mariane). As for your mother, she is not altogether unreasonable, and we might perhaps prevail upon her and induce her to transfer to the son the gift which she wished to make to the father. (*To* Cléante). But the mischief in it is, that your father is your father.

Cléante. Of course.

Frosine. I mean that he will bear malice if he finds that he is refused, and that he will not be of a mind afterwards to give his consent to your marriage. To do well, the refusal ought to come from himself, and she ought to try, by some means, to inspire him with a disgust towards her.

Cléante. You are right.

Frosine. Yes, I am right; I know that well enough. That is what is wanted, but how the deuce can we find the means? Stop! Suppose we had some woman a little advanced in age who had my talent, and acted sufficiently well to counterfeit a lady of quality, by the help of a retinue made up in haste, and with an eccentric name of a marchioness or a viscountess, whom we will suppose to come from Lower Brittany, I would have skill enough to make your father believe that she was a person possessed of a hundred thousand crowns in ready money, besides her houses; that she was distractedly enamoured of him, and had so set her mind upon being his wife, that she would make all her property over to him by marriage-contract. I do not doubt that he would lend an ear to this proposal. For, after all, he loves you much, I know it, but he loves money a little more; and when, dazzled with this bait, he had once given his consent in what concerns you, it would matter very little if he were afterwards disabused, when he wished to see more clearly into the property of our marchioness.

Cléante. All this is very well conceived.

Frosine. Let me manage. I just recollect one of my friends who will suit us.

Cléante. Be assured of my gratitude, Frosine, if you carry out this matter. But, charming Mariane, let us begin, I pray you, by gaining over your mother; it is doing much, at any rate, to break off this match. Make every possible effort on your part, I entreat you. Employ all the power which her tenderness for you gives you over her. Show her unreserved, the eloquent graces, the all-powerful charms, with which Heaven has endowed your eyes and your lips; and please do not overlook any of these tender words, of these sweet prayers, and of these winning caresses to which, I am persuaded, nothing can be refused.

Mariane. I will do my best, and forget nothing.

SCENE II.—HARPAGON, CLÉANTE, MARIANE, ELISE, FROSINE.

Harpagon (aside, without being seen). Hey day! my son kisses the hand of his intended stepmother; and his intended stepmother does not seem to take it much amiss! Can there be any mystery underneath this?

Elise. Here is my father.

Harpagon. The carriage is quite ready; you can start as soon as you like.

Cléante. Since you are not going, father, permit me to escort them.

Harpagon. No: remain here. They will do well enough by themselves, and I want you.

SCENE III.—HARPAGON, CLÉANTE.

Harpagon. Now, tell me, apart from becoming your stepmother, what think you of this lady.

Cléante. What do I think of her.

Harpagon. Yes, of her air, of her figure, of her beauty, of her mind?

Cléante. So, so.

Harpagon. That is no answer.

Cléante. To speak to you candidly, I have not found her what I expected. Her air is that of a downright coquette, her figure is sufficiently awkward, her beauty very so-so, and her mind quite ordinary. Do not think, father, that this is said to give you a distaste to her; for, stepmother for stepmother, I would as soon have her as any other.

Harpagon. You said to her just now, however . . .

Cléante. I have said some sweet nothings to her in your name, but it was to please you.

Harpagon. So much so, that you would not feel any inclination towards her.

Cléante. I? not at all.

Harpagon. I am sorry for it; for it does away with an idea that came into my head. In seeing her here, I have reflected upon my age; and I thought that people might find something to cavil at in seeing me marry so young a girl. This consideration has made me abandon the plan; and as I have made the demand of her hand, and am engaged to her by my word, I would have given her to you, had it not been for the aversion which you show.

Cléante. To me?

Harpagon. To you.

Cléante. In marriage?

Harpagon. In marriage.

Cléante. Listen. It is true that she is not much to my taste; but to please you, father, I would make up my mind to marry her, if you wish it.

Harpagon. I, I am more reasonable than you give me credit for. I will not force your inclination.

Cléante. Pardon me; I will make this effort for your sake.

Harpagon. No, no. No marriage can be happy where there is no inclination.

Cléante. Perhaps it will come afterwards, father; they say that love is often the fruit of wedlock.

Harpagon. No. From the side of the man, one must not risk such a thing; it generally brings grievous consequences, to which I do not care to commit myself.

Had you felt any inclination for her, it would have been
a different thing; I should have made you marry her
instead of me; but, that not being the case, I will follow
up my first plan, and marry her myself.

Cléante. Well! father, since matters are so, I must
lay open my heart to you; I must reveal our secret to
you. The truth is, I love her, since, on a certain day, I
saw her walking; that my plan was, a short while ago,
to ask her to become my wife, and that nothing restrained
me but the declaration of your sentiments, and the fear
of displeasing you.

Harpagon. Have you paid her any visits?

Cléante. Yes, father.

Harpagon. Many times?

Cléante. Just enough, considering the time of our
acquaintance.

Harpagon. Have you been well received?

Cléante. Very well, indeed, but without her knowing
who I was; and that is what just now caused the surprise of Mariane.

Harpagon. Have you declared your passion to her,
and the design you had to marry her?

Cléante. Indeed yes; and I even made some over-
tures to her mother about it.

Harpagon. Has she listened to your proposal for her
daughter?

Cléante. Yes, very civilly.

Harpagon. And does the girl much reciprocate your
love?

Cléante. If I am to believe appearances, I flatter myself, father, that she has some affection for me.

Harpagon (softly, to himself). I am glad to have
found out such a secret; that is just what I wished.
(*Aloud.*) Hark you, my son, do you know what you
will have to do. You must think, if you please, of getting rid of your love, of ceasing from all pursuits of a

person whom I intend for myself, and of marrying shortly
the one who has been destined for you.

Cléante. So, father; it is thus that you trick me!
Well! since matters have come to this pass, I declare to
you, that I will not get rid of my love for Mariane; that
there is nothing from which I shall shrink to dispute with
you her possession; and that, if you have the consent of
a mother on your side, I have other resources, perhaps,
which will combat on mine.

Harpagon. What, hang-dog, you have the audacity
to poach on my preserves!

Cléante. It is you that are poaching on mine. I am
the first comer.

Harpagon. Am I not your father, and do you not owe
me respect?

Cléante. This is not a matter in which a child is
obliged to defer to his father, and love is no respecter of
persons.

Harpagon. I will make you respect me well enough
with some sound cudgel-blows.

Cléante. All your threats will do nothing.

Harpagon. You shall renounce Mariane.

Cléante. I shall do nothing of the kind.

Harpagon. Give me a stick immediately.

Scene IV.—Harpagon, Cléante, Master Jacques.

Jacques. Eh, eh, eh, gentlemen, what is all this?
what are you thinking about?

Cléante. I do not care a straw.

Jacques (*to* Cléante). Come, Sir, gently.

Harpagon. To speak to me with such impertinence!

Jacques (*to* Harpagon). Pray, Sir, pray!

Cléante. I will not bate a jot.

Jacques (*to* Cléante). Eh what! to your father?

Harpagon. Let me alone.

Jacques (*to* HARPAGON). What! to your son? I could overlook it to myself.

Harpagon. I will make yourself, Master Jacques, judge in this affair, to show you that I am in the right.

Jacques. I consent. (*To* CLÉANTE). Get a little farther away.

Harpagon. I love a girl whom I wish to marry; and the hang-dog has the insolence to love her also, and to aspire to her hand in spite of my commands.

Jacques. He is wrong there.

Harpagon. Is it not a dreadful thing for a son to wish to enter into rivalry with his father? and ought he not, out of respect, to abstain from meddling with my inclinations?

Jacques. You are right. Let me speak to him, while you remain here.

Cléante (*to* MASTER JACQUES, *who is approaching him*). Well! yes, since he chooses you as judge, I shall not draw back; it matters not to me who it may be; and I am willing to refer to you, Master Jacques, in this our quarrel.

Jacques. You do me much honour.

Cléante. I am smitten with a young girl who returns my affection, and tenderly accepts the offer of my love: and my father takes it into his head to come and trouble our passion, by asking for her hand.

Jacques. He is assuredly wrong.

Cléante. Is he not ashamed at his age to think of marrying? Does it still become him to be in love, and should he not leave this pastime to young people?

Jacques. You are right. He is only jesting. Let me speak a few words to him. (*To* HARPAGON.) Well! your son is not so strange as you make him out, and he is amenable to reason. He says that he knows the respect which he owes you, that he was only carried away by momentary warmth; and that he will not refuse to submit to your pleasure, provided you will treat him better than you do, and give him some one for a wife with whom he shall have reason to be satisfied.

Harpagon. Ah! tell him, Master Jacques, that, if he looks at it in that way, he may expect everything of me and that, except Mariane, I leave him free to choose whom he likes.

Jacques. Let me manage it. (*To* CLÉANTE.) Well! your father is not so unreasonable as you make him out; and he has shown me that it was your violence that made him angry; that he objects only to your behaviour; and that he will be very much disposed to grant you what you wish, provided you shall do things gently, and show him the deference, the respect, and the submission which a son owes to his father.

Cléante. Ah! Master Jacques, you may assure him that if he grants me Mariane, he will always find me the most submissive of beings, and that I never shall do anything except what he wishes.

Jacques (*to* HARPAGON). That is done. He consents to what you say.

Harpagon. Then things will go on in the best possible way.

Jacques (*to* CLÉANTE). Everything is arranged; he is satisfied with your promises!

Cléante. Heaven be praised!

Jacques. Gentlemen, you have but to talk the matter over: you are agreed now, and you were going to quarrel for want of understanding each other.

Cléante. My dear Master Jacques, I shall be obliged to you all my life.

Jacques. Do not mention it, Sir.

Harpagon. You have given me great pleasure, Master Jacques; and that deserves a reward. (HARPAGON *fumbles in his pockets;* MASTER JACQUES *holds out his*

hand, but HARPAGON *only draws out his handkerchief.*)
Go now, I shall remember this, I assure you.

Jacques. I kiss your hands.

SCENE V.—HARPAGON, CLÉANTE.

Cléante. I ask your pardon, father, for the passion which I have displayed.

Harpagon. Never mind.

Cléante. I assure you that I regret it exceedingly.

Harpagon. And I, I have the greatest delight in seeing you reasonable.

Cléante. How good of you to forget my fault so quickly!

Harpagon. The faults of children are easily forgotten, when they return to their duty.

Cléante. What! not retain any resentment for all my extravagance?

Harpagon. You compel me to it, by the submission and the respect to which you pledge yourself.

Cléante. I promise you, father, that I shall carry the recollection of your goodness to my grave with me.

Harpagon. And I, I promise you, that you may obtain anything from me.

Cléante. Ah! father, I ask for nothing more; you have given me enough by giving me Mariane.

Harpagon. How!

Cléante. I say, father, that I am too well pleased with you, and that I find everything in your kindness in giving me Mariane.

Harpagon. Who says anything to you of giving you Mariane?

Cléante. You, father.

Harpagon. I!

Cléante. Undoubtedly.

Harpagon. What! it is you who have promised to renounce her.

Cléante. I renounce her!

Harpagon. Yes.

Cléante. Not at all.

Harpagon. You have not given up your pretensions to her?

Cléante. On the contrary, I am more determined than ever upon them.

Harpagon. What! hang-dog, you begin afresh?

Cléante. Nothing can change my mind.

Harpagon. Let me get at you, wretch.

Cléante. Do what you like.

Harpagon. I forbid you ever to come within my sight.

Cléante. All right.

Harpagon. I abandon you.

Cléante. Abandon as much as you like.

Harpagon. I disown you as my son.

Cléante. Be it so.

Harpagon. I disinherit you.

Cléante. Whatever you please.

Harpagon. And I give you my malediction.

Cléante. I want none of your gifts.

Scene VI.—Cléante, La Flèche.

La Flèche (coming from the garden with a casket under his arm). Ah! Sir, I find you in the nick of time! Follow me quickly.

Cléante. What is the matter?

La Flèche. Follow me, I tell you; we are all right.

Cléante. How?

La Flèche. Here is your affair.

Cléante. What?

La Flèche. I kept my eye upon this the whole day.

Cléante. What is it?

La Flèche. Your father's treasure, which I have laid hands on.

Cléante. How did you manage?

La Flèche. You shall know all. Let us fly; I hear his shouts.

SCENE VII.—HARPAGON, *aloud, shouting in the garden, rushing in without his hat.*

Thieves! Thieves! Murder! Stop the murderers! Justice! just Heaven! I am lost! I am killed; they have cut my throat; they have stolen my money. Who can it be? What has become of him? Where is he? Where does he hide himself? What shall I do to find him? Where to run? Where not to run? Is he not there? Who is it? Stop! (*To himself, pressing his own arm*). Give me back my money. scoundrel . . . Ah, it is myself! My senses are wandering, and I do not know where I am, who I am, and what I am doing. Alas! my poor money! my poor money! my dearest friend, they have deprived me of you; and as you are taken from me, I have lost my support, my consolation, my joy: everything is at an end for me, and I have nothing more to do in this world. Without you, life be· comes impossible. It is all over; I am utterly exhausted; I am dying; I am dead; I am buried. Is there no one who will resuscitate me by giving me back my beloved money, or by telling me who has taken it? Eh! what do you say? There is no one. Whoever he is who has done this, he must have carefully watched his hour; and he has just chosen the time when I was speaking to my wretch of a son. Let us go. I must inform the authori· ties, and have the whole of my household examined; fe- male-servants, male-servants, son, daughter, and myself also. What an assembly! I do not look at any one whom I do not suspect, and every one seems to be my thief. Eh! what are they speaking of yonder? of him who has robbed me? What noise is that up there? Is it my thief who is there? For pity's sake, if you know any news of my thief, I implore you to tell me. Is he not hidden among you? They are all looking at me, and laughing in my face. You will see that they have, no doubt, a share in the robbery. Come quickly, magistrates, police-officers, provosts, judges, instruments of torture, gibbets, and executioners. I will have the whole world hanged; and if I do not recover my money, I will hang myself afterwards.

ACT V

Scene I.—Harpagon, a Magistrate.

Magistrate. Let me manage it; I know my busi. ness, thank Heaven. To-day is not the first time that I am engaged in discovering robberies; and I should like to have as many bags of a thousand francs as the number of people I have helped hang.

Harpagon. Every magistrate must have an interest in taking this matter in hand; and, if they do not enable me to find my money again, I shall demand justice upon the authorities themselves.

Magistrate. We must take all the needful steps. You said that there was in this box . . .

Harpagon. Ten thousand crowns in cash.

Magistrate. Ten thousand crowns!

Harpagon (crying). Ten thousand crowns.

Magistrate. The robbery is considerable!

Harpagon. There is no punishment great enough for the enormity of this crime; and, if it remain unpunished. the most sacred things are no longer safe.

Magistrate. And in what coin was this sum?

Harpagon. In good louis d'or and pistoles without a flaw.

Magistrate. Whom do you suspect of this robbery?

Harpagon. Every one; and I wish you to arrest the town and the suburbs.

Magistrate. You must, if you will take my opinion, scare nobody, but endeavour gently to collect some proofs, in order to act afterwards, by severer process, to recover the coin which has been taken from you.

349

Scene II.—Harpagon, a Magistrate, Master
Jacques.

Jacques (*at the far end of the stage, turning towards
the door by which he entered*). I am coming back directly. Let its throat be cut immediately; let them singe
me its feet; let them put it in boiling water, and let them
hang it from the ceiling.

Harpagon. Who? he who has robbed me?

Jacques. I am speaking of a sucking pig which your
steward has just sent in, and I wish to dress it for you
after my own fancy.

Harpagon. There is no question of that; and this is
a gentleman to whom you must speak of something else.

Magistrate (*to* Master Jacques). Do not be alarmed.
I am not the man to cause any scandal, and matters will
be managed in a gentle way.

Jacques. Is this gentleman of the supper party?

Magistrate. In this case, dear friend, you must hide
nothing from your master.

Jacques. Upon my word, Sir, I shall show all I know,
and I shall treat you in the best possible way.

Harpagon. That is not the question.

Jacques. If I do not dish you up something as good
as I could wish, it is the fault of your Master Steward,
who has clipped my wings with the scissors of his economy.

Harpagon. You wretch! it concerns something else
than the supper; and I wish you to give me some information respecting the money that has been stolen from
me.

Jacques. They have stolen some money from you?

Harpagon. Yes, you scoundrel; and I shall have you
hanged if you do not give it me back again.

Magistrate (*to* Harpagon). Good Heavens! do not
ill-use him. I perceive by his face that he is an honest

man, and that, without having him locked up, he will inform you of what you wish to know. Yes, my friend, if you confess the matter to me, no harm will come to you, and you will be suitably rewarded by your master. He has been robbed of his money to-day; and it is scarcely possible that you do not know something of the matter.

Jacques (*aside to himself*). This is just what I wish, in order to revenge myself on our steward. Since he has set foot in this house, he is the favourite; his counsels are the only ones listened to; and the cudgel-blows, just now received, are also sticking in my throat.

Harpagon. What are you muttering to yourself about?

Magistrate (*to* HARPAGON). Leave him alone. He is preparing to give you satisfaction; and I told you that he was an honest man.

Jacques. If you wish me to tell you things as they are, Sir, I believe that it is your dear steward who has done this.

Harpagon. Valère!

Jacques. Yes.

Harpagon. He! who seemed so faithful to me?

Jacques. Himself. I believe that he is the one who robbed you.

Harpagon. And upon what do you base your belief?

Jacques. Upon what?

Harpagon. Yes.

Jacques. I believe it . . . because I believe it.

Magistrate. But it is necessary to mention the evidence which you have.

Harpagon. Have you seen him hang about the spot where I had put my money?

Jacques. Yes, indeed. Where was your money?

Harpagon. In the garden.

Jacques. That is just where I have seen him **hanging** about, in the garden. And what was this money in?

Harpagon. In a cash-box.

Jacques. The very thing. I have seen him **with a** cash-box.

Harpagon. And this cash-box, how is it made? I shall soon see if it be mine.

Jacques. How is it made?

Harpagon. Yes.

Jacques. It is made . . . it is made like a cash-box.

Magistrate. Of course. But just describe it a little, that I may see.

Jacques. It is a large cash-box.

Harpagon. The one that has been stolen from me is a small one.

Jacques. Eh! Yes, it is small, if you take it in that way; but I call it large on account of its contents.

Magistrate. And what colour is it?

Jacques. What colour?

Magistrate. Yes.

Jacques. It is of a colour . . . of a certain colour. Could you not help me to say?

Harpagon. Ah!

Jacques. Is it not red?

Harpagon. No, grey.

Jacques. Yes, that is it, greyish-red; that is what I meant.

Harpagon. There is no longer any doubt; it is the one assuredly. Write down, Sir, write down his deposition. Heavens! whom is one to trust henceforth! One must no longer swear to anything; and I verily believe, after this, that I am the man to rob myself.

Jacques (*to* HARPAGON). He is just coming back, Sir. Do not tell him, at least, that it is I who have revealed all this.

SCENE III.—HARPAGON, MAGISTRATE, VALÈRE, MASTER JACQUES.

Harpagon. Come near, and confess to the blackest deed, the most horrible crime that ever was committed.

Valère. What do you wish, Sir?

Harpagon. How, wretch! you do not blush for your crime.

Valère. Of what crime are you talking?

Harpagon. Of what crime am I talking, infamous monster! as if you did not know what I mean! It is in vain that you attempt to disguise it; the thing has been discovered, and I have just learned all. How could you thus abuse my kindness, and introduce yourself into my house expressly to betray me, to play me a trick of that sort?

Valère. Since everything has been revealed to you, Sir, I will not prevaricate, and deny the matter to you.

Jacques (*aside*). Oh! Oh! could I unconsciously have guessed aright!

Valère. It was my intention to speak to you about it, and I wished to wait for a favourable opportunity; but, since matters are so, I implore you not to be angry, and to be willing to listen to my motives.

Harpagon. And what pretty motives can you advance, infamous thief?

Valère. Ah! Sir, I have not deserved these names. It is true that I have committed an offence against you; but after all, the fault is pardonable.

Harpagon. How! pardonable? A trap, a murder like that.

Valère. For pity's sake, do not get angry. When you have heard me, you will see that the harm is not so great as you make it.

Harpagon. The harm is not so great as I make it! What! my blood, my very heart, hang-dog!

Valère. Your blood, Sir, has not fallen into bad hands. I am of a rank not to do it any injury; and there is nothing in all this but what I can easily repair.

Harpagon. That is what I intend, and that you should restore to me what you have robbed me of.

Valère. Your honour shall be amply satisfied, Sir.

Harpagon. There is no question of honour in it. But tell me, who has driven you to such a deed?

Valère. Alas! need you ask me?

Harpagon. Yes, indeed, I do ask you.

Valère. A god who carries his excuse for all he makes people do. Love.

Harpagon. Love?

Valère. Yes.

Harpagon. A pretty love, a pretty love, upon my word! the love for my gold pieces!

Valère. No, Sir, it is not your wealth that has tempted me; it is not that which has dazzled me; and I protest that I have not the slightest design upon your property, provided you leave me that which I have got.

Harpagon. No, by all the devils I shall not leave it to you. But see what insolence to wish to keep that of which he has robbed me!

Valère. Do you call that robbery?

Harpagon. If I call it a robbery? a treasure like that!

Valère. It is a treasure, that is true, and the most precious which you have got, no doubt; but it would not be losing it to leave it to me. I ask you for it on my knees, this treasure full of charms? and to do right, you should grant it to me.

Harpagon. I shall do nothing of the kind. What does it all mean?

Valère. We have pledged our faith to each other, and have sworn never to part.

Harpagon. The oath is admirable, and the promise rather funny.

Valère. Yes, we have bound ourselves to be all in all to each other for ever.

Harpagon. I shall hinder you from it, I assure you.

Valère. Nothing but death shall separate us.

Harpagon. It is being devilishly enamoured of my money.

Valère. I have told you already, Sir, that interest did not urge me to do what I have done. My heart did not act from the motives which you imagine; a nobler one inspired me with this resolution.

Harpagon. You shall see that it is from Christian charity that he covets my property! But I shall look to that; and the law will give me satisfaction for all this, you bare-faced rogue.

Valère. You shall act as you like, and I am ready to bear all the violence you please; but I implore you to believe, at least, that if harm has been done, I only am to be blamed, and that in all this, your daughter is in nowise culpable.

Harpagon. Indeed, I believe you! it would be very strange if my daughter had had a part in this crime. But I will have my property back again, and I will have you confess where you have carried it away to.

Valère. I? I have not carried it away at all. It is still in your house.

Harpagon (*aside*). O! my beloved cash-box! (*Aloud*). Then it has not gone out of my house?

Valère. No, sir.

Harpagon. Just tell me that you have not made free with it?

Valère. I make free with it! Ah! you wrong us both; and it is with a wholly pure and respectable ardour that I burn.

Harpagon (*aside*). Burn for my cash-box!

Valère. I would sooner die than show her any offensive thought: she is too prudent and honourable for that.

Harpagon (*aside*). My cash-box too honourable!

Valère. All my wishes are confined to enjoy the sight of her; and nothing criminal has profaned the passion with which her beautiful eyes have inspired me.

Harpagon (*aside*). The beautiful eyes of my cash-box! He speaks of her as a lover speaks of his mistress.

Valère. Mistress Claude, Sir, knows the truth of this affair; and she can testify to it.

Harpagon. What! my servant is an accomplice in the matter?

Valère. Yes, Sir; she was a witness to our engagement; and it is after having known the honourable intent of my passion, that she has assisted me in persuading your daughter to plight her troth, and receive mine.

Harpagon (*aside*). He? Does the fear of justice make him rave? (*To* VALERE.) What means all this gibberish about my daughter?

Valère. I say, Sir, that I have had all the trouble in the world to bring her modesty to consent to what my love wished for.

Harpagon. The modesty of whom?

Valère. Of your daughter; and it is only yesterday that she could make up her mind to sign a mutual promise of marriage.

Harpagon. My daughter has signed you a promise of marriage?

Valère. Yes, Sir, as I have signed her one.

Harpagon. O Heaven! another disgrace!

Jacques (*to the* MAGISTRATE). Write, Sir, write.

Harpagon. More harm! additional despair! (*To the* MAGISTRATE). Come, Sir, do the duty of your office; and draw up for him his indictment as a felon and a suborner.

Jacques. As a felon and a suborner

Valère. These are names that do not belong to me; and when people shall know who I am . . .

SCENE IV.—HARPAGON, ELISE, MARIANE, VALÈRE, FROSINE, MASTER JACQUES, A MAGISTRATE.

Harpagon. Ah! graceless child! daughter unworthy of a father like me! it is thus that you carry out the lessons which I have given you? You allow yourself to become smitten with an infamous thief; and you pledge him your troth without my consent! But you shall both find out your mistake. (*To* ELISE). Four strong walls will answer for your conduct; (*to* VALÈRE,) and a good gibbet will give me satisfaction for your audacity.

Valère. It will not be your passion that shall judge this matter; and I shall get at least a hearing before being condemned.

Harpagon. I have made a mistake in saying a gibbet; and you shall be broken alive on the wheel.

Elise (*at* HARPAGON'S *knees*). Ah! father, show a little more humanity in your feelings, I beseech you, and do not push matters with the utmost violence of paternal power. Do not give way to the first movements of your passion, and give yourself time to consider what you do. Take the trouble to know better him whom you believe to have offended you. He is quite different from what he appears in your eyes; and you will find it less strange that I have given myself to him, when you know that, had it not been for him, you would long ago have had me no longer. Yes, father, it is he who saved me from the great peril I was in when I fell into the water, and to whom you owe the life of that very daughter, who . . .

Harpagon. All that is nothing; and it would have been much better for me. had he allowed you to be drowned, than to do what he has done.

Elise. I implore you, father, by your paternal love, to . . .

Harpagon. No, no; I will hear nothing, and justice must have its course.

Jacques. You shall pay me my cudgel-blows.

Frosine (*aside*). What strange confusion is this!

SCENE V.—ANSELME, HARPAGON, ELISE, MARIANE, FROSINE, VALÈRE, MAGISTRATE, MASTER JACQUES.

Anselme. What is the matter, M. Harpagon? I find you quite upset.

Harpagon. Ah! M. Anselme, I am the most unfortunate of men; and there is a great deal of trouble and disorder connected with the contract which you have come to sign! I am attacked in my property, I am attacked in my honour; and behold a wretch, a scoundrel who has violated the most sacred rights; who has introduced himself into my house as a servant to rob me of my money, and to tamper with my daughter.

Valère. Who is thinking of your money, of which you make such a cock-and-bull story?

Harpagon. Yes, they have given each other a promise of marriage. This insult concerns you, M. Anselme, and it is you who ought to take up the cudgels against him, and employ all the rigours of the law, to revenge yourself upon him for his insolence.

Anselme. It is not my intention to make any one marry me by compulsion, and to lay claim to a heart which has already pledged itself; but, as far as your interests are concerned, I am ready to espouse them, as if they were my own.

Harpagon. This gentleman here is an honest magistrate who will forget nothing, from what he has said to me, of the duties of his office. (*To the* MAGISTRATE) Charge him, Sir, in the right fashion, and make matters very criminal.

Valère. I do not see what crime can be made out against me of the affection which I entertain for your daughter, and to what punishment you think I can be condemned on account of our engagement when it shall be known who I am . . .

Harpagon. I do not care about any of these stories; in our days the world is full of these assumed noblemen; of these impostors, who take advantage of their obscurity, and with the greatest insolence adopt the first illustrious name which comes into their head.

Valère. I would have you to know that I am too upright to deck myself with anything that does not belong to me; and that all Naples can bear testimony to my birth.

Anselme. Gently! take care what you are going to say. You run a greater risk in this than you think; you are speaking before a man to whom all Naples is known, and who can easily see through your story.

Valère (proudly putting his hat on). I am not the man to fear anything; and if you know Naples, you know who was Don Thomas d'Alburci.

Anselme. No doubt, I know; and few people have known him better than I.

Harpagon. I do not care for Don Thomas nor Don Martin. (*Seeing two candles burning, blows one out*).

Anselme. Pray let him speak; we shall hear what he means to say about him.

Valère. I mean to say that to him I owe my birth.

Anselme. To him?

Valère. Yes.

Anselme. Come; you are jesting. Invent some other story which may succeed better, and do not attempt to save yourself by this imposture.

Valère. Learn to speak differently. It is not an imposture, and I advance nothing but what can be easily proved by me.

Anselme. What! you dare call yourself the son of Don Thomas d'Alburci?

Valère. Yes, I dare; and I am prepared to maintain this truth against any one.

Anselme. The audacity is marvellous! Learn to your confusion, that it is sixteen years at least since the man you speak of perished at sea with his wife and children, while endeavouring to save their lives from the cruel persecutions which accompanied the troubles at Naples, and which caused the exile of several noble families.

Valère. Yes; but learn, to your confusion, you, that his son, seven years of age, with a servant, was saved from the wreck by a Spanish vessel, and that this son, who was saved, is the person who speaks to you. Learn that the captain of that ship, pitying my misfortune, conceived a friendship for me; that he had me educated as his own son, and that I was trained to the profession of arms ever since I was old enough; that I have learned lately that my father is not dead, as I always believed; that passing through here to go in search of him, an accident, arranged by Heaven, brought me into contact with the charming Elise; that the sight of her made me a slave to her beauty, and that the violence of my passion and the harshness of her father made me resolve to introduce myself into his house, and to send some one else in quest of my parents.

Anselme. But what other proofs than your words can guarantee to us that this is not a fable based upon truth?

Valère. The Spanish captain; a ruby seal which belonged to my father; an agate bracelet which my mother had on her arm; old Pedro, the servant, who was saved with me from the wreck.

Mariane. Alas! to your words I can answer, I, that you are not imposing, and all that you say shows me clearly that you are my brother.

Valère. You, my sister!

Mariane. Yes. My heart was touched the moment you opened your lips; and our mother, who will be overjoyed at seeing you, has thousands of times related to me the misfortunes of our family. Heaven also permitted us not to perish in this dreadful shipwreck; but our lives were saved only at the cost of our liberty; and they were pirates that picked us up, my mother and me, on a plank of our vessel. After ten years of slavery, a happy accident regained for us our freedom; and we returned to Naples, where we found all our property sold, without being able to gather any news of our father. We then travelled to Genoa, whither my mother went to pick up some miserable remains of an inheritance of which she had been despoiled; and thence, flying from the barbarous injustice of her relatives, she came hither, where she has barely been able to drag on her life.

Anselme. O Heaven! how great is the evidence of thy power! and how well shewest thou that it belongs only to thee to perform miracles! Embrace me, my children, and share your joys with those of your father.

Valère. You are our father?

Mariane. It is you whom my mother has so much bewailed.

Anselme. Yes, my daughter, yes, my son; I am Don Thomas d'Alburci, whom Heaven saved from the waves, with all the money which he carried with him, and who, believing you all dead during more than sixteen years, prepared, after long journeying, to seek, in the union with a gentle and discreet girl, the consolation of a new family. The little safety which I found for my life in Naples, has made me for ever abandon the idea of returning; and having found means to sell all that I possessed there, I became used to this place, where, under the name of Anselme, I wished to get rid of the sorrows of this other name, which caused me so many misfortunes

Harpagon (*to* ANSELME). Is this your son?

Anselme. Yes.

Harpagon. Then I hold you responsible for paying me ten thousand crowns of which he has robbed me.

Anselme. He has robbed you!

Harpagon. Himself.

Valère. Who tells you this?

Harpagon. Master Jacques.

Valère (*to* MASTER JACQUES). Is it you who say this?

Jacques. You see that I say nothing.

Harpagon. Yes. There is the Magistrate who has received his deposition.

Valère. Can you believe me capable of so base an action?

Harpagon. Capable or not capable, I want my money back again.

SCENE VI.—HARPAGON, ANSELME, ELISE, MARIANE, CLÉANTE, VALÈRE, FROSINE, A MAGISTRATE, MASTER JACQUES, LA FLÈCHE.

Clèante. Do not worry yourself any longer, father, and accuse no one. I have discovered tidings of your affair; and I have come to tell you, that if you will make up your mind to let me marry Mariane, your money shall be returned to you.

Harpagon. Where is it?

Cléante. Do not grieve about that. It is in a spot for which I answer; and everything depends upon me. It is for you to say what you resolve; and you can choose, either to give me Mariane, or to lose your cash-box.

Harpagon. Has nothing been taken out?

Cléante. Nothing at all. Now make up your mind whether you will subscribe to this marriage, and join your consent to that of her mother, who leaves her free to choose between us two.

Mariane (*to* CLÉANTE). But you do not know that this consent is no longer sufficient; and that Heaven restores to me not only a brother (*pointing to* VALÈRE) but also (*pointing to* ANSELME) a father, from whom you must obtain me.

Anselme. Heaven has not restored me to you, my children, to go contrary to your desires. M. Harpagon, you are well aware that the choice of a young girl will fall upon the son rather than upon the father; come, do not oblige people to say what it is not necessary to hear; and consent, as well as I do, to this double match.

Harpagon. To be well advised, I must see my cash-box.

Cléante. You shall see it safe and sound.

Harpagon. I have no money to give my children in marriage.

Anselme. Well! I have some for them; do not let that trouble you.

Harpagon. Will you undertake to defray all the expenses of these two weddings?

Anselme. Yes, I undertake it. Are you satisfied?

Harpagon. Yes, provided that you will order me a suit for the nuptials.

Anselme. That is agreed. Let us go and rejoice in the happiness which this day brings us.

Magistrate. Hullo! gentlemen, hullo! Gently, if you please. Who is to pay for my writing?

Harpagon. We have nothing to do with your writings.

Magistrate. Yes! but I do not pretend to have written for nothing.

Harpagon (*pointing to* MASTER JACQUES). For your payment, there is a man of whom I make you a present; and you may hang him.

Jacques. Alas! how must one act? I get cudgel-blows for speaking the truth; and they wish to hang me for telling a lie!

Anselme. M. Harpagon, you must forgive him this imposture.

Harpagon. Will you pay the magistrate, then?

Anselme. Be it so. Come let us go quickly to share our joy with your mother.

Harpagon. And I, to see my dear cash-box.

THE END